Databricks ML in Action

Learn how Databricks supports the entire ML lifecycle end to end from data ingestion to the model deployment

Stephanie Rivera

Anastasia Prokaieva

Amanda Baker

Hayley Horn

Databricks ML in Action

Group Product Manager: Ali Abidi
Publishing Product Manager: Sanjana Gupta
Content Development Editor: Priyanka Soam
Technical Editor: Kavyashree K S
Copy Editor: Safis Editing
Project Coordinator: Shambhavi Mishra
Proofreader: Priyanka Soam
Indexer: Rekha Nair
Production Designer: Jyoti Kadam
Marketing Coordinator: Nivedita Singh

First published: May 2024

Production reference: 1240424

Published by Packt Publishing Ltd.
Grosvenor House
11 St Paul's Square
Birmingham
B3 1RB, UK.

ISBN 978-1-80056-489-3

www.packtpub.com

*To the strong women who have come before me, for their sacrifices and for exemplifying
the power of determination. To the memory of my grandmother, Hazel Adolph, for being
my best friend and cheerleader.*

– Stephanie Rivera

*To females who pursued a STEM career and did not give up no matter what obstacles occurred
on their way. Some would say science it's not for girls, well, prove them wrong.*

- Anastasia Prokaieva

*To my mother, Mary Baker. Thank you for showing me what true strength is, for being both
a voice of reason and unbridled support, and for believing in me no matter what.*

– Amanda Baker

*This is dedicated to the women who inspired me to lead by example, to my mom, Susan Charba,
who reminded me that I could be the one who inspires, and to the women still working their way up.
I'll send the elevator back down. There is plenty of room for us all.*

– Hayley Horn

Contributors

About the authors

Stephanie Rivera has worked in big data and machine learning since 2011. She collaborates with teams and companies as they design their data intelligence platform as a senior solutions architect for Databricks.

Previously, Stephanie was the VP of data intelligence for a global company, ingesting 20+ terabytes of data daily. She led the data science, data engineering, and business intelligence teams.

Her data career has also included contributing to and leading a team creating software that teaches people how to explore fictional planets using data science algorithms. Stephanie authored numerous sections of Booz Allen Hamilton's publication *The Field Guide to Data Science*.

I want to thank my loving partner, Rami Alba Lucio, Databricks coworkers, family, and friends for their unwavering support.

Anastasia Prokaieva began her career 9 years ago as a research scientist at CEA (France), focusing on large data analysis and satellite data assimilation, treating terabytes of data. She has been working within the big data analysis and machine learning domain since then. In 2021, she joined Databricks and became the regional AI subject matter expert.

On a daily basis, Anastasia is a consultant Databricks users on best practices for implementing AI projects end to end. She also delivers training and workshops to democratize AI. Anastasia holds two MSc degrees in theoretical physics and energy science.

I would like to thank my partner, Julien, and my family for their tremendous support. My gratitude to my talented teammates all around the globe, as you inspire me every day!

Amanda Baker began her career in data 8 years ago. She loves leveraging her skills as a data scientist to orchestrate transformative journeys for companies across diverse industries as a solutions architect for Databricks. Her experiences have brought her from large corporations to small start-ups and everything in between. Amanda is a graduate of Carnegie Mellon University and the University of Washington.

Thank you to my partner, Emmanuel, my parents, sisters, and friends for their enduring love and support.

Hayley Horn started her data career 15 years ago as a data quality consultant on enterprise data integration projects. As a data scientist, she specialized in customer insights and strategy. Hayley has presented at data science and AI conferences in the US and Europe. She is currently a senior solutions architect for Databricks, with expertise in data science and technology modernization.

A graduate of the MS data science program at Southern Methodist University in Dallas, Texas, USA, she is now a capstone advisor to students in their final semesters of the program.

I'd like to thank my husband, Kevin, and my sons, Dyson and Dalton, for their encouragement and enthusiastic support.

About the reviewers

Jeanne Choo studied plant biology and zoology at college, teaching herself how to code while doing so, to understand better how genes evolve over time. She was then hired by AI Singapore, a Singaporean government entity, as their first AI engineer. At AI Singapore, she was key in building the technical consulting practice, apprenticeship program, and technical stack from nothing. She set up the AI Apprenticeship Program, which won the Talent Accelerator Award Asia-Pacific IDC Digital Transformation Awards.

Most of Jeanne's work has focused on challenges specific to the Asia-Pacific region. Some past projects include building ML pipelines for Japanese search query understanding, training speech recognition models for Singlish, and building NLP models and corpora for Indonesian. At Databricks, she advises customers on best practices related to all things MLOps and generative AI.

Clever Anjos is a principal solutions architect at Qlik, a data analytics and data integration software company.

He has been working for Qlik since 2018 but has been around the Qlik ecosystem as a partner and customer since 2009. He is a business discovery professional with several years of experience working with Qlik, AWS, Google Cloud, Databricks, and other BI technologies.

He is a highly active member of Qlik Community, with over 8,000 posts and 4,500 page views.

In May 2022, he was named Qlik Community's featured member.

Clever is also a writer and has published a book called *Hands-On Business Intelligence With Qlik*. The book is a practical guide to using Qlik to build and deploy business intelligence applications.

Amreth is an engineering leader in the cloud, AI/ML engineering, observability, and SRE. Over the last few years, Amreth has played a key role in cloud migration, generative AI, AIOps, observability, and ML adoption at various organizations. Amreth is also co-creator of the Conducktor Platform, serving T-Mobile's over 100 million customers, and a tech/customer advisory board member at various companies on observability. Amreth has also co-created and open sourced Kardio.io, a service health dashboard tool. Amreth has been invited to and spoken at several key conferences and has won several awards.

I would like to thank my wife, Ashwinya, and my son, Athvik, for their patience and support provided during my review of this book.

Databricks subject matter experts, *we want to extend our heartfelt gratitude to each of you who took the time to review the text and code. The speed at which Databricks evolves with technology makes it an incredible feat to be current. Your guidance and support throughout this journey has been invaluable. Your contributions have not only enhanced the technical accuracy and depth of our book but have also provided invaluable context and perspective rooted in your firsthand experiences at Databricks.*

- Stephanie Rivera
- Anastasia Prokaieva
- Amanda Baker
- Hayley Horn

Table of Contents

3

Building Out Our Bronze Layer   51

Part 2: Heavily Use Case-Focused

4

Getting to Know Your Data   79

5

Feature Engineering on Databricks   111

6

Searching for a Signal   143

7

Productionizing ML on Databricks   163

8

Monitoring, Evaluating, and More   203

Preface

In this book, you will discover what makes the Databricks Data Intelligence Platform the go-to choice for top-tier machine learning solutions. *Databricks ML in Action* presents cloud-agnostic, end-to-end examples with hands-on illustrations of executing data science, machine learning, and generative AI projects on the Databricks Platform. You'll develop expertise in Databricks' managed MLflow, Vector Search, AutoML, Unity Catalog, and Model Serving as you learn to apply them practically in everyday workflows. This Databricks book not only offers detailed code explanations but also facilitates seamless code importation for practical use. You'll discover how to leverage the open source Databricks platform to enhance your learning, boost your skills, and elevate your productivity with supplemental resources. By the end of this book, you'll have mastered the use of Databricks for data science, machine learning, and generative AI, enabling you to deliver outstanding data products.

Who this book is for

This book is for machine learning engineers, data scientists, and technical managers seeking hands-on expertise in implementing and leveraging the Databricks Data Intelligence Platform and its lakehouse architecture to create data products.

What this book covers

Chapter 1, *Getting Started with This Book and Lakehouse Concepts*, covers the different techniques and methods for data engineering and machine learning. The goal is not to unveil insights into data never seen before. If that were the case, this would be an academic paper. Instead, the goal of this chapter is to use open and free data to demonstrate advanced technology and best practices. You will list and describe each dataset present in the book.

Chapter 2, *Designing Databricks: Day One*, covers workspace design, model life cycle practices, naming conventions, what not to put in DBFS, and other preparatory topics. The Databricks platform is simple to use. However, there are many options available to cater to the different needs of different organizations. During my years as a contractor and my time at Databricks, I have seen teams succeed and fail. I will share with you the successful dynamics as well as any configurations that accompany those insights in this chapter.

Chapter 3, *Building Out Our Bronze Layer*, begins your data journey in the Databricks DI Platform by exploring the fundamentals of the Bronze layer of the Medallion architecture. The Bronze layer is the first step in transforming your data for downstream projects, and this chapter will focus on the Databricks features and techniques you have available for the necessary transformations. We will start by introducing you to Auto Loader, a tool to automate data ingestion, which you can implement with or without **Delta Live Tables** (**DLT**) to insert and transform your data.

Chapter 4, *Getting to Know Your Data*, explores the features within the Databricks DI Platform that help improve and monitor data quality and facilitate data exploration. There are numerous approaches to getting to know your data better with Databricks. First, we cover how to oversee data quality with DLT to catch quality issues early and prevent the contamination of entire pipelines. We will take our first close look at Lakehouse Monitoring, which helps us analyze data changes over time and can alert us to changes that concern us.

Chapter 5, *Feature Engineering on Databricks*, progresses from *Chapter 4*, where we harnessed the power of Databricks to explore and refine our datasets, to delve into the components of Databricks that enable the next step – feature engineering. We will start by covering **Databricks Feature Engineering** (**DFE**) in Unity Catalog to show you how you can efficiently manage engineered features using Unity Catalog. Understanding how to leverage DFE in UC is crucial for creating reusable and consistent features across training and inference. Then, you will learn how to leverage Structured Streaming to calculate features on a stream, which allows you to create stateful features needed for models to make quick decisions.

Chapter 6, *Searching for a Signal*, examines how to use data science to search for a signal hidden in the noise of data. We will leverage the features we created within the Databricks platform during the previous chapter. We will start by using AutoML in a basic modeling approach, providing auto-generated code and quickly enabling data scientists to establish a baseline model to beat. When searching for a signal, we experiment with different features, hyperparameters, and models. Historically, tracking these configurations and their corresponding evaluation metrics is a time-consuming project in and of itself. A low-overhead tracking mechanism, such as the tracking provided by MLflow, an open source platform for managing data science projects and supporting MLOps, will reduce the burden of manually capturing configurations. More specifically, we'll introduce MLflow Tracking, an MLflow component that significantly improves tracking each permutation's many outputs. However, that is only the beginning.

Chapter 7, *Productionizing ML on Databricks*, explores productionizing a machine learning model using Databricks products, which makes the journey more straightforward and cohesive by incorporating functionality such as the Unity Catalog Registry, Databricks Workflows, Databricks Asset Bundles, and Model Serving capabilities. This chapter will cover the tools and practices to take your models from development to production.

Chapter 8, *Monitoring, Evaluating, and More*, covers how to create visualizations for dashboards in both the new Lakeview dashboards and the standard DBSQL dashboards. Deployed models can be shared via a web application. Therefore, we will not only introduce Hugging Face Spaces but also deploy the RAG chatbot using a Gradio app to apply what we have learned.

To get the most out of this book

Software/hardware covered in the book	Operating system requirements
Databricks	Windows, macOS, or Linux
Python and its associated libraries	Windows, macOS, or Linux

If you are using the digital version of this book, we advise you to type the code yourself or access the code from the book's GitHub repository (a link is available in the next section). Doing so will help you avoid any potential errors related to the copying and pasting of code.

This book contains a few long screenshots which have been captured to show the overview of workflows and also the UI. Due to this, the content in this images may appear small at 100% zoom. Please check out the PDF copy provided with the book to zoom in for clearer images.

Download the example code files

You can download the example code files for this book from GitHub at `https://github.com/PacktPublishing/Databricks-ML-In-Action`. If there's an update to the code, it will be updated in the GitHub repository.

We also have other code bundles from our rich catalog of books and videos available at `https://github.com/PacktPublishing/`. Check them out!

Conventions used

There are a number of text conventions used throughout this book.

`Code in text`: Indicates code words in text, database table names, folder names, filenames, file extensions, pathnames, dummy URLs, user input, and Twitter handles. Here is an example: " For example, you could select the `ml_in_action.favorita_forecasting.train_set` table."

Bold: Indicates a new term, an important word, or words that you see on screen. For instance, words in menus or dialog boxes appear in **bold**. Here is an example: " Once you have a dataset, return to the **Canvas** tab."

> **Tips or important notes**
> Appear like this.

Get in touch

Feedback from our readers is always welcome.

General feedback: If you have questions about any aspect of this book, email us at customercare@ packtpub.com and mention the book title in the subject of your message.

Errata: Although we have taken every care to ensure the accuracy of our content, mistakes do happen. If you have found a mistake in this book, we would be grateful if you would report this to us. Please visit www.packtpub.com/support/errata and fill in the form.

Piracy: If you come across any illegal copies of our works in any form on the internet, we would be grateful if you would provide us with the location address or website name. Please contact us at copyright@packtpub.com with a link to the material.

If you are interested in becoming an author: If there is a topic that you have expertise in and you are interested in either writing or contributing to a book, please visit authors.packtpub.com.

Share Your Thoughts

Once you've read *Databricks ML in Action*, we'd love to hear your thoughts! Scan the QR code below to go straight to the Amazon review page for this book and share your feedback.

https://packt.link/r/1-800-56489-9

Your review is important to us and the tech community and will help us make sure we're delivering excellent quality content.

Download a free PDF copy of this book

Thanks for purchasing this book!

Do you like to read on the go but are unable to carry your print books everywhere?

Is your eBook purchase not compatible with the device of your choice?

Don't worry, now with every Packt book you get a DRM-free PDF version of that book at no cost.

Read anywhere, any place, on any device. Search, copy, and paste code from your favorite technical books directly into your application.

The perks don't stop there, you can get exclusive access to discounts, newsletters, and great free content in your inbox daily

Follow these simple steps to get the benefits:

1. Scan the QR code or visit the link below

https://packt.link/free-ebook/978-1-80056-489-3

2. Submit your proof of purchase

3. That's it! We'll send your free PDF and other benefits to your email directly

Part 1: Overview of the Databricks Unified Lakehouse Platform

The goal of this part is not to unveil insights into data never seen before. If that were the case, this would be an academic paper. Instead, the goal is to use open and free data to demonstrate advanced technology and best practices. This part will list and describe each dataset present in the book. It also introduces you to the successful dynamics as well as any configurations that accompany the insights in this part. This part covers workspace design, model life cycle practices, naming conventions, what not to put in DBFS, and other preparatory topics.

This part has the following chapters:

- *Chapter 1, Getting Started with This Book and Lakehouse Concepts*
- *Chapter 2, Designing Databricks: Day One*
- *Chapter 3, Building Out Our Bronze Layer*

Getting Started with This Book and Lakehouse Concepts

"Give me six hours to chop down a tree, and I will spend the first four sharpening the axe."

– *Abraham Lincoln*

We will start with a basic overview of how **Databrick's Data Intelligence Platform** (**DI**) is an open platform on a **lakehouse** architecture and the advantages of this in developing **machine learning** (**ML**) applications. For brevity, we will use terms such as *Data Intelligence Platform* and *Databricks* interchangeably throughout the book. This chapter will introduce the different projects and associated datasets we'll use throughout the book. Each project intentionally highlights a function or component of the DI Platform. Use the example projects as hands-on lessons for each platform element we cover. We progress through these projects in the last section of each chapter – namely, applying our learning.

Here is what you will learn in this chapter:

- The components of the Data Intelligence Platform
- Advantages of the Databricks Platform
- Applying our learning

The components of the Data Intelligence Platform

The Data Intelligence Platform allows your entire organization to leverage your data and AI. It's built on a lakehouse architecture to provide an open, unified foundation for all data and governance layers. It is powered by a **Data Intelligence Engine**, which understands the context of your data. For practical purposes, let's talk about the components of the Databricks Data Intelligence Platform:

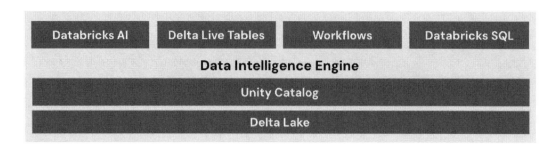

Figure 1.1 – The components of the Databricks Data Intelligence Platform

Let's check out the following list with the descriptions of the items in the figure:

- **Delta Lake**: The data layout within the Data Intelligence Platform is automatically optimized based on common data usage patterns

- **Unity Catalog**: A unified governance model to secure, manage, and share your data assets

- **Data Intelligence Engine**: This uses AI to enhance the platform's capabilities

- **Databricks AI**: ML tools to support end-to-end ML solutions and **generative AI** capabilities, including creating, tuning, and serving LLMs

- **Delta live tables**: Enables automated data ingestion and **data quality**

- **Workflows**: A fully integrated orchestration service to automate, manage, and monitor multi-task workloads, queries, and pipelines

- **Databricks SQL (DBSQL)**: An SQL-first interface, similar to how you would interact with a data warehouse, and with functionality such as text-to-SQL, which lets you use natural language to generate queries

Now that we have our elements defined, let's discuss how they help us achieve our ML goals.

The advantages of the Databricks Platform

Databricks' implementation of a lakehouse architecture is unique. Databricks' foundation is built on a Delta-formatted data lake that Unity Catalog governs. Therefore, it combines a data lake's scalability and cost-effectiveness with a data warehouse's governance. This means not only are table-level permissions managed through **access control lists** (**ACLs**) but file and object-level access are also regulated. This change in architecture from a data lake and/or a data warehouse to a unified platform is ideal – a lakehouse facilitates a wide range of new use cases for analytics, business intelligence, and data science projects across an organization. See the *Introduction to Data Lakes* blog post in the *Further reading* section for more information on lakehouse benefits.

This section will discuss the importance of open source frameworks and two critical advantages they provide – transparency and flexibility.

Open source features

How open source features relate to the Data Intelligence Platform is unique. This uniqueness lies in the concepts of openness and transparency, often referred to as the "glass box" approach by Databricks. It means that when you use the platform to create assets, there's no inscrutable black box that forces you to depend on a specific vendor for usage, understanding, or storage. A genuinely open lakehouse architecture uses open data file formats to make accessing, sharing, and removing your data simple. Databricks has optimized the managed version of Apache Spark to leverage the open data format Delta (which we'll cover in more detail shortly). This is one of the reasons why the Delta format is ideal for most use cases. However, nothing stops you from using something such as the CSV or Parquet format. Furthermore, Databricks introduced **Delta Lake Universal Format** (**Delta Lake UniForm**) to easily integrate with other file formats such as Iceberg or Hudi. For more details, check out the *Further reading* section at the end of this chapter.

Figure 1.2 illustrates the coming together of data formats with UniForm.

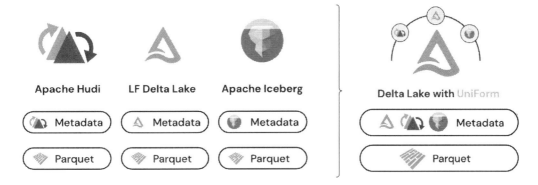

Figure 1.2 – Delta Lake UniForm makes consuming Hudi and
Iceberg file formats as easy as consuming Delta

The ability to use third-party and open source software fuels rapid innovation. New advances in data processing and ML can be quickly tested and integrated into your workflow. In contrast, proprietary systems often have longer wait times for vendors to incorporate updates. Waiting for a vendor to capitalize on open source innovation may seem rare, but it is the rule rather than the exception. This is especially true for data science. The speed of software and algorithmic advances is incredible. Evidence of this frantic pace of innovation can be seen daily on the Hugging Face community website. Developers share libraries and models on Hugging Face; hundreds of libraries are updated daily on the site alone.

Delta, Spark, the Pandas API on Spark (see *Figure 1.3*), and MLflow are notable examples of consistent innovation, largely driven by their transparency as open source projects. We mention these specifically because they were all initially created by either the founders of Databricks or company members following its formation.

ML developers benefit significantly from this transparency, as it provides them with unparalleled flexibility, easy integration, and robust support from the open source community – all without the overhead of maintaining an open source full stack.

Starting development as a contractor using Databricks is super-fast compared to when companies require a fresh development environment to be set up. Some companies require a service request to install Python libraries. This can be a productivity killer for data scientists. In Databricks, many of your favorite libraries are pre-installed and ready to use, and of course, you can easily install your own libraries as well.

Additionally, there is a large and vibrant community of Databricks users. The Databricks community website is an excellent resource to ask and answer questions about anything related to Databricks. We've included a link in the *Further reading* section at the end of this chapter.

```
1    import pandas as pd
2
3    df = pd.read_csv(r'/folder/single.csv', sep=',', decimal='.')
4    df.columns = ['a', 'b', 'c']
5    df['a2'] = df.a * df.a
6    spark.createDataFrame(df).write.saveAsTable("pandas_as_table")
```

```
1    import pyspark.pandas as ps
2
3    df = ps.read_csv(r'/folder-of-csv-files/', sep=',', decimal='.')
4    df.columns = ['a','b','c']
5    df['a2'] = df.a * df.a
6    df.to_table("pyspark_pandas_as_table")
```

Figure 1.3 – The pandas API on Spark

The pandas API on Spark is nearly identical syntax to standard pandas, making distributed computing with Spark easier to learn for those who have written pandas code in Python

While continuing with a focus on transparency, let's move on to Databricks **AutoML**.

Databricks AutoML

Databricks refers to its AutoML solution as a **glass box**. This terminology highlights the fact that there is nothing hidden from the user. This feature in the Data Intelligence Platform leverages an open source library, Hyperopt, in conjunction with Spark for hyperparameter tuning. It intelligently explores different model types in addition to optimizing the parameters in a distributed fashion. The use of Hyperopt allows each run within the AutoML experiment to inform the next run, reducing the overall number of runs needed to reach an optimal solution compared to a grid search. Each run in the experiment has an associated notebook with the code for the model. This method increases productivity, reduces unnecessary computing, and lets scientists perform experiments instead of writing boilerplate code. Once AutoML has converged on the algorithmically optimal solution, there is a "best notebook" for the best scoring model. We'll expand on AutoML in several chapters throughout this book.

Reusability and reproducibility

As data scientists, transparency is especially important. We do not trust black box models. How do you use them without understanding them? A model is only as good as the data going in. In addition to not trusting the models, black boxes create concerns about our research's reproducibility and model drivers' explainability.

When we create a model, who does it belong to? Can we get access to it? Can we tweak, test, and, most importantly, reuse it? The amount of time put into the model's creation is not negligible. Databricks AutoML gives you everything to explain, reproduce, and reuse the models it creates. In fact, you can take the model code or model object and run it on a laptop or wherever. This open source, glass-box, reproducible, and reusable methodology is our kind of open.

Open file formats give you flexibility

Flexibility is also an essential aspect of the Databricks platform, so let's dive into the file format Delta, an open source project that makes it easy to adapt to many different use cases. For those familiar with Parquet, you can think of Delta as Parquet-plus – Delta files are Parquet files with a transaction log. The transaction log is a game changer. The increased reliability and optimizations make Delta the foundation of Databricks' lakehouse architecture. The data lake side of the lakehouse is vital to data science, streaming, and unstructured and semi-structured data formats. Delta has also made the warehouse side possible. There are entire books on Delta; see the *Further reading* section for some examples. We are focusing on the fact that it is an open file format with key features that support building data products.

Integration and control

Having an open file format is essential to maintain ownership of your data. Not only do you want to be able to read, alter, and open your data files, but you also want to keep them in your cloud tenant. Maintaining control over your data is possible in the Databricks Data Intelligence Platform. There is no need to put the data files into a proprietary format or lock them away in a vendor's cloud. Take a look at *Figure 1.4* to see how Delta is part of the larger ecosystem.

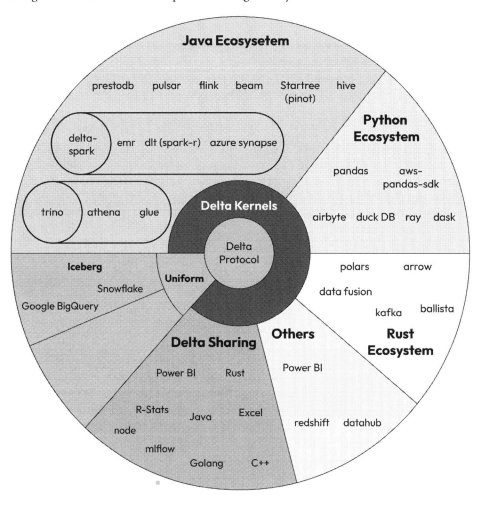

Figure 1.4 – The Delta Kernel connection ecosystem

The Delta Kernel introduces a fresh approach, offering streamlined, focused, and reliable APIs that abstract away the intricacies of the Delta protocol. By simply updating the Kernel version, connector developers can seamlessly access the latest Delta features without needing to modify any code.

Time-travel versioning in Delta

The freedom and flexibility of open file formats make it possible to integrate with new and existing external tooling. Delta Lake, in particular, offers unique support to create data products thanks to features such as time-travel versioning, exceptional speed, and the ability to update and merge changes. Time travel, in this context, refers to the capability of querying different versions of your data table, allowing you to revisit the state of the table before your most recent changes or transformations (see *Figure 1.5*). The more obvious use is to back up after making a mistake rather than writing out multiple copies of the table as a safety measure. A possibly less obvious use for time travel is reproducible research. You can access the data your model was trained on in the previous week without creating an additional copy of the data. Throughout the book, we will detail features of the Data Intelligence Platform you can use to facilitate reproducible research. The following figure shows you how the previous version of a table, relative to a timestamp or a version number, can be queried.

```
1    -- view table as it was by timestamp
2    SELECT * FROM ml_in_action.favorita_forecasting.favorita_transactions TIMESTAMP AS OF '2023-09-29 22:57:25';
3
4    -- view table as it was by version
5    SELECT * FROM lakehouse_in_action.favorita_forecasting.favorita_transactions VERSION AS OF 1;
```

Figure 1.5 – A code example of the querying techniques to view previous versions of a table

The speed of Databricks' optimized combination

Next, let us discuss the speed of Databricks' lakehouse architecture. In November 2021, Databricks set a new world record for the gold standard performance benchmark for data warehousing. The Barcelona Computing Group shared their research supporting this finding. This record-breaking speed resulted from the Databricks' engines (Spark and Photon) paired with Delta (see the *Databricks Sets Official Data Warehousing Performance Record* link in the *Further reading* section).

The additional benefits of Delta

Delta's impressive features include **change data feed (CDF)**, **change data capture (CDC)**, and **schema evolution**. Each plays a specific role in data transformation in support of ML.

Starting with Delta's CDF capability, it is exactly what it sounds like – a feed of the changed data. Let's say you have a model looking for fraud, and that model needs to know how many transaction requests have occurred in the last 10 minutes. It is not feasible to rewrite the entire table each time a value for an account needs to be updated. The feature value, or in this case, the number of transactions that occurred in the last 10 minutes, needs to be updated only when the value has changed. The use of CDF in this example enables updates to be passed to an **online feature store**; see *Chapters 5* and *6* for more details.

Finally, let's talk about change data capture, a game-changer in the world of data management. Unlike traditional filesystems, CDC in Delta has been purposefully designed to handle data updates efficiently. Let's take a closer look at CDC and explore its capabilities through two practical scenarios:

- **Scenario 1 – effortless record updates**: Picture a scenario involving Rami, one of your customers. He initially made a purchase in Wisconsin but later relocated to Colorado, where he continued to make purchases. In your records, it's essential to reflect Rami's new address in Colorado. Here's where Delta's CDC shines. It effortlessly updates Rami's customer record without treating him as a new customer. CDC excels at capturing and applying updates seamlessly, ensuring data integrity without any hassles.

- **Scenario 2 – adapting to evolving data sources**: Now, consider a situation where your data source experiences unexpected changes, resulting in adding a new column containing information about your customers. Let's say this new column provides insights into the colors of items purchased by customers. This is valuable data that you wouldn't want to lose. Delta's CDC, combined with its schema evolution feature, comes to the rescue.

Schema evolution, explored in depth in *Chapter 3*, enables Delta to gracefully adapt to schema changes without causing any disruptions. When dealing with a new data column, Delta smoothly incorporates this information, ensuring your data remains up to date while retaining its full historical context. This ensures that you can leverage valuable insights for both present and future analyses.

Applying our learning

This book is heavily project-based. Each chapter starts with an overview of the important concepts and Data Intelligence Platform features that will prepare you for the main event – the *Applying our learning* sections. Every *Applying our learning* section has a *Technical requirements* section so that you know what technical resources you will need, in addition to your Databricks workspace and GitHub repository, to complete the project work in the respective chapter.

Technical requirements

Here are the technical requirements needed to get started with the hands-on examples used throughout this book:

- We use Kaggle for two of our datasets. If you do not already have an account, you will need to create one.

- Throughout the book, we will refer to code in GitHub. Create an account if you do not already have one.

Getting to know your data

There are four main projects that progress sequentially throughout the book. In each subsequent chapter, the code will expand upon the code in previous chapters. We chose these projects to highlight a variety of Data Intelligence Platform features across different ML projects. Specifically, we include streaming data into your lakehouse architecture, forecasting sales, building a **deep learning** (**DL**) model for computer vision, and building a chatbot using **Retrieval Augmented Generation** (**RAG**) techniques. Read through the descriptions of each project to get an idea of what it will cover. If some of the concepts and features are unfamiliar, don't worry! We'll explain them in the following chapters.

Project – streaming transactions

This first project is a data solution for the streaming transactions dataset we will generate. The transaction data will include information such as the customer ID and transaction time, which we'll use to simulate transactions streaming in real time; see the sample data in *Figure 1.6*.

Amount	CustomerID	Label	Product	TransactionTimestamp
10.0	1240	0	Product A	2023-12-12T23:36:16.284Z
250.01	1253	0	Product A	2023-12-12T23:36:16.284Z
10.0	1254	0	Product A	2023-12-12T23:36:16.284Z
250.01	1253	0	Product A	2023-12-12T23:36:16.284Z
69.99	1244	0	Product A	2023-12-12T23:36:16.284Z
10.0	1247	0	Product A	2023-12-12T23:36:16.284Z
250.01	1242	0	Product A	2023-12-12T23:36:16.284Z

Figure 1.6 – A sample of the synthetic streaming transactions data

Our goal with this project is to demonstrate how flexible the Data Intelligence Platform is compared to proprietary data warehouses of the past, which were more rigid for data ingestion. Additionally, we want to highlight important Databricks capabilities such as **Spark Structured Streaming**, **Auto Loader**, schema evolution, Delta Live Tables, and **Lakehouse Monitoring**.

When we generate the transactions, we also generate a label based on statistical distributions (note that the label is random and only used for learning purposes). This is the label we will be predicting. Our journey includes generating transaction records as multiline JSON files, formatting the files to a Delta table, creating a streaming feature for our ML model, wrapping a **Light Gradient-Boosting Machine** (**LightGBM** or **LGBM**) model in a Python function (`pyfunc`) with the preprocessing steps, and deploying the model wrapper via a workflow. Take a look through the project pipeline in *Figure 1.7* to understand how we'll progress through this project.

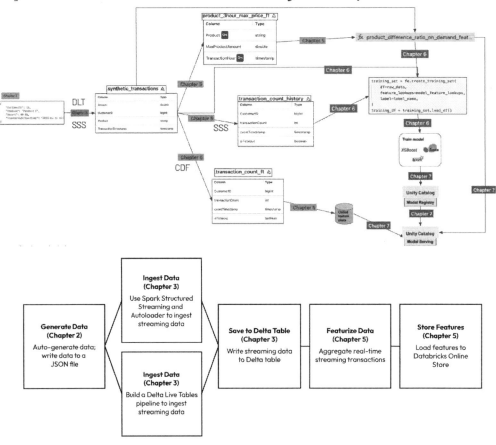

Figure 1.7 – The project pipeline for the streaming transactions project

That concludes the streaming transaction project explanation. Next, we will look at the forecasting project.

Project – Favorita sales forecasting

This is a typical forecasting project. Our dataset is hosted on the Kaggle website (see the *Further reading* section). We will use the data to build a model to predict the total sales amount for a family of goods at a specific Favorita store in Ecuador. The data includes train, test, and supplementary data. This project will use Databricks' AutoML for data exploration and to create a baseline model. Take a look through the project pipeline in *Figure 1.8* to understand how we'll progress through this project. The store sales dataset is a rich time-series dataset, and we encourage you to build on the project framework we provide using your favorite time-series library.

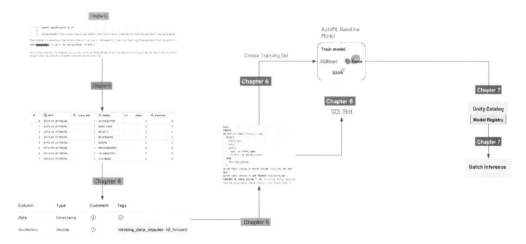

Figure 1.8 – The project pipeline for the Favorita store sales project

That concludes the forecasting project explanation. Next, we will look at the DL project.

Project – multilabel image classification

This project is a DL data solution that uses another Kaggle dataset. We will use these datasets images to fine-tune a deep-learning model, using PyTorch and Lightning to predict a corresponding label. We will implement MLflow code for experiment and model tracking, Spark for fast training and **inference**, and Delta for data version control. We will deploy the model as we would for a real-time scenario by creating a model wrapper, similar to the wrapper we use for the streaming transactions project. Take a look through the project pipeline in *Figure 1.9* to understand how we'll progress through this project.

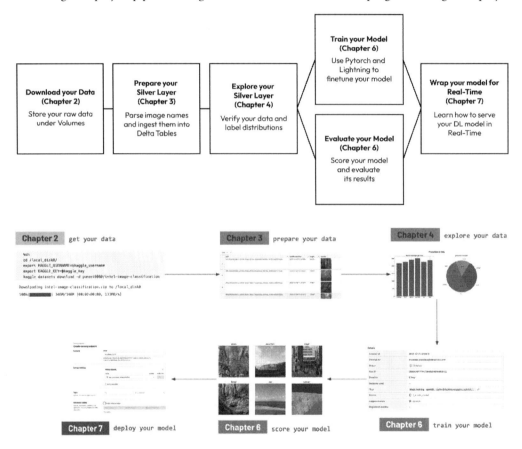

Figure 1.9 – The project pipeline for the multilabel image classification project

That concludes the image classification project explanation. Next, we will look at the chatbot project.

Project – a retrieval augmented generation chatbot

This project is a RAG chatbot. The dataset we use comes from the *arXiv* website. We have selected a few research articles about the impact of generative AI on humans and labor. We will download and store them in a volume in *Chapter 2*. After we download the PDF documents, we will extract and prepare the text through a process of chunking and tokenization, creating embeddings of the documents to be referenced in the chatbot. We will use Databricks Vector Search to store the embeddings. Then, we will use the new Foundation Model API to generate answers when text is retrieved. The final bot will be deployed as an application using **Databricks Model Serving**. This example allows you to build a chatbot from start to finish! Take a look through the project pipeline in *Figure 1.10* to understand how we'll progress through this project.

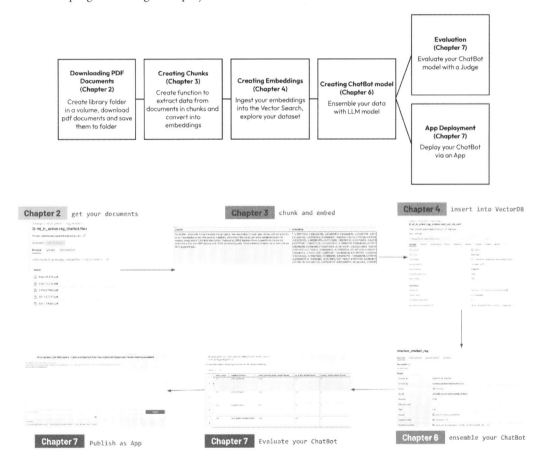

Figure 1.10 – The project pipeline for the chatbot project

The four projects are hands-on examples that can be implemented on Databricks. *Databricks ML in Action* provides best practices and recommendations from an ML perspective based on our experiences and supplements online documentation. All the code and solutions presented in this book have been developed and tested on the full version of Databricks. However, we understand that accessibility matters. There is also a free community version of the Databricks Data Intelligence Platform available, enabling everyone to follow along with the examples to a certain point before considering an upgrade.

Summary

In this chapter, we introduced you to *Databricks ML in Action*. We emphasized that the Databricks Data Intelligence Platform is designed with openness, flexibility, and tooling freedom in mind, which greatly accelerates productivity. Additionally, we've given you a sneak peek at the projects and the associated datasets that will be central to this book.

Now that you've gained a foundational understanding of the Data Intelligence Platform, it's time to take the next step. In the upcoming chapter, we'll guide you through setting up your environment and provide instructions on downloading the project data. This will prepare you for the practical, hands-on ML experiences that lie ahead in this journey.

Questions

Let's test ourselves on what we've learned by going through the following questions:

1. How will you use this book? Do you plan to go cover to cover or pick certain sections out? Have you chosen sections of interest?

2. We covered why transparency in modeling is critical to success. How does Databricks' glass-box approach to AutoML support this?

3. Databricks has developed a new way of uniting the open data formats, called UniForm. Which data formats does UniForm unite?

4. Delta is the foundation of the lakehouse architecture. What is one of the benefits of using Delta?

5. What is the main advantage of using the Delta file format for large-scale data processing over simple Parquet files in Databricks?

Answers

After putting thought into the questions, compare your answers to ours:

1. We cannot answer this question, but we hope you learn something you can use in your career soon!

2. The glass-box approach supports transparency by providing the code run for each run in the experiment and the best run, thus enabling reusability and reproducibility.

3. Apache Iceberg, Apache Hudi, and Linux Foundation Delta Lake (an open source/unmanaged version of Delta).

4. There are several. Here are a few:

   * Open protocol (no vendor lock-in)

   * Speed

   * Change data capture

   * Time travel

5. While Parquet also provides columnar storage and has efficient read/write operations, its lack of ACID transaction capabilities distinguishes Delta Lake.

Further reading

In this chapter, we introduced vital technologies. Look at these resources to go deeper into the areas that interest you most:

* YouTube video – *Introduction to Databricks Data Intelligence Platform*: `https://youtu.be/E885Ld3N2As?si=1NPg85phVH8RhayO`

* *Introduction to Data Lakes*: `https://www.databricks.com/discover/data-lakes`

* *5 Steps to a Successful Data Lakehouse* by Bill Inmon, father of the data warehouse: `https://www.databricks.com/resources/ebook/building-the-data-lakehouse`

* *Delta Lake: Up & Running* by O'Reilly: `https://www.databricks.com/resources/ebook/delta-lake-running-oreilly`

* *Delta Lake: The Definitive Guide*: `https://www.oreilly.com/library/view/delta-lake-the/9781098151935/`

* *Comparing Apache Spark and Databricks*: `https://www.databricks.com/spark/comparing-databricks-to-apache-spark`

* *Databricks MLflow*: `https://www.databricks.com/product/managed-mlflow`

* *Databricks Community Edition FAQ*: `https://www.databricks.com/product/faq/community-edition#:~:text=What%20is%20the%20difference%20between,ODBC%20integrations%20for%20BI%20analysis`

* *Delta 2.0 - The Foundation of your Data Lakehouse is Open*: `https://delta.io/blog/2022-08-02-delta-2-0-the-foundation-of-your-data-lake-is-open/`

* *Delta Lake Integrations*: `https://delta.io/integrations/`

- *Delta vs Iceberg*: https://databeans-blogs.medium.com/delta-vs-iceberg-performance-as-a-decisive-criteria-add7bcdde03d

- *UniForm*: https://www.databricks.com/blog/delta-uniform-universal-format-lakehouse-interoperability

- *Delta Kernel: Simplifying Building Connectors for Delta*: https://www.databricks.com/dataaisummit/session/delta-kernel-simplifying-building-connectors-delta/

- *Databricks Community Website*: https://community.cloud.databricks.com

- *Podcast: Delta Lake Discussions with Denny Lee*: https://open.spotify.com/show/6YvPDkILtWfnJNTzJ9HsmW?si=214eb7d808d84aa4

- *Databricks Sets Official Data Warehousing Performance Record*: https://www.databricks.com/blog/2021/11/02/databricks-sets-official-data-warehousing-performance-record.html

- *LightGBM*: https://github.com/microsoft/LightGBM https://lightgbm.readthedocs.io/en/latest/

- *Kaggle | Store Sales*: https://www.kaggle.com/competitions/store-sales-time-series-forecasting/overview

- *Kaggle | Multi Label Image Classification*: https://www.kaggle.com/datasets/meherunnesashraboni/multi-label-image-classification-dataset

- *Store Sales - Time Series Forecasting*: Kaggle.com/competitions/store-sales-time-series-forecasting/overview

- *arXiv website*: https://arxiv.org

2
Designing Databricks: Day One

"Design is not just what it looks like and feels like. Design is how it works."

- Steve Jobs

This chapter will introduce concepts and topics that engineers, data scientists, and people in similar roles should know to set themselves up for success in the Databricks Data Intelligence Platform. When setting up your data and AI platform, in our case, Databricks, there are always best practices to follow. We share those in this chapter to give you a better understanding of the setup options and their impacts; these can be strategic decisions that impact the entire data product workflow, as well as simply matters of preference. We start by explaining Databrick's general architecture and key terminology, then cover the most important decisions to be made during platform setup, and conclude with code examples and configurations to download the data for our example projects. We also introduce a variety of platform features and components throughout the chapter, which we will cover in more detail throughout the rest of this book. Here is what you will learn as part of this chapter:

Here is what you will learn about as part of this chapter:

- Planning your platform
- Defining a workspace
- Selecting the metastore
- Discussing data preparation
- Planning to create features
- Modeling in Databricks
- Applying learning

Planning your platform

This section covers topics for discussion before and during the DI Platform setup process. The role of the data team often determines the platform setup. One of Databricks' ideal attributes is that the technology stack is unified, making the setup and collaboration between teams more straightforward. The data team reporting structure frequently determines the border where one role ends and another begins, rather than the actual data product workflow. Luckily, we do not have to worry because the DI Platform serves data engineers, scientists, and analysts alike.

In *Figure 2.1*, you can see an end-to-end lakehouse architecture and the components in Databricks.

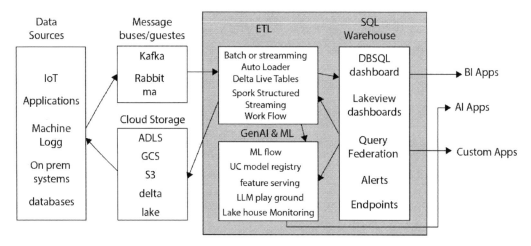

Figure 2.1 – Overview of a lakehouse architecture and how Databricks DI Platform fits this paradigm

The DI Platform consists of one or more Databricks accounts. Most of the time, companies only have one. However, there are situations where companies require extra environment isolation, and having separate accounts for development, staging, and production is an option. Discussion about multiple accounts for levels of isolation is outside of this book's scope, but if you have questions or want to know more, please check out the resources in *Further reading*.

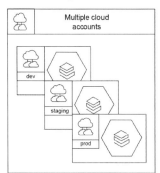 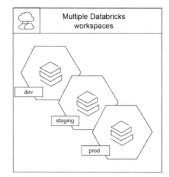 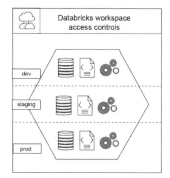

Figure 2.2 – Visual representation of the environment isolation options

We separate our environments using different catalogs. Most of this book's project work occurs using the ml_in_action catalog. For the production version of some models, we use the ml_in_prod catalog. Setting up multiple workspaces is another way to separate environments. We recommend using documentation and your company policies to guide your isolation setup. Let's move on to what precisely a workspace is in the context of Databricks.

Defining a workspace

It's important to know that Databricks uses the word **workspace** to refer to two distinct components: an instance of Databricks (meaning your hosted Databricks deployment that you access via your unique URL address) and the folder environment for accessing your work products, like notebooks, queries, and dashboards.

Let's go through the two components:

- **Workspace as an instance**: A Databricks account can have multiple workspaces attached to it, meaning instances of the DI Platform are deployed and often accessible from a browser, as mentioned previously, but are also accessible via an SDK or a REST API.

- **Workspace as a folder**: Workspace also refers to the folder that contains your user's home folder, repositories, projects, and a shared folder that is visible to all users on the workspace instance. Often, users set their main system path to their Workspace folder to store their MLFlow experiments or Terraform states for pipeline deployment. You can also create and store notebooks outside source control in your home and project folders.

We now have a clearer understanding of a workspace. Now let's discuss why we choose **Unity Catalog (UC)** as our preferred metastore.

Selecting the metastore

A metastore is a system that stores metadata for a data platform and can be thought of as the top-level container of objects. It registers a variety of information about databases, tables, views, **User-Defined Functions (UDFs)**, and other data assets. Metadata includes details such as storage location and the permissions that govern access to each asset.

Two types of metastores are natively available in the DI Platform: **Unity Catalog (UC)** and the **Hive Metastore (HMS)**. UC has a three-level namespace consisting of a catalog, a database (also called a schema), and a table name. In contrast, the HMS only uses a two-level namespace containing just a database and table name. A metastore is required for your Databricks Workspace instance, as this is the component that organizes and governs data access. Deciding on the right metastore is an early decision in your DI Platform journey, and we recommend Unity Catalog. Let's talk about why.

Notice in *Figure 2.3* that you can have multiple workspaces assigned to the same metastore. **Access Controls** and **User Management** are scoped to the account level, as shown in the figure. A UC **Metastore**, a group of catalogs, is scoped to a region with precisely one metastore per region. Within the region, you can easily share **Data**, **Features**, **Volumes** access, **Functions**, and **Models**.

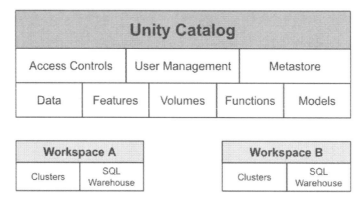

Figure 2.3 – The Design of Unity Catalog with multiple workspaces

Unity Catalog is more than a group of data assets. UC also tracks who has accessed assets, which makes auditing a simple exercise. Using UC allows companies to administer privileges and secure data and objects easily while being able to share them between various workspaces. Securely sharing between environments is one of the reasons why we recommend using the UC metastore.

The HMS design is less centralized than that of UC. For example, historically, workspaces have been created as data and code isolation, meaning there is a separate workspace for separate isolation levels. This design often required a centralized model registry workspace in addition to development, staging, and production workspaces. If not using UC, each workspace requires its own HMS and user and group management. In contrast, UC governs all assets at the account level rather than the individual workspace level; see *Figure 2.3*, *Figure 2.4*, and *Further reading*. The centralized governance model provides the ability to integrate multiple workspaces more seamlessly.

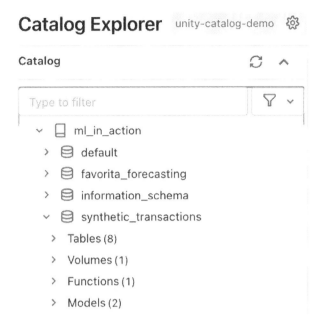

Figure 2.4 – UC governs all assets under catalogs, including
databases, tables, volumes, functions, and models

Deciding on your metastore does not have to be a permanent choice. However, migrating later could become a headache. UC is continually improving and integrating with new Databricks features. The list of reasons to choose UC over HMS continues to grow, and our recommendation is to begin with and stick with UC.

To determine whether Unity Catalog is the right choice for you and your company, you can check out the shrinking list of limitations for choosing UC in *Further reading*. As UC continues to expand in capability, it is the path of the future. Specifically, for machine learning, there is an integration with the Feature Engineering client and the new Model Registry. Using the UC Model Registry for model sharing and governing is simpler. We will cover more about the Model Registry in Unity Catalog and Databricks Feature Engineering Client in *Chapters 5, 6,* and *7,* but if you're curious and eager to learn more now, you can check out Manage model lifecycle in Unity Catalog in the Further reading section. Given the ever-growing number of reasons to use UC, all project code in this book will use UC.

Defining where the data lives, and cloud object storage

All data products start with data, and so how we make the data accessible for data teams is another important early design choice. Databricks is a cloud-based platform that connects to cloud object storage – **Azure Data Lake Storage (ADLS)**, Amazon **Simple Storage Service (S3)**, or **Google Cloud Storage (GCS)**. There is a separation of compute and storage. Databricks orchestrates compute; the data is in cloud object storage.

Originally, data had to be in cloud object storage before being utilized on the DI Platform. Now, **Query Federation** allows customers to query their data no matter where it resides (see the documentation for any possible limitations) without first worrying about ingestion and data engineering from that remote system. However, that is data in memory, not persistent data. You can land your data in cloud storage in various ways. There are many documentation sources and external tools for the actual landing of data in cloud storage. These may depend on your cloud service provider of choice. Despite best practices of storing data in your cloud storage, using the **Databricks File System** (**DBFS**) to store the data for this book's example projects is also possible.

DBFS is a shared filesystem provided by Databricks that all users of a given workspace can access. Any data stored in DBFS is potentially accessible to all users, regardless of their group, role, or permissions. Therefore, only non-sensitive and non-production data you are willing to share openly across your organization should be in DBFS. An example of non-sensitive data would be the publicly available *Kaggle* datasets. This lack of governance is why we recommend storing data in Databricks volumes, where you can apply governance. We will cover more on volumes in the last section of this chapter.

When it comes to cloud storage, the optimal format for structured data is almost always Delta, which we talked about in detail in *Chapter 1*. When a table is stored in the Delta format, we refer to it as a Delta table. You can choose tables to be "managed" or "external" tables. We use both types of tables in this book (the choice is justified when required). Please see the resources in *Further reading* for more information on the two types of tables.

Discussing source control

Whether or not to use a source control is usually not the question. The question is how should someone use it? Databricks has a few features that can aid in source control.

The first is the version history that is built into notebooks. The history of changes for each notebook is tracked even before submitting it to a remote repository using Git. Version tracking is beneficial as we are not always ready to make a Git commit but still want to track progress and collaborate. It's also a game changer if you accidentally pull someone's code into your working remote branch and forget to push your code before it. The notebook's history will keep your edited copy so you can simply roll back in time and restore all your work!

The second feature is the ease of connecting notebooks and files in your workspace to a remote Git repository. Historically, saving Jupyter notebooks to remote repositories was a technical nightmare for code reviews, sharing, and diffs. The Databricks code repository integration allows Databricks notebooks to contain multiple languages (Python, Scala, SQL) and track them as nicely as a typical Python file. This ability to track notebooks in source as a standard file is an improvement for data engineers and scientists wanting to review notebooks compared to previously converting files to Python and losing all output and images. The days of setting up hooks to automatically save your notebook as a regular Python file every time you save your notebook are over.

Of course, you can store standard file formats such as markdown, delimiter separated, JSON, or YML for a whole reproducibility approach. Note that we do not recommend keeping data under repos unless it's a data sample for testing.

Within a repository, how a team defines the expected folder structure for each project is generally less important than the consistent use of that structure. However, defining your project structure is still important. We recommend reading through *Big Book of MLOps* (Joseph Bradley, Rafi Kurlansik, Matthew Thomson, and Niall Turbitt, 2023, *Big Book of MLOps, second edition*, `https://www.databricks.com/resources/ebook/the-big-book-of-mlops`) to determine the best structure for your team or organization. As we will see in future chapters, MLflow and repositories are essential for **reproducible research**. In the world of data science and machine learning specifically, we want to ensure the reproduction of models and experiments.

Discussing data preparation

Generally, the first step for any data science project is to explore and prepare the data. We will refer to this process as moving the data from "Bronze" to "Silver" layers in reference to the Medallion architecture methodology. You might think of this type of data transformation exclusively as a data engineering task, but it's also essential for data science and machine learning.

If you aren't familiar with this architecture terminology, the **Medallion architecture** is a data design pattern used to organize data logically in a warehouse. This architecture is also commonly called "multi-hop" architecture. It aims to incrementally and progressively improve the structure and quality of data as it flows through each layer. The Medallion architecture has three layers: Bronze, Silver, and Gold, listed as follows:

- The **Bronze** layer is the raw data layer. It contains all the raw, unprocessed data ingested from the source systems. This data still needs to be cleaned or transformed.

- The **Silver** layer is the validated data layer. It contains data that has been cleaned and is subject to various validation and transformation steps. This data is ready to be used for analysis and modeling.

- The **Gold** layer is the enriched data layer. It is the highest level and contains data enriched with additional information, such as business intelligence metrics and key performance indicators, to meet the requirements of the business users.

The Medallion architecture is a flexible and customizable architecture that can meet the specific needs of each organization. The Medallion architecture is compatible with the concept of Data Mesh. Data Mesh is an architectural and organizational paradigm to ensure value from data. Lakehouse and Data Mesh are complementary, paradigms. See *Further reading* for blog posts on leveraging a data mesh with the DI Platform. This distributed data architecture enables organizations to unlock the value of their data by making it accessible and usable by everyone in the organization.

Communication and collaboration are vital for the data preparation process. This step involves identifying and correcting errors, filling in missing values, and resolving inconsistencies in the data. The actions you take should be discussed as a team and documented. This is especially important when working collaboratively across data teams because data engineers and data scientists often have different perspectives on how data should be prepared. For example, we have seen situations where an engineer imputed all the missing values in a column with a zero. The rationalization made sense; many zeros were already in the column, making the KPIs' values come out correctly. However, from a modeling perspective, missing data differs from zeros, especially if there are already zeros in the dataset. The approach of replacing nulls with zeros is not necessarily incorrect; it simply needs to be discussed with the downstream consumers of the data. One helpful communication tool is the column tagging functionality from the Databricks Catalog UI. See *Figure 2.5* for an example:

Column	Type	Comment	Tags
date	timestamp	⊕	⊕
dcoilwtico	double	⊕	**missing_data_imputer**: fill_forward

Figure 2.5 – Example of how to use tagging in a catalog to communicate
the transformation performed on a column to all table users

This implementation of an incorrect imputation method also serves as an example of wanting to go back and reprocess history. Luckily, using the Medallion architecture methodology is a saving grace. In the situation mentioned previously, the chosen imputation would only be present in the Silver and Gold data layers. Meanwhile, the Bronze layer still contains the original raw data, so the source of truth is not lost, and reprocessing is possible.

One of the ways that the Databricks Platform boosts productivity and collaboration is the feature of real-time collaboration support for notebooks. This feature allows two or more people to simultaneously see and edit a notebook. The ability to pair-program virtually during the pandemic was a lifesaver for many. We're big fans of people who have worked remotely for much of our careers. Collaborative editing of a notebook is much easier than sharing code via video call. While there are many options for reviewing code, historically, reviewing code in notebooks has been difficult, particularly when committing notebooks to source control.

After completing transformations, documentation is easy using markdown in notebooks. Even if the resulting notebook is not not itself designated for production ETL, documenting the how and why of your data transformations is important for all downstream users. To read more about Databricks notebooks, see the documentation in *Further reading*.

Planning to create features

A data engineer may build Gold tables from Silver tables for consumption by the business. At the same time, a data scientist is building features from the same Silver tables for models. If we aren't careful, two people working separately without communication can create different versions of the same metrics. When architecting your unified DI Platform, be sure to think about reusability and maintainability. For this reason, with features specifically, the features-as-code approach is our recommendation. Features-as-code refers to the software development practice *everything is code*, with a focus on creating a repository of reusable code to define features rather than features stored in tables.

You can implement features-as-code in various ways. Initially, we mainly focus on function reusability. You can place functions you execute in multiple notebooks or scripts in a folder within the repository root directory. In the *Applying our learning* section, you will see this is where we store functions even when not calculating a feature per se. We call these the utils. You will be referencing the `mlia_utils` notebook throughout the example projects.

You can find the `mlia_utils` functions in the root folder of the GitHub repository (`https://github.com/PacktPublishing/Databricks-Lakehouse-ML-In-Action`). We walk through pulling the GitHub repository into Databricks in the *Applying our learning* section. In it, you will find Python files containing useful functions we will use in the projects. It is best practice to save, share, and track functions so that the metrics and features we calculate are consistent. Note the empty `__init__.py` file is also in the `utils` folder. Having an `__init__.py` file is required. With this structure, we can use all functions as imports, for example, from `mlia_utils.rag_funcs` import `extract_doc_text`.

Features-as-code is not only a way to reduce duplicative work by reusing functions. It is also a great way to ensure consistent business metrics. For example, online advertising often has complex calculations for the different types of revenue. Therefore, if other people or teams calculate business-critical metrics differently, it will be hard to establish the true metric value. Instead, you can often avoid this confusion by providing executive-approved functions for use. We will talk about this again in *Chapters 5* and *6*. In addition to features being centrally located and thus easier to find, Databricks offers easy ways to document your data assets.

Creating a business process requiring the team to document tables and functions with descriptions makes current and previous efforts more discoverable. In the Databricks Catalog UI, you should see *AI-generated* suggestions to fill in your table and column descriptions, so you don't have to start from scratch. Another great way to document transformations performed on a data table would be using tags. Tags can help with documentation and communication. Recall the example of missing data being imputed (*Figure 2.5*).

Focusing on ML features more specifically, you will learn how to store and serve feature functions to simplify your final deployment process. You will create an on-demand feature function and use it in your model. We also will show you how to leverage saved feature tables to create training sets. If you want to jump ahead right away, see *Chapter 5*, where we cover topics such as on-demand feature functions, feature lookups, syncing to the online store, and the Databricks Feature Engineering client.

Modeling in Databricks

After features have been created and stored as feature tables, we create training sets and focus on model training. We will cover modeling in terms of leveraging Databricks to facilitate the model lifecycle in *Chapter 6*. In *Chapter 7*, we'll discuss the Unity Catalog Registry and how to use it to track an enormous amount of information from the associated experiments, in addition to details such as model lineage. You can register multiple versions of a model at every stage and can give these different versions aliases, such as **champion** and **challenger**, or a more specific alias referring to versions A and B in an A/B test. See aliasing in *Figure 2.6*.

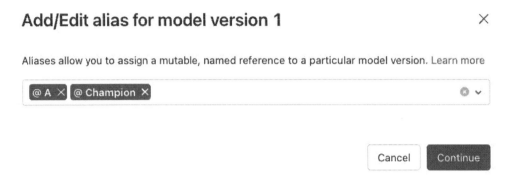

Figure 2.6 – A user can alias a model with specific names for A/B testing or multi-armed bandits

In *Chapter 7*, we demonstrate how to trigger a testing script to test every model before having a human review it. Testing models is an efficient practice to reduce the time to production when used consistently and with intention. We suggest defining the criteria for successfully transitioning models/code through isolation environments (from development to stage to production). Clearly defined environments are one of the practices that enable you to create clear and consistent model quality expectations across all models. Be sure to consult *The Big Book of MLOps* on best practices for isolation and model promotion. No matter where your environment is, it is beneficial to incorporate logging into model experimentation.

We discuss logging in the ML context rather than the software development sense. Logging for ML is focused on reproducible research and is also known as experiment tracking. It is common practice to track the following:

- The input data used to train a model
- The parameters used to train a model
- The accuracy and speed performance of a model during training and inference
- The errors that occur during training and inference
- The runtime environment of a model

When using MLflow, you have access to a powerful feature called automatic logging, or autologging. Autologging is excellent because it makes it easy to track the parameters, metrics, and artifacts of your machine learning experiments without explicit instructions.

> **Note**
>
> Auto logging only tracks flavors supported by MLflow. Custom *pyfunc* models are not supported. For more information, check *Further reading*.

MLflow auto logging logs parameter values and models for each run in a single experiment. Every time you train and evaluate your model, MLflow logs your standard metrics and parameters. If you have custom metrics to track with your models, you can also easily add them. We demonstrate tracking custom metrics in *Chapter 6*, when we log parameters for the streaming transactions model.

An admin can enable auto logging for all notebooks attached to interactive clusters at the workspace level. At the cluster level, you can add `spark.databricks.mlflow.autologging.enabled=true` to the advanced section of your cluster configuration to turn on auto logging with a cluster scope. It is less common but possible to enable auto logging within a notebook scope by adding `mlflow.autolog()` to a Python cell in a notebook. Be sure to check the list of modeling flavors supported by autolog.

By default, MLflow saves the tracked items in the managed folder in DBFS (which will be in UC in the future). You can also set `artifact_location` to point to a volume path, which is what we do in the example projects. You also have the option to set the location to another cloud storage location, although doing so eliminates the ability to see your experiments in the MLflow UI.

The MLflow UI makes it incredibly easy to compare each trail; see *Figures 2.7* and *2.8*.

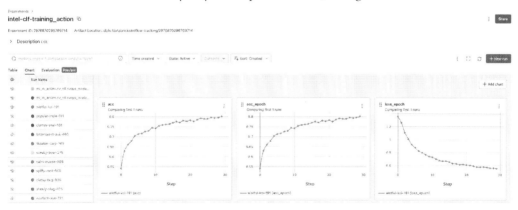

Figure 2.7 – Comparison of experiment runs using the MLflow UI

There are numerous options for visualizing the results of experiments tracked using MLflow.

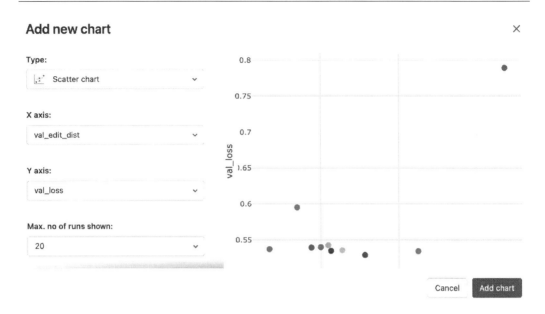

Figure 2.8 – Graphically comparing parameters and model performance in the MLflow UI

We've examined how to compare parameters and model performance in your experiment using the MLflow UI. Next, we'll look at how to use model monitoring (Lakehouse monitoring) to keep track of your model's performance over time.

Monitoring data and models

When we think about model monitoring and how to implement it, it becomes less about the actual model itself and more about the model's input and output. For this reason, Databricks Lakehouse Monitoring focuses on monitoring a model's input and output, which is simply data. The computation of table metrics occurs in the background using serverless compute, or as we like to call it, managed compute. Fully managed compute abstracts away the complexities and optimization so users focus on which tables to monitor, known as primary tables, rather than how. Lakehouse Monitoring is currently in public preview, meaning not all information is ready for release. For the latest on this feature, check out the Lakehouse Monitoring product page. We demonstrate how to use Lakehouse Monitoring in *Chapters 4 and 7*.

We've touched on a wide variety of topics so far, from the earliest design decisions when setting up your Databricks Data Intelligence Platform to the key topics we'll cover throughout the rest of this book. Now let's dive into the example projects. Get ready to follow along in your own Databricks workspace as you work through setting up your workspace.

Applying our learning

This chapter's *Applying our learning* section focuses on getting your Databricks workspace set up and ready for each project we'll be working through. We'll also go over getting set up in Kaggle so that you can download the datasets we will use throughout the rest of this book. Let's get started!

Technical requirements

Before we begin setting up a workspace, please review the technical requirements needed to complete the hands-on work in this chapter:

- We utilize a Python package, `opendatasets`, to download the data we need from the Kaggle API easily.

- We use the Databricks Labs Python library, `dbldatagen`, to generate synthetic data.

- To use the Kaggle API, you must download your credential file, `kaggle.json`.

- A GitHub account is beneficial for connecting Databricks and the code repository for the book (`https://github.com/PacktPublishing/Databricks-ML-In-Action`). In addition to a GitHub account, it is ideal to fork the book repository into your GitHub account. You will see that each chapter has a folder, and each project has a folder under the chapters. We will refer to the notebooks by name throughout the project work.

- We will use the Databricks Secrets API to save both Kaggle and OpenAI credentials. The Secrets API requires the Databricks CLI. We will walk through this setup. However, you will need to create a **personal access token** (**PAT**) on your own for the configuration step: `https://docs.databricks.com/en/dev-tools/auth/pat.html`

- The compute clusters we use are as follows (they vary slightly depending on your data cloud):

  - Single-node CPU configuration

Figure 2.9 – Single-node CPU cluster configuration, DBR ML 14.2

This will work for most workloads in this book.

Setting up your workspace

As defined previously, the workspace discussed in this section refers to the deployment instance. Here, we will discuss workspace setup recommendations, project setup files, and download instructions for each dataset used throughout this book.

There is comprehensive documentation on deploying your workspace for the first time. If you do not already have a Databricks account and deployed workspace, then you have a couple of places to start from. One method is going into your cloud account and activating Databricks through the marketplaces. Another method is to begin on the Databricks website. For more advanced users, consider using Terraform. Given the amount of documentation and the ever-changing world of technology, we leave the exercise of activating a workspace up to you.

Once we have a workspace deployed, we can begin setting it up. Generally, we start with user groups and governance. The experience of setting up Unity Catalog is frequently updated for simplicity. Therefore, we recommend you watch the latest video documentation on how to do so (see *Further reading*). The process is the same, regardless of the data persona using the platform. Please be sure to complete metastore and governance setup before going forward.

Kaggle setup

You will need a Kaggle account to download the Kaggle datasets we'll be using, which require an API token for authentication. There is an official Kaggle API, but, there are numerous other ways to connect to Kaggle to download data and interact with the Kaggle site as well. All methods require downloading your API credentials file, `kaggle.json`, from the Kaggle website. Before downloading data, you need to make your credentials accessible. Here are three methods for accomplishing this:

- **Option 1**: Upload the `kaggle.json` file to your project folder. If you choose to do this, be aware that your credentials are viewable to others, even if only admins. Also, add `kaggle.json` to your `.gitignore` file to prevent committing your credentials to the repository and ensure you do not commit your credentials to a Git repository.

- **Option 2**: Paste your credentials into a notebook with the same concerns as option one. Keeping secret API keys in your Databricks notebook is far from best practice, but it is the simplest option and you can lock down your notebook access and add a configuration notebook to your `.gitignore` file to prevent committing your credentials to the repository. However, the ability to remove other users' access may not be in your control, depending on your role. Furthermore, in general, admins can see all files.

```
1   import os
2   os.environ['kaggle_username'] = 'YOUR KAGGLE USERNAME HERE'
3
4   os.environ['kaggle_key'] = 'YOUR KAGGLE KEY HERE'
```

Figure 2.10 – Passing user credentials to the notebook

- **Option 3**: Use Databricks secrets to store and retrieve your username and token, for optimal security, as shown in *Figure 2.11*. This is the method we use for downloading images.

```
1   import os
2
3   os.environ['kaggle_username'] = dbutils.secrets.get("lakehouse-in-action",
    "kaggle_username")
4
5   os.environ['kaggle_key'] = dbutils.secrets.get("lakehouse-in-action", "kaggle_key")
```

Figure 2.11 – Using secrets to store and retrieve your username and token

This code is in global_setup.py, but you could also put it in the notebook itself

- **Option 4**: Use the `opendatasets` library to paste your credentials in at the time of download. This is a safe way to download data, so we demonstrate this with the Favorita Sales data.

We'll will walk through `global-setup.py` later. The last section of the file is setting your Kaggle credentials. We recommend setting up a secret scope with your credentials. We will show you how to set this up once you have a cluster running, so there is no need to jump around. Simply download your Kaggle credentials for now.

Setting up our GitHub repository

The first thing is to pull the code you will work with throughout the book from the GitHub repository.

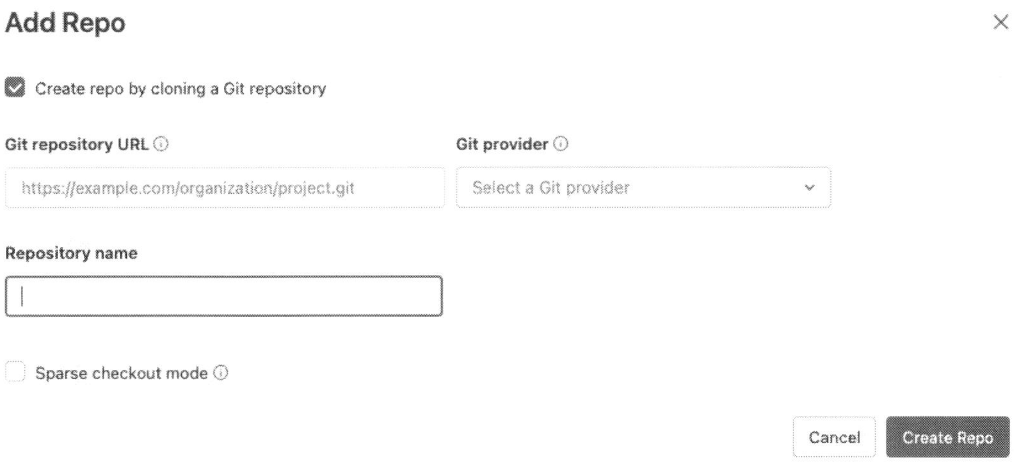

Add Repo   ✕

☑ Create repo by cloning a Git repository

Git repository URL ⓘ   **Git provider** ⓘ

| https://example.com/organization/project.git | | Select a Git provider   ⌄ |

Repository name

☐ Sparse checkout mode ⓘ

Cancel   Create Repo

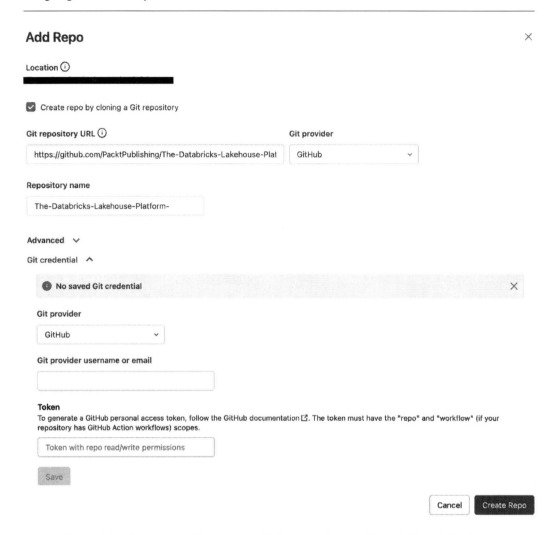

Figure 2.12 – Setting up a Git repository: Workspace > Repos > Home folder > Add > Repo

Navigate to your fork of the Book's GitHub repository, as mentioned in the *Technical requirements* section under the *Applying our learning* section. You can copy and paste the HTTPS link into the **Add Repo** screen's URL section, shown in *Figure 2.12*. Next, you will link your GitHub account. If you are unsure how to do this, follow the documentation linked in *Further reading* titled *About personal access tokens* and *Set up Databricks Repos*. Once your repository is ready, you can create a cluster if no one has done so yet.

Creating compute

We provide the cluster configurations we use for this project in the *Technical requirements* section. You can use the same configuration if you like. There are several options to choose from when creating a new cluster configuration. It might seem complicated for new users, but stay calm when trying to choose the right one. We highly recommend the *Best Practices for Cluster Configuration* linked in *Further reading* for guidance, especially if you are responsible for setting up compute for one or more teams. Let's talk about some of the compute options as they relate to ML and this book:

- **Multi-node versus single-node**: Multi-node is excellent for distributed projects (think Spark). Single-node is suitable for projects or workloads that are performed on the driver (think scikit-learn or pandas).

- **Access mode**: Some cluster configurations support Unity Catalog, and some don't. Choose a cluster that supports UC for the projects in this book.

- **Databricks Runtime (DBR) and Python packages**: The DBR is part of the managed service of Databricks. A DBR is a group of commonly used packages bundled and pinned to a release version and then versioned as a DBR. There are two significant variations of a DBR: standard and ML. Data engineering workloads often utilize the standard DBR. The ML DBR, as the name implies, is for DS and ML workloads. Think of the greatest hits of ML Packages – sklearn, pandas, numpy, and seaborn, as well as the latest CUDA libraries for GPU clusters, and so on, these are included in the ML runtime, which means they are pre-installed and ready to be used in your code. DBRs provide the benefit of reproducibility as well as reducing the engineering development time of packaging and pinning versions. When adding additional libraries, you can add them to your notebook, cluster, or workspace.

The best practice for production is to install cluster-scoped libraries rather than notebook-scoped libraries. However, notebook-scoped libraries are great for interactive use and development (please note that if you opt for notebook-scoped libraries, every notebook will require you to re-install non-default libraries each time, as one notebook represents a unique pyenv). You will install libraries both at the cluster level and in a couple of project notebooks. You can see the **Libraries** tab in *Figure 2.13*. Simply click **Install new** to install a new library.

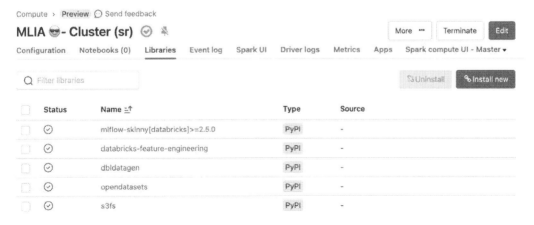

Figure 2.13 – Adding libraries to the Machine Learning in Action (MLIA) cluster configuration

This is the ideal time to install the libraries you will need. Install via `PyPI opendatasets`, `dbldatagen`, `databricks-feature-engineering`, and `mlflow-skinny[data-bricks]>=2.5.0`. These libraries are used across multiple notebooks throughout the book.

- **Photon acceleration**: Photon is an acceleration engine that speeds up ETL and SQL workloads. Photon currently is not advantageous for standard ML modeling.

- **VM types**: There are many VMs to pick from. You can choose VMs by family from the drop-down list. You can start with a VM in the *General Purpose* group if you need more clarification or are just starting.

- **Min and max workers**: The rule of thumb is to start with a few max workers and increase the number of workers as your workload increases. Keep in mind that your cluster will autoscale for you. However, we still recommend starting smaller and growing out for only the more compute-heavy examples, such as certain notebooks in the Multilabel Image Classification deep learning project.

You now have your development environment set up. You are ready to lock down your credentials for safe use in your code.

Setting up the Databricks CLI and secrets

The Databricks CLI is the command line interface for Databricks. We recommend using the web terminal from your cluster to install Databricks CLI as well as create Databricks secrets. As we mentioned earlier in the chapter, there are other options to get access to Kaggle datasets, but we walk you through the steps to set up secrets here. Please see the documentation in *Further reading* for more details on the CLI, installation, usage, and secrets.

1. Go to the **Apps** tab of the compute cluster you set up in the last section. You can refer to *Figure 2.13* to see the location of the **Apps** tab. Apps are only available while the cluster is, so it may be greyed out initially. You will have to start your cluster to proceed.

2. Select the web terminal.

3. Install the latest version of the CLI. `curl -fsSL https://raw.githubusercontent.com/databricks/setup-cli/main/install.sh | sudo sh`

4. Check your Databricks version to be sure it's greater than `0.2`. We had to point to the updated version in the location installed by curl. `/usr/local/bin/databricks-v.`

5. Next, you need to configure the connection. You need your PAT for this:

   ```
   /usr/local/bin/databricks configure
   ```

6. Create a secret scope for storing credentials related to this book:

   ```
   /usr/local/bin/databricks secrets create-scope "machine-
   learning-in-action"
   ```

7. Create a secret for storing your Kaggle username:

```
/usr/local/bin/databricks secrets put-secret --json '{"scope":
"machine-learning-in-action",
"key": "kaggle_username",
"string_value": "readers-username"
}'
```

8. Create a secret for storing your Kaggle API key:

```
/usr/local/bin/databricks secrets put-secret --json '{
"scope": "machine-learning-in-action",
"key": "kaggle_key",
"string_value": "readers-api-key"
}'
```

9. Last, list your secrets to make sure everything works as expected:

```
/usr/local/bin/databricks secrets list-secrets "machine-
learning-in-action"
```

In *Chapter 8*, we'll create another scope to hold an OpenAI API key, but for now we just need the Kaggle credentials. Now that we have our secrets set up, let's get our codebase ready!

Setting up your code base

We use a setup file to help keep variables consistent across multiple project notebooks. You will run the setup file each time you run the project notebooks using a magic command, %run. This command brings everything into the memory of your notebook session. The global-setup.py file has numerous components to it. Let's walk through each section. Feel free to edit the file to fit your needs.

> **Note**
>
> It's possible you'll receive an error message: py4j.security.Py4JSecurityException:
> Method public scala.collection.immutable.Map com.databricks.
> backend.common.rpc.CommandContext.tags() is not whitelisted on
> class class com.databricks.backend.common.rpc.CommandContext
>
> This is because you are on a shared compute cluster. You can simply hardcode current_user to your username.

Passing variables via widgets

Widgets pass variables to notebooks similarly to how command-line arguments pass variables to Python scripts. The code block in *Figure 2.14* creates the widgets needed to pass variables from the Run command to the global-setup.py file using Databricks Utilities or dbutils. You can read more about the dbutils capabilities in the Databricks Utilities documentation in *Further reading*. These widgets create, pass, and access parameters. The arguments are the variable name, default value, and verbose name in respective order.

```
# RUN TIME ARGUMENTS
dbutils.widgets.text("env", "dev", "Environment")

#ignored if db is set (we force the databse to the given value in this case)
dbutils.widgets.text("project_name", "", "Project Name")

#Empty value will be set to a database scoped to the current user using project_name
dbutils.widgets.text("db", "", "Database")
```

```
1   # RUN TIME ARGUMENTS
2   # Minimum Databricks Runtime version allowed for notebooks attaching to a cluster
3   dbutils.widgets.text("min_dbr_version", "13.0", "Min required DBR version")
4
5   dbutils.widgets.text("catalog", "ml_in_action", "Catalog")
6
7   #ignored if db is set (we force the databse to the given value in this case)
8   dbutils.widgets.text("project_name", "", "Project Name")
9
10  #Empty value will be set to a database scoped to the current user using project_name
11  dbutils.widgets.text("db", "", "Database")
```

Figure 2.14 – Creating widgets for accepting notebook-specific variables

You can pass each variable while running the file by adding a single line cell with appropriate parameters at the top of the notebook, as shown in *Figure 2.15*.

```
1   %run ../../global-setup $project_name=synthetic_transactions
```

Figure 2.15 – Running project-specific variables in our global setup file

Running global-setup.py saves all the variables defined in the script in memory for easy reference.

Checking for compatibility

Next, in global-setup.py, we run checks for compatibility between the code base and the cluster attached to the notebook.

The compatibility code block checks the following:

- A project name was submitted as a variable.

- The cluster is configured with an ML runtime and meets the minimum version. To be sure all features in the code are available in the runtime used, we set a minimum.

Once all checks pass, we assign a user and paths.

Setting a default catalog and project-specific database

This book provides code that uses the Unity Catalog catalog. Your default catalog is set based on your environment. If you do not set the environment or you set it to dev, then the catalog is named ml_in_action. When the environment is prod, the catalog is ml_in_prod. The default name for the database is always the project name. However, you can provide a different name if you desire by entering a project variable for the database name.

```
74   # With parallel execution this can fail the time of the initialization. add a few
     retries to fix these issues
75   for i in range(10):
76     try:
77       spark.sql(f"""USE `{catalog}`.`{database_name}`""")
78       break
79     except Exception as e:
80       time.sleep(1)
81       if i >= 9:
82         raise e
```

Figure 2.16 – Using the defined variables to set the default with retries

We want to be sure that the catalog and database are set to the notebooks' defaults. Occasionally, with parallel execution, this command can fail during initialization; therefore, we add a few retries to work around this issue, as shown in *Figure 2.16*.

Granting permissions

Now that we've set our catalog and database defaults, we can grant permissions.

```
84    # Granting UC permissions to account users - change if you want your data private
85    if catalog != 'hive_metastore':
86      try:
87        spark.sql(f"GRANT CREATE, SELECT, USAGE on SCHEMA {catalog}.{database_name} TO
          `account users`")
88        spark.sql(f"ALTER SCHEMA {catalog}.{database_name} OWNER TO `account users`")
89      except Exception as e:
90        print("Couldn't grant access to the database for all users:"+str(e))

# Granting UC permissions to account users - change if you want your data private
spark.sql(f"GRANT CREATE, SELECT, USAGE on SCHEMA {catalog}.{database_name} TO `account users`")
```

Figure 2.17 – Granting permissions to the catalog and database

We grant the group `account users` permission. If you do not want to make your assets available to others, remove this or comment it out.

> **Important note**
>
> Be sure to use tick marks around your group name or email address when granting permission. If you use single quotes instead, you will get an error message.

The catalog and database are ready for tables. However, not all data we use in machine learning goes into a table. For other data, files, and objects, we have volumes.

Setting up volumes

Volumes are views of cloud object storage. We create project-specific volumes. Use them for path-based access to structured or unstructured data. Volumes sit under a database in a catalog and are used to manage and provide access to data files. You can govern access to volumes using GRANT statements. Volumes provide scalable file-based storage without sacrificing governance. Often, we use unstructured, semi-structured, or non-tabular data in machine learning. Images are a good example of unstructured, non-tabular data that we will use for the Multilabel Image Classification project. To work with these images, the Multilabel Image Classification project uses volumes.

```
1    import os
2    os.environ['kaggle_username'] = 'YOUR KAGGLE USERNAME HERE'
3
4    os.environ['kaggle_key'] = 'YOUR KAGGLE KEY HERE'
```

```
1    import os
2
3    os.environ['kaggle_username'] = dbutils.secrets.get("lakehouse-in-action",
     "kaggle_username")
4
5    os.environ['kaggle_key'] = dbutils.secrets.get("lakehouse-in-action", "kaggle_key")
```

Figure 2.18 – EndpointApiClient class

Starting the projects

We have planned our platform and set up our workspace environment. Next, let's work through each project. In GitHub, you will see that each chapter has a folder containing folders corresponding to each project. When we refer to the notebooks by name, we assume you are in the appropriate chapter and project folder. For example, this chapter has the first notebook:

```
Chapter 2: Designing Databricks: Day One/
  Project: Favorita Store Sales - TimeSeries Forecasting/
CH2-01-Downloading_Sales_Forecast_Data
```

We refer to the notebook by only the filename itself, CH2-01-Downloading_Sales_Forecast_Data. Let's jump into the first project.

Project: Favorita store sales – time series forecasting

Recall from *Chapter 1* that we use a Kaggle-provided dataset to forecast sales. In this chapter, we download our data from the Kaggle website. To follow along in your workspace, please open the following notebook:

- CH2-01-Downloading_Sales_Forecast_Data

In the notebook, and as well as the code here in *Figures 2.19 and 2.20*, we set our path and download our data from Kaggle.

First, we designate raw_data_path to store the files.

```
1    raw_data_path = volume_file_path + 'raw_data'
2
3    dbutils.fs.mkdirs(raw_data_path)
```

Figure 2.19 – Setting the path for our volume

In the following code block (*Figure 2.20*), we use the Python package opendatasets, a library specifically created to download data from the Kaggle API. You can find more information in the *Further reading* section.

```
1    import opendatasets as od
2
3    od.download("https://www.kaggle.com/competitions/
     store-sales-time-series-forecasting/data",raw_data_path)
```

Figure 2.20 – Downloading Favorita data from opendatasets

That is all for the *Favorita Store Sales* project in this chapter! Now, we can focus on generating data for our `Streaming Transactions` project.

Project: Streaming Transactions

Your goal with the Streaming Transactions project is to build a model to classify transactions. The dataset consists of JSON-formatted transactions with `Transaction`, `timestamp`, `Label`, `Amount`, and `CustomerID`.

In later chapters, you will add a product column to demonstrate schema evolution. In this chapter, you'll create the first version of transaction data used throughout the rest of the book. To follow along in your workspace, please open the following notebook:

- `CH2-01-Generating_Records_Using_DBKS_Labs_Datagen`

You can run each cell of the notebook as we work through them or run them all at once. After the setup commands, we set notebook variables to establish the number of rows generated per batch of transactions (`nRows`), the number of positively labeled rows per batch (`nPositiveRows`), the path to the volume where you will store the JSON dataset (`destination_path`), a temporary path (`temp_path`), and the number of seconds between each batch of data you generate (`sleepIntervalSeconds`).

The following code block accesses the value of the `Reset` widget. Any data already written to the volume will be deleted if the widget is set to `True` (its default value).

```
                          Check the Reset Widget Value

1    if bool(dbutils.widgets.get('Reset')):
2        dbutils.fs.rm(temp_path, recurse=True)
3        dbutils.fs.rm(destination_path, recurse=True)
4        dbutils.fs.mkdirs(destination_path)
```

Figure 2.21 – Checking the Reset widget

Next, we set the parameter values used in the data generator to create the transactions. We set the minimum and maximum values for each `CustomerID`. We also create a dictionary of product types and set `min`, `max`, `mean`, `alpha`, and `beta` variables, which you use to generate random transaction amounts according to a distribution.

```
CustomerID_vars = {"min": 1234, "max": 1260}

Product_vars = {"None": {"min": 1000, "max": 25001, "mean": 15520, "alpha": 4, "beta": 10}}
```

```
                              Data Variables
1    CustomerID_vars = {"min": 1234, "max": 1260}
2
3    Product_vars = {"None": {"min": 1000, "max": 25001, "mean": 15520,
     "alpha": 4, "beta": 10},
4                   "A": {"min": 1000, "max": 25001, "mean": 15520, "alpha":
                    4, "beta": 10},
5                   "B": {"min": 1000, "max": 5501, "mean": 35520, "alpha":
                    10, "beta": 4},
6                   "C": {"min": 10000, "max": 40001, "mean": 30520, "alpha":
                    3, "beta": 10}}
```

Figure 2.22 – Dictionaries to hold variables for use within the define_specs function

With the variables set, we build out the functions to create the transaction data, starting with the `define_specs` function. The function accepts as input a product type (defined in the dictionary in *Figure 2.22*), a positive or negative label, and a timestamp; it returns a dollar amount for the transaction. *Figure 2.23* shows a portion of the code; the rest is in the accompanying notebook.

```
1    import dbldatagen as dg
2    from datetime import datetime
3    import dbldatagen.distributions as dist
4    from pyspark.sql.types import IntegerType, FloatType, StringType
5
6    def define_specs(Product, Label, currentTimestamp = datetime.now()):
7      pVars = Product_vars[Product]
8      if Product == "None":
9        if Label:
10         return (dg.DataGenerator(spark, name="syn_trans", rows=nRows, partitions=4)
11           .withColumn("CustomerID", IntegerType(), nullable=False,
12                   minValue=CustomerID_vars["min"], maxValue=CustomerID_vars["max"], random=True)
13           .withColumn("TransactionTimestamp", "timestamp",
14                   begin=currentTimestamp, end=currentTimestamp,nullable=False,
15                   random=False)
16           .withColumn("Amount", FloatType(),
17                   minValue=pVars["min"],maxValue=pVars["max"],
18                   distribution=dist.Beta(alpha=pVars["alpha"], beta=pVars["beta"]), random=True)
19           .withColumn("Label", IntegerType(), minValue=1, maxValue=1)).build()
20       else:
21         return (dg.DataGenerator(spark, name="syn_transs", rows=nRows, partitions=4)
22           .withColumn("CustomerID", IntegerType(), nullable=False,
23                   minValue=CustomerID_vars["min"], maxValue=CustomerID_vars["max"], random=True)
24           .withColumn("TransactionTimestamp", "timestamp",
25                   begin=currentTimestamp, end=currentTimestamp,nullable=False,
26                   random=False)
27           .withColumn("Amount", FloatType(),
28                   minValue=pVars["min"],maxValue=pVars["max"],
29                   distribution=dist.Normal(mean=pVars["mean"], stddev=.001), random=True)
30           .withColumn("Label", IntegerType(), minValue=0, maxValue=0)).build()
31     else:
32       if Label:
33         return (dg.DataGenerator(spark, name="syn_trans", rows=nRows, partitions=4)
34           .withColumn("CustomerID", IntegerType(), nullable=False,
35                   minValue=CustomerID_vars["min"], maxValue=CustomerID_vars["max"], random=True)
36           .withColumn("TransactionTimestamp", "timestamp",
37                   begin=currentTimestamp, end=currentTimestamp,nullable=False,
38                   random=False)
39           .withColumn("Product", StringType(), template=f"Pro\duct \{Product}")
40           .withColumn("Amount", FloatType(),
41                   minValue=pVars["min"],maxValue=pVars["max"],
42                   distribution=dist.Beta(alpha=pVars["alpha"], beta=pVars["beta"]), random=True)
43           .withColumn("Label", IntegerType(), minValue=1, maxValue=1)).build()
```

Figure 2.23 – Defining the define_specs function to generate transaction records

Next, we write a function to generate a single record by calling `define_specs` and including the current timestamp.

```
1    from pyspark.sql.functions import expr
2    from functools import reduce
3    import pyspark
4    import os
5
6    # Generate a record
7    def generateRecord(Product,Label):
8      return (define_specs(Product=Product, Label=Label, currentTimestamp=datetime.now()))
```

Figure 2.24 – Defining a function to generate a single transaction record

We then build `generateRecordSet` to generate the `recordCount` number of records in each batch. Notice that in this notebook, we're using the `None` product type, so the records generated will only have four features: `CustomerID`, `TransactionTimestamp`, `Amount`, and `Label` (this will be important in the next chapter!).

```
10   # Generate a list of records
11   def generateRecordSet():
12     Products = ["None"]
13     Labels = [0,1]
14     recordSet = []
15     for Prod in Products:
16       for Lab in Labels:
17         recordSet.append(generateRecord(Prod, Lab))
18     return reduce(pyspark.sql.dataframe.DataFrame.unionByName, recordSet)
```

Figure 2.25 – The generateRecordSet function creates a record for each
product and each label. Each record contains nRows transactions

Finally, we write a function to generate a set of data, convert the data to a DataFrame, and write it out as one JSON file to a temporary path. Then, we move that file to the final volume destination.

```
23   def writeJsonFile(destination_path):
24     recordDF = generateRecordSet()
25     recordDF = recordDF.withColumn("Amount", expr("Amount / 100"))
26     recordDF.coalesce(1).write.format("json").save(temp_path)
27
28     tempJson = os.path.join(temp_path, dbutils.fs.ls(temp_path)[3][1])
29     dbutils.fs.cp(tempJson, destination_path)
30     dbutils.fs.rm(temp_path, True)
```

Figure 2.26 – The writeJsonFile function generates a set of records

The set contains amounts generated as integers, so we divide by 100 to turn the amounts into dollars and type float. The function writes out the JSON file to a `temp` directory and then moves the single file to the final directory.

With everything set up, create the dataset with the code provided. Feel free to increase the iterations to build a larger dataset. Then, move on to the next project!

Project: Retrieval-Augmented Generation Chatbot

The RAG Chatbot project will ingest PDF documents to build the knowledge base for the chatbot. We use a volume to store the PDFs. To follow along in your workspace, please open the following notebook:

- `CH2-01-Downloading_PDF_Documents`

Files can be uploaded to a volume directly in the Databricks console via the user interface, as shown in *Figure 2.27*; however, this project uses the code provided in the notebook to download and save the data to a volume programmatically.

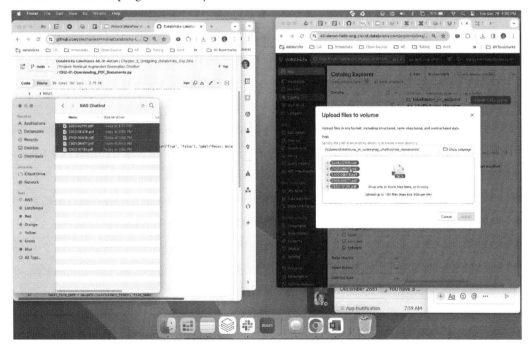

Figure 2.27 – Manually uploading documents into a volume

The code for this chapter begins with setup cells and helper functions, and in *Figure 2.28* we designate library_folder where we will save the PDFs we download.

```
1    library_folder = "{}/raw_documents".format(volume_file_path)
2
3    user_agent = "mlaction_book"
```

Figure 2.28 – Designating the library folder to hold the files for this project

We are using open articles published on the **Arxiv** page that relate to **Generative AI** (**GenAI**) and how it can impact human labor markets and economics. We pass the URLs to be used as documents for our chatbot and load these files into our volume.

```
                                                              Python  ⁙ ▶▾ ∨ − ✕
# we are getting our documents, you could directly upload it to the volumes using UI
pdfs = {'2203.02155.pdf':'https://arxiv.org/pdf/2203.02155.pdf',
        '2302.09419.pdf': 'https://arxiv.org/pdf/2302.09419.pdf',
        '2303.10130.pdf':'https://arxiv.org/pdf/2303.10130.pdf',
        '2302.06476.pdf':'https://arxiv.org/pdf/2312.00506.pdf',
        '2302.06476.pdf':'https://arxiv.org/pdf/2302.06476.pdf',
        '2303.10130.pdf':'https://arxiv.org/pdf/2303.10130.pdf',
        '2209.07753.pdf':'https://arxiv.org/pdf/2209.07753.pdf',
        '2304.07683.pdf':'https://arxiv.org/pdf/2304.07683.pdf'}

for pdf in pdfs.keys():
    load_file(pdfs[pdf], pdf, library_folder)
```

Figure 2.29 – Download PDF files and save them to our volume

Now that we have the documents downloaded and, they are ready to be processed for our chatbot. With that completed, we can move on to our final project: **Multilabel Image Classification**.

Project: Multilabel Image Classification

The MIC project ingests images into Delta tables to fine-tune a pre-trained model from the *Restnet* family to improve its accuracy. We will programmatically download the images from Kaggle and save the data to a volume. To follow along in your workspace, please open the CH2-01-Downloading_Images notebook:

```
%sh
cd /local_disk0/
kaggle datasets download -d puneet6060/intel-image-classification
 %sh
 cd /local_disk0/
 export KAGGLE_USERNAME=$kaggle_username
 export KAGGLE_KEY=$kaggle_key
 kaggle datasets download -d puneet6060/intel-image-classification
```

Figure 2.30 – Downloading data from Kaggle using Databricks magic commands

Now we create the volume folder and unzip the images for our classification project into our volumes. It will take around one hour (as it contains 80K images!) to extract the images from ZIP to Volumes.

```
!mkdir {volume_file_path}/intel_image_clf/
!mkdir {volume_file_path}/intel_image_clf/raw_images

# this can take up to a few hours
# or load a few examples to UC on your own if time is a constraint
!unzip -n /local_disk0/intel-image-classification.zip -d /Volumes/
{catalog}/{database_name}/files/intel_image_clf/raw_images
```

Figure 2.31 – Unzipping images into the volumes for this project

We have downloaded or generated all four datasets, and they are ready to be brought into our Bronze layer in the next chapter.

Summary

This chapter covered a wide range of setup decisions, options, and processes for planning your Data Intelligence Platform. We took you through an overview of the main components of the DI Platform, from early design choices to important features that we will dive into further in upcoming chapters. You also learned how to set up your workspace and project code base. We hope you feel more comfortable with the basics of the platform. With Databricks ready and the project data downloaded, we are now ready to get into what it means to build out the Bronze data layer.

In *Chapter 3*, we cover the essentials of building out the Bronze data layer within the Databricks Intelligence Platform. We will format our data into the most optimized format, learn about schema evolution, change data capture using Delta, and more.

Questions

The following questions are meant to solidify key points to remember and tie the content back to your own experience.

1. How do Databricks runtimes enable stability?

2. How can we make our data more discoverable?

3. What are some common steps needed to set up a Databricks workspace?

Answers

After putting thought into the questions, compare your answers to ours.

1. Databricks runtimes enable stability by providing a consistent set of libraries.

2. Utilizing the built-in functionality for metadata, such as table and column descriptions, makes our data more discoverable.

3. Some common steps for setting up a workspace are activating Databricks through the marketplace and setting up user groups and governance.

Further reading

In this chapter, we identified specific libraries, technical features, and options. Please take a look at these resources to delve deeper into the areas that interest you most:

*   *What is Unity Catalog?*: `https://docs.databricks.com/data-governance/unity-catalog/index.html`

*   *Lakehouse Monitoring demo*: `https://youtu.be/3TLBZSKeYTk?t=560`

*   *UC has a more centralized method of managing the model lifecycle than HMS*: `https://docs.databricks.com/machine-learning/manage-model-lifecycle/index.html`

*   *Share Models across workspaces*: `https://docs.databricks.com/en/machine-learning/manage-model-lifecycle/multiple-workspaces.html`

*   *In-depth UC setup on Azure*: `https://youtu.be/itGKRVHdNPo`

*   *Connecting external HMS to UC*: `https://www.databricks.com/blog/extending-databricks-unity-catalog-open-apache-hive-metastore-api`

*   *Unity Catalog limitations*: `https://docs.databricks.com/en/data-governance/unity-catalog/index.html#unity-catalog-limitations`

*   *Best practices: Cluster configuration | Select Cloud in the dropdown*: `https://docs.databricks.com/clusters/cluster-config-best-practices.html`

*   *Databricks Notebooks*: `https://docs.databricks.com/en/notebooks/index.html`

*   *Databricks Autologging | Select Cloud in the dropdown*: `https://docs.databricks.com/mlflow/databricks-autologging.html#security-and-data-management`

*   *Kaggle API GitHub*: `https://github.com/Kaggle/kaggle-api`

*   *Lakehouse Monitoring product page*: `https://www.databricks.com/product/machine-learning/lakehouse-monitoring`

- *System Tables*: `https://www.databricks.com/resources/demos/tutorials/governance/system-tables`

- *Opendatasets Python package*: `https://pypi.org/project/opendatasets/`

- *Kaggle API*: `https://www.kaggle.com/docs/api`

- *GitHub*: `https://github.com/`

- *Databricks ML in Action GitHub Repository*: `https://github.com/PacktPublishing/Databricks-ML-In-Action`

- *Databricks Secrets API*: `https://docs.databricks.com/en/security/secrets/secrets.html`

- *Databricks CLI*: `https://docs.databricks.com/en/dev-tools/cli/index.html`

- *Databricks Utilities*: `https://docs.databricks.com/en/dev-tools/databricks-utils.html`

- *Workspace libraries*: `https://docs.databricks.com/en/libraries/workspace-libraries.html`

- *Data Mesh and the DI Platforms Blog Posts*: `https://www.databricks.com/blog/2022/10/10/databricks-lakehouse-and-data-mesh-part-1.html`, `https://www.databricks.com/blog/2022/10/19/building-data-mesh-based-databricks-lakehouse-part-2.html`

- *Short YouTube video on managed vs external tables in UC*: `https://youtu.be/yt9vax_PH58?si=dVJRZHAOnrEUBdkA`

- *Query Federation*: `https://docs.databricks.com/en/query-federation/index.html`

- *Centralized model registry workspace for HMS*: `https://docs.databricks.com/applications/machine-learning/manage-model-lifecycle/multiple-workspaces.html`

- *Manage model lifecycle in Unity Catalog*: `https://docs.databricks.com/machine-learning/manage-model-lifecycle/index.html`

- *Terraform https*: `https://github.com/databricks/terraform-provider-databricks`

- *Widgets*: `https://docs.databricks.com/notebooks/widgets.html`

- *Kaggle API GitHub*: `https://github.com/Kaggle/kaggle-api.`

3

Building Out Our Bronze Layer

"Data is a precious thing and will last longer than the systems themselves."

– Tim Berners-Lee, generally credited as the inventor of the World Wide Web

In this chapter, you'll embark on the beginning of your data journey in the Databricks platform, exploring the fundamentals of the Bronze layer. We recommend employing the Medallion design pattern within the lake house architecture (as described in *Chapter 2*) to organize your data. We'll start with **Auto Loader**, which you can implement with or without **Delta Live Tables** (**DLT**) to insert and transform data in your architecture. The benefits of using Auto Loader include quickly transforming new data into the Delta format and enforcing or evolving schemas, which are essential for maintaining consistent data delivery to the business and customers. As a data scientist, strive for efficiency in building your data pipelines and ensuring your data is ready for the steps in the machine learning development cycle. You will best learn these topics through the example projects, so the *Applying our learning* section is the main focus of this chapter.

Let's see what topics you will cover in this chapter:

- Revisiting the Medallion architecture pattern
- Transforming data to Delta with Auto Loader
- DLT, starting with Bronze
- Maintaining and optimizing Delta Tables
- Applying our learning

Revisiting the Medallion architecture pattern

We introduced the Medallion architecture in *Chapter 2*. As a reminder, this refers to the data design pattern used to organize data logically. It has three layers – Bronze, Silver, and Gold. There are also cases where additional levels of refinement are required, so your Medallion architecture could be extended to Diamond and Platinum levels if needed. The Bronze layer contains raw data, the Silver layer contains cleaned and transformed data, and the Gold layer contains aggregated and curated data. Curated data refers to the datasets selected, cleaned, and organized for a specific business or modeling purpose. This architecture is a good fit for data science projects. Maintaining the original data as a source of truth is important, while curated data is valuable for research, analytics, and machine learning applications. By selecting, cleaning, and organizing data for a specific purpose, curated data can help improve its accuracy, relevance, and usability.

> **Note**
>
> This book will introduce quite a few project tasks, such as *building curated datasets*, that often fall under the domain of a data engineer. There will also be tasks that machine learning engineers, data analysts, and so on commonly perform. We include all of this work in our examples because roles are blurred in today's fast-moving world and will vary by company. Titles and expectations quickly evolve. Therefore, it's imperative to have a handle on the entire end-to-end workflow.

Maintaining a Bronze layer allows us to go back to the original data when we want to create a different feature, solve a new problem that requires us to look at historical data from another point of view, or simply maintain the raw level of our data for governance purposes. As the world of technology evolves, it's crucial to stay current and follow trends, but the core principles will remain for years. For the remainder of this chapter, we will cover DI platform features that facilitate building the Bronze layer.

Transforming data to Delta with Auto Loader

Harness the power of Auto Loader to automate your data ingestion process, significantly enhancing your data product's workflow efficiency. It can ingest data from cloud storage and streaming data sources. You can configure Auto Loader to run on a schedule or be triggered manually.

Here are some benefits of using Databricks' Auto Loader:

- **It keeps data up to date**: Auto Loader maintains checkpoints, removing the need to know which data is new. Auto Loader handles all that on its own.

- **It improves data quality**: Auto Loader can automatically detect schema changes and rescue any new data columns, so you can be confident that your data is accurate.

- **It increases data agility**: Auto Loader can help you quickly and easily ingest new data sources so that you can be more agile in responding to changes in your business.
- **Flexible ingestion**: Auto Loader can stream files in batches or continuously. This means it can consume batch data as a stream to reduce the overhead of a more manual batch pipeline.

Auto Loader is a powerful tool. It can be used standalone, as the underlying technology for DLT, or with **Spark Structured Streaming**. Spark Structured Streaming is a near-real-time processing engine; we will cover how to create a real-time feature in *Chapter 5*. This chapter also covers an example of streaming ingestion in the streaming transactions project. Let's discuss Auto Loader's ability to evolve a schema over time.

Schema evolution

Auto Loader's schema evolution allows you to add or modify fields in streaming data seamlessly. Databricks automatically adjusts relevant data to fit the new schema while preserving existing data integrity. This automated schema handling makes it easy to evolve your data schema over time as your business needs and data sources change, without having to worry about data loss or downtime. Furthermore, schema handling reduces the amount of work and headache associated with managing data pipelines that could change unexpectedly.

The new schema includes an additional column in the *Applying our learning* section. We will show how no data is lost despite a schema changing without notice. In our case, the default schema evolution mode for Auto Loader, `.option("cloudFiles.schemaEvolutionMode", "addNewColumns")`, in combination with `.option("mergeSchema", "true")`, perform schema evolution. Auto Loader will handle changes in the schema for us. Auto Loader tracking the changes is beneficial when new data fields become available with or without prior notice; code changes are unnecessary.

There's documentation on all schema options. The method we use for our project is the only option for automatic schema evolution. Every other option will require manual intervention. For example, you can use "rescue" mode to rescue data from being lost. Alternatively, you can use "failOnNewColumns" mode to cause the pipeline to fail and keep the schema unchanged until the production code is updated. There are numerous options and patterns for Auto Loader. Check out the *Common loading patterns with Auto Loader* link in the *Further reading* section for more information.

DLT, starting with Bronze

As we touched upon in a previous chapter, remember that DLT actively simplifies your pipeline operations, empowering you to focus on setting clear objectives for your pipeline rather than getting bogged down in operational details. Building on this foundation, we will now delve into DLT's capabilities. Auto Loader's schema evolution is integrated with DLT, underscoring its utility in handling dynamic data schemas with minimal manual intervention.

DLT benefits and features

DLT is a sophisticated framework designed to construct reliable data pipelines. DLT automates and streamlines complex operations such as orchestration and cluster management, significantly boosting the efficiency of data workflows. All you need to do is specify your transformation logic to be up and running. We will focus on just a few of the benefits of DLT as they pertain to creating your Bronze data layer, but we've included a link to DLT documentation in the *Further reading* section at the end of this chapter as well. DLT is another great tool in your toolbox for ingesting data. It provides several benefits over traditional ETL pipelines, including the following:

- **Declarative pipeline development**: DLT allows you to define your data pipelines using SQL or Python, which makes them easier to understand and maintain

- **Automatic data quality testing**: DLT can automatically apply your tests to your data, preventing quality issues, which helps to ensure that your pipelines are producing accurate results

- **Deep visibility for monitoring and recovery**: DLT provides detailed tracking and logging information, making troubleshooting problems and recovering from failures easier

- **Cost-effective streaming through efficient compute autoscaling**: DLT can automatically scale your compute resources up or down based on demand, which helps to reduce costs

DLT is a powerful tool for building reliable and scalable data pipelines in batch or streaming. It can help you improve the quality, efficiency, and visibility of your data processing workflows.

Here are some of the specific features of DLT that provide these benefits:

- **Streaming tables**: DLT uses streaming and live tables to process data in real time and to keep your pipelines up to date with the latest data.

- **Materialized views**: DLT uses materialized views to create snapshots of your data. You can query your data in real time and use it for downstream processing.

- **Expectations**: DLT uses expectations to test your data for quality issues automatically and to take action if the data does not meet your expectations.

- **Autoscaling**: DLT can automatically scale your compute resources up or down based on demand, reducing costs and improving the performance of your pipelines.

DLT is a good way to build reliable, scalable, and testable data pipelines. Next, we will focus on DLT in the context of the Bronze layer.

Bronze data with DLT

DLT uses Auto Loader to support schema evolution, offering significant benefits in terms of data quality, a key aspect of the Bronze layer in a Medallion architecture. In this architecture, the Bronze layer serves as the foundational stage where raw data is initially ingested and stored. DLT contributes to this layer by ensuring that each transformation applied to the raw data is precisely captured and managed. As a data scientist, understanding these transformations is crucial for maintaining the integrity of the data processing workflow. A powerful feature of DLT is its ability to automatically generate an accurate workflow Directed Acyclic Graph (**DAG**). This DAG not only visualizes the sequence and relationships of these data transformations but also enhances the reliability of the entire data pipeline.

The following screenshot shows the DLT pipeline workflow:

Figure 3.1 – The DLT pipeline workflow for the transactional dataset in this chapter

In *Figure 3.1*, there is one task in the DLT workflow, but it can accommodate a complex workflow with multiple dependencies.

Once we get data landed in Delta, there are actions we can take to ensure we take full advantage of Delta's benefits.

Maintaining and optimizing Delta tables

While the primary focus of this book is not on the intricate details of Delta table optimization, understanding these techniques is crucial for developing a data-centric machine learning solution. Efficient management of Delta tables directly impacts the performance and reliability of ML models, as these models heavily rely on the quality and accessibility of the underlying data. Employ techniques such as VACUUM, liquid clustering, OPTIMIZE, and bucketing to store, access, and manage your data with unparalleled efficiency. Optimized tables ensure that the data feeding into ML algorithms is processed efficiently. We'll cover these briefly here, but we also suggest that you refer to the Delta Lake documentation for a comprehensive understanding of each technique.

VACUUM

The VACUUM command is crucial in managing resources within Delta tables. It works by cleaning up invalidated files and optimizing the metadata layout. If your Delta table undergoes frequent **Data Manipulation Language** (**DML**) operations (update, insert, delete, and merge), we recommend running the VACUUM operation periodically. DML operations can generate numerous small files over time. Failure to run VACUUM may result in several small files with minimal data remaining online, leading to poor performance.

Note that VACUUM doesn't run automatically; you must explicitly schedule it. Consider scheduling VACUUM at regular intervals, such as weekly or monthly, depending on your data ingestion frequency and how often you update the data. Additionally, you have the option to configure the retention period to optimize storage and query performance. The delta.logRetentionDuration Delta configuration command allows you to control the retention period by specifying the number of days you want to keep the data files. This means you will delete all transaction log data for a table that goes back beyond the retention setting (e.g., only the last seven days of metadata remain). This way, you can control the duration the Delta table retains data files before the VACUUM operation removes them. The retention duration affects your ability to look back in time to previous versions of a table. Keep that in mind when deciding how long you want to retain the metadata and transaction log. Additionally, the transaction log is not very big.

Liquid clustering

Liquid clustering is a great alternative to partitioning; see how to implement it in *Figure 3.2*. Frequently, data gets over-partitioned, leaving too few files in a partition or unbalanced partitions. You do not need partitioning unless a table is a terabyte or larger. In addition to replacing partitioning, liquid clustering also replaces Z-ordering on Delta tables. Z-ordering is not compatible with clustered tables. When choosing columns to cluster on, include high cardinality columns that you use to query filters. Another commonly given example is a timestamp column. Instead of creating a derived column date to minimize the cardinality, simply cluster on the timestamp. Liquid clustering benefits Delta tables with skewed data distribution or changing access patterns. It allows a table to adapt to analytical needs by redefining clustering keys without rewriting data, resulting in optimized query performance and a flexible, maintenance-efficient structure. With liquid clustering enabled, you must use DBR 13.3+ to create, write, or optimize Delta tables.

```
1    CREATE TABLE my_clustered_table (id INT, name STRING, timestamp TIMESTAMP)
2    USING DELTA
3    CLUSTER BY (id, timestamp);
```

Figure 3.2 – Example code to create a table optimized with liquid clustering

OPTIMIZE

The OPTIMIZE command will trigger clustering. This is extra important when streaming data, as tables are not clustered on write. OPTIMIZE also compacts data files, which is vital for Delta tables with numerous small files. It merges these files into larger ones, enhancing read query speed and storage efficiency, which is especially beneficial for large datasets.

Predictive optimization

Predictive optimization is a feature that runs VACUUM and OPTIMIZE for you. Your admin can enable it in settings if you have the premium version, serverless enabled, and Unity Catalog set up.

Now that we've covered the basics of the Medallion architecture, Auto Loader, DLT, and some techniques to optimize your Delta tables, get ready to follow along in your own Databricks workspace as we work through the *Chapter 3* code by project.

Applying our learning

You will ingest the data before diving into each project's core "data science" aspects. We've discussed how Auto Loader, schema evolution, and DLT can format your data in storage. You'll notice that the following projects use different patterns to load data into the Bronze layer. The streaming transactions project uses Auto Loader to ingest incoming JSON files. You will transform the data with DLT and Structure Streaming independently, allowing you to get experience with both methods.

Technical requirements

Before we begin, review the technical requirements needed to complete the hands-on work in this chapter.

Databricks ML Runtime includes several pre-installed libraries useful for ML and data science projects. For this reason, we will use clusters with an ML runtime.

Project – streaming transactions

The next step in our streaming transactions project is to build out the Bronze layer, or the raw data we'll eventually use in our classification model. We specifically created this streaming project to practice using Auto Loader, schema evolution, Spark Structured Streaming, and DLT features, so we'll use those throughout this part of the project. To follow along in your workspace, open the following notebooks:

- CH3-01-Auto_Loader_and_Schema_Evolution
- CH3-02-Generating_Records_and_Schema_Change
- delta_live_tables/CH3-03-Formatting_to_Delta_with_DLT

Here's where we are in the project flow:

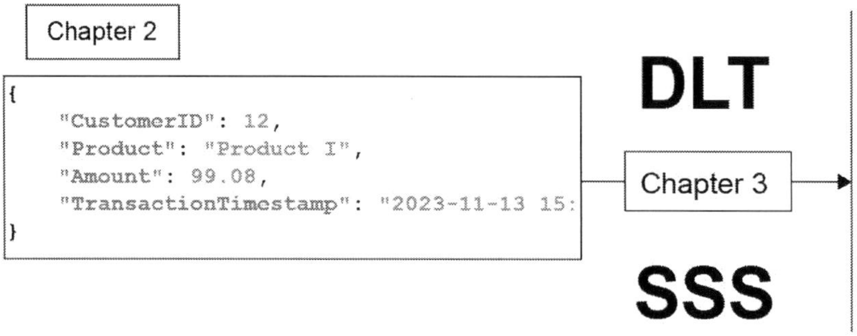

Figure 3.3 – The project plan for the synthetic streaming transactions project

In *Chapter 2*, we generated and stored our synthetic transaction data in JSON files. Now, we will read that data into a Delta table. We'll also update the data generation notebook to add a product string column, which will demonstrate schema evolution, as mentioned previously in the *Schema evolution* section. Let's walk through two options for reading and writing the data stream to a Delta table. Both options use Auto Loader to ingest. The files are then handled and written out by either Spark Structured Streaming or DLT. There are two notebooks for this section. We will start with CH3-01-Auto_Loader_and_Schema_Evolution.

Continuous data ingestion using Auto Loader with Structured Streaming

The code in this section uses Auto Loader to format the incoming JSON files as Delta. The table name we are using is synthetic_transactions. Before processing data, we create a widget (see *Figure 3.4*) to determine whether we want to reset the schema and checkpoint history. Resetting the history can be helpful when altering or debugging pipelines. If you reset (remove) your checkpoint history, you will reprocess all historical data.

```
1   dbutils.widgets.dropdown(name='Reset', defaultValue='False', choices=['True', 'False'], label="Reset Checkpoint and Schema")
```

Figure 3.4 – Creating a widget to reset the checkpoint and schema

Next, we set our variables for the script, which are mainly paths:

```
table_name = "synthetic_transactions"
raw_data_location = f"{volume_file_path}/schema_change_data/"
schema_location = f"{volume_file_path}/{table_name}/schema"
checkpoint_location = f"{volume_file_path}/{table_name}/checkpoint"
```

Figure 3.5 – Setting the path variables

The setup file provides us with `volume_file_path`, where we store the synthetic data, schema, and checkpoint folders.

As shown in *Figure 3.6*, we add spark configurations to optimize and reduce the sample size for inference:

```
1   spark.conf.set("spark.databricks.delta.optimizeWrite.enabled", True)
2   spark.conf.set("spark.databricks.delta.autoCompact.enabled", True)
3   spark.conf.set("spark.databricks.cloudFiles.schemaInference.sampleSize.numFiles",1)
4   spark.conf.set("spark.databricks.delta.schema.autoMerge.enabled", True)
```

Figure 3.6 – Setting configurations to optimize and reduce the sample size

You can set these Spark configurations in the cluster's advanced options. These configurations will automatically compact sets of small files into larger files for optimal read performance.

Configuring stream for data ingestion

The stream command is relatively long, so let's walk through each chunk of the code:

1. We are creating a stream to read from the synthetic dataset. The format option references the stream format. The `cloudFiles` refers to the files located in cloud storage. In this case, we generate data and write it to cloud storage. However, creating a stream with `.format("kafka")` is possible, which ingests directly from the stream without writing to cloud storage first. We also designate the file format as JSON.

```
stream = spark.readStream \
    .format("cloudFiles") \
    .option("cloudFiles.format", "json") \
```

Figure 3.7 – Creating the stream using CloudFiles and the JSON file format

2. The default is to set column types to `string`. However, we can provide schema hints so that the columns we are sure about get typed appropriately. While inferring the schema, we also want to infer the column types. The new column is a `string`, so we do not see this option in action, as new columns default to a `string`.

```
.option("cloudFiles.schemaHints","CustomerID int, Amount double,
TransactionTimestamp timestamp") \
.option("cloudFiles.inferColumnTypes","true") \
```

Figure 3.8 – Setting schema hints to reduce possible type mismatches. We
want to infer the data type for columns not in the schema hint

3. Auto Loader uses the `rescue` column to catch the change and quickly puts the new column into play without data loss! Note that the stream will fail and need to be restarted. The schema location is needed if we want Auto Loader to keep track of the schema and evolve it over time.

```
.option("cloudFiles.schemaEvolutionMode", "addNewColumns") \
.option("cloudFiles.schemaLocation", schema_location) \
```

Figure 3.9 – Setting schema evolution to add new columns and designating the schema location so that Auto Loader keeps track of schema changes over time

4. Next, we load the location of the raw data files. We need to select the fields we want. We will select all data fields, but you could be selective on the fields you pull in.

5. The following lines of code begin the "write" portion of the stream. Here, we start `writeStream`. Delta is the default data format, but we prefer to explicitly set it. We also designate that this stream is append-only, as we are not performing any updates or inserts.

6. A checkpoint is a mechanism in Spark Structured Streaming that allows you to save the state of your stream. If your stream fails, when it restarts, it uses the checkpoint to resume processing where it left off. The mergeSchema option is essential. Merging the schema adds the new columns as they arrive without intervention.

```
.option("checkpointLocation", checkpoint_location) \
.option("mergeSchema", "true") \
```

Figure 3.10 – Creating our checkpoint location and setting merge schema

7. The next step is to set the trigger. The trigger setting refers to the processing pace and has two main modes. Per the following code, you can specify the time-based trigger interval in seconds. Our data from the generation notebook is continuous. Here, we efficiently handle it with micro-batches. We provided a select statement in *step 4*. We can now write the result of that statement to Delta files in the `destination_location` path.

In *step 7*, we use a trigger with a processing time of 10 seconds. The processing time means micro-batches of data will be processed every 10 seconds. Suppose you do not require micro-batches. If you need your data processed once an hour or once per day, then the `trigger.availableNow` option is best. If you want to process whatever new data has arrived in the last hour, use `trigger.AvailableNow` in your pipeline, and schedule the pipeline to kick off in workflows using a job cluster every hour. At that time, Auto Loader will process all data available and then shut down.

8. Next, to show schema evolution, we update our data generation notebook from *Chapter 2* to include an additional data column. You'll find the new version, CH3-02-Generating_ Records_and_Schema_Change, in the *Chapter 3* folder. Note that we provide a list of possible products to writeJsonFile. The result is an additional field, Product, with a product string for the record (*Figure 3.11*).

```
1    import time
2
3    Products = ["None"]
4    t=1
5    total = 100
6    while(t<total):
7      writeJsonFile(destination_path,Products=Products)
8      t = t+1
9      if not (t % 4):
10       print(f"t={t}")
11     time.sleep(sleepIntervalSeconds)
12     if (t > total/4):
13       Products = ["A","B","C"]
```

Figure 3.11 – The updated method for generating data with or without a product string

As a result of our changes, you now have a stream of data that adds an additional column midstream. You can start the Auto Loader notebook to see the schema evolution in action. The stream stops when it detects the extra column, providing an exception – [UNKNOWN_FIELD_EXCEPTION. NEW_FIELDS_IN_RECORD_WITH_FILE_PATH]. Don't worry; upon restart, the schema evolution takes over. Run the cell with the stream in it again to restart.

You are finished reading and writing with Auto Loader with Spark Structured Streaming. Next, we'll show you how to accomplish the same task with DLT (using less code!).

Continuous data ingestion using Auto Loader with DLT

This section uses the Auto Loader code to read the stream of JSON files and then DLT to write the files to a table. This notebook is in the delta_live_tables folder and titled CH3-03-Formatting_to_Delta_with_DLT.

The only import you need is DLT – import dlt. The DLT code is relatively short, partly because the pipeline configuration occurs in the pipeline object rather than the code. Before we look through our source code, let's navigate to the **Databricks Workflows** pane in the left-hand navigation bar, select **Delta Live Tables**, and click **Create Pipeline**, which opens the pipeline settings page, as shown in *Figure 3.12*.

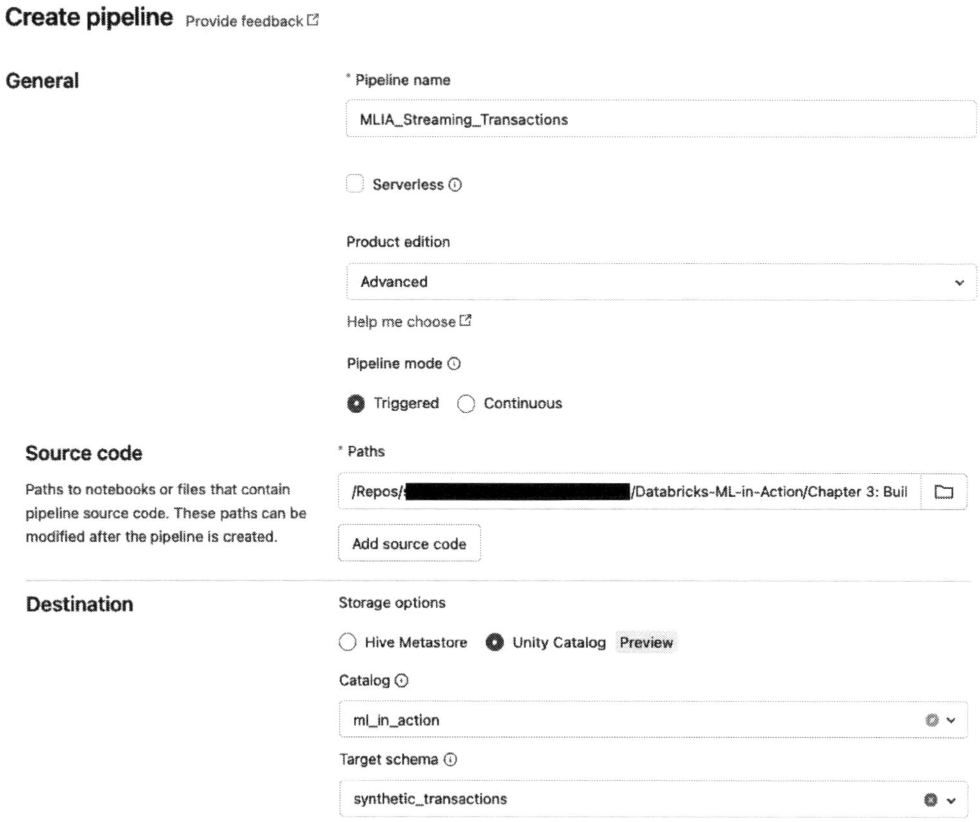

Create pipeline Provide feedback �

General	* Pipeline name

MLIA_Streaming_Transactions

☐ Serverless ⓘ

Product edition

Advanced ⌄

Help me choose �

Pipeline mode ⓘ

● Triggered   ○ Continuous

Source code

Paths to notebooks or files that contain
pipeline source code. These paths can be
modified after the pipeline is created.

* Paths

/Repos/█████████████████/Databricks-ML-in-Action/Chapter 3: Buil   🗀

Add source code

Destination

Storage options

○ Hive Metastore   ● Unity Catalog Preview

Catalog ⓘ

ml_in_action

Target schema ⓘ

synthetic_transactions

Figure 3.12 – The DLT pipeline setup in the workflow UI

Pipeline configuration for DLT

The pipeline settings are minimal, given that DLT does the optimization, so the setup instructions are minimal. The parameters entered into the pipeline configuration are accessible in the pipeline code using spark.conf.get, as shown in *Figures 3.13* and *3.14*:

1. Enter a pipeline name. We will use MLIA_Streaming_Transactions.

2. For **Product edition**, select **Advanced**. This DLT edition comes with the most features, including DLT's expectation rules.

3. For **Pipeline mode**, select **Triggered**. This will ensure that the pipeline stops processing after a successful run.

4. For **Paths**, select this notebook from the repository for the source code:

```
Databricks-ML-in-Action/
Chapter 3: Building Out Our Bronze Layer/
```

```
Project: Streaming Transactions/
delta_live_tables/
CH3-03-Formatting_to_Delta_with_DLT
```

5. Select **Unity Catalog** as your storage option.

6. Select `ml_in_action` for the catalog and `synthetic_transactions_dlt` as the target schema.

7. Enter `table_name` and `synthetic_transactions_dlt` as configurations in the **Advanced** section. Additionally, specify your `raw_data_location` as follows (as shown in *Figure 3.13*):

```
/Volumes/ml_in_action/
synthetic_transactions/files/
synthetic_transactions,
```

Configuration

table_name	synthetic_transactions_dlt	✕
raw_data_location	/Volumes/ml_in_action/synthetic_trans	✕
Add configuration		

Channel ⓘ

| Current | ⌄ |

Figure 3.13 – Advanced pipeline configuration settings for variables

Methods in the DLT pipeline

Now that we have filled in the pipeline UI, let's focus on the methods used in the source code of the pipeline. In this function, we mostly reuse our previous code (*Figure 3.14*). Note that we do not use the setup file in this notebook. Instead, we use the variables we set in the pipeline settings' advanced configuration section.

```
1  def build_autoloader_stream():
2      raw_data_location = spark.conf.get('raw_data_location')
3      return spark.readStream.format('cloudFiles') \
4          .option("cloudFiles.format", "json") \
5          .option("cloudFiles.inferColumnTypes","true") \
6          .option("cloudFiles.schemaEvolutionMode", "addNewColumns") \
7          .option("cloudFiles.schemaHints","CustomerID bigint, Amount double, TransactionTimestamp timestamp") \
8          .load(f"{raw_data_location}")
```

Figure 3.14 – The autoloader stream method details

Generating the bronze table in a DLT pipeline

The `generate_table()` function feeds the read stream created using Auto Loader into DLT. We use `spark.conf.get('variable_name')` to access the variable values we defined in the pipeline's advanced settings (*Figure 3.13*). In the notebook, you will see the final step, a one-line cell called `generate_table()`.

```
1   def generate_table():
2     table_name = spark.conf.get('table_name')
3     @dlt.table(name=f'{table_name}',table_properties={"quality":"bronze"})
4     def create_table():
5       return build_autoloader_stream()
```

Figure 3.15 – Generating the Bronze table in a DLT pipeline

DLT is unique. It is not code you run line by line, so you don't execute the pipeline in the notebook. Back in the DLT UI, we save and click the **Start** button. After the setup process, you will see a graph that includes our table. **Start** not only starts the pipeline but creates it as well. Once it finishes, you will have a screen like the one shown in *Figure 3.1*.

Querying streaming tables created with DLT

You can query a streaming table created with DLT just like you query other tables. This is handy for populating dashboards, which we will cover in *Chapter 8, Monitoring, Evaluating, and More*.

> **Important note**
>
> If in a notebook you try to query your streaming table, you may get this error:
>
> `ExecutionException: org.apache.spark.sql.AnalysisException: 403: Your token is missing the required scopes for this endpoint.`
>
> This is because to query streaming tables created by a DLT pipeline, you must use a shared cluster using Databricks Runtime 13.1 and above, or a SQL warehouse. Streaming tables created in a Unity Catalog-enabled pipeline cannot be queried from assigned or no-isolation clusters. You can change your cluster or use the DBSQL query editor.

The pipeline creates our Bronze table, wrapping up this project on streaming transaction data.

Project – Favorita store sales – time series forecasting

You downloaded the *Favorita Sales Forecasting* dataset from Kaggle using `opendatasets` in the last chapter. We will use that data now to create Delta tables. To follow along in your own workspace, open the `CH3-01-Loading_Sales_CSV_Data_as_Delta` notebook.

The downloaded data is in single CSV files. We use pandas to read the datasets and Spark to write to a Delta table. We demonstrate this for only the first file in the following code block (*Figure 3.16*).

```
1   df = pd.read_csv(f'{cloud_storage_path}/holidays_events.csv', sep=',', decimal='.')
2   df['date'] = pd.to_datetime(df['date'])
3   spark.createDataFrame(df).write.mode("overwrite").saveAsTable("holiday_events")
4   display(df)
```

Figure 3.16 – Reading in the sales holiday events datasets with Pandas

We utilized the data profile capability (*Figure 3.17*) to check the data types before writing to a table. Profiling shows the inferred data type for the date field is a string rather than a date or timestamp. Therefore, we alter the data type before writing to a Delta table.

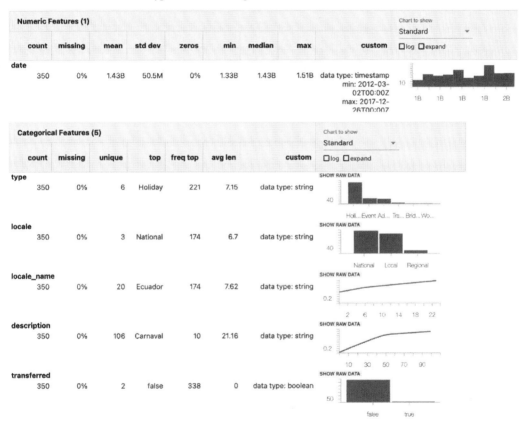

Figure 3.17 – Utilizing display(df), we can click + to see the data profile.
This lets us look at the data types and distributions quickly

Each table for the Favorita project is transformed into Delta tables similarly. As a result, we only include the first table in the book's pages. However, the code that transforms each of the tables is, of course, in the repository.

Project – a retrieval augmented generation chatbot

RAG stands for **Retrieval Augmented Generation**. A RAG system often consists of your data, a vector database, a search algorithm, and a **generative AI** model to generate an answer to a user's query. *Figure 3.18* shows the pipeline we will build throughout this book.

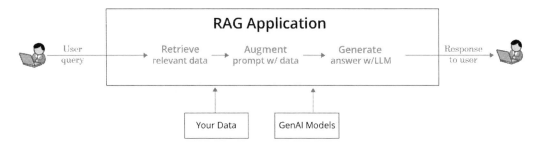

Figure 3.18 – A pipeline example that we will try to replicate through the book

We can see from *Figure 3.18* that we need to retrieve relevant data according to the user query. This is where our search method would access a vector database and conduct a semantic or hybrid search. At this stage in the RAG chatbot project, we have our PDFs in their raw, unstructured form. We want our users to access this knowledge via our chatbot, so we have to bring relevant content with information from all the PDFs into our chatbot, running in real time. To do so, we'll convert all our PDFs into a machine-readable format. This chapter shows how to extract unstructured data from PDF files, chunk it, and transform your text into embeddings. Then, we store the embeddings in a Delta table:

1. Our first step for data preparation is to extract unstructured information from PDF files. To follow along in your workspace, open the CH3-01-Creating_EmbeddedChunks notebook.

2. To start building the Bronze data layer, create an empty Delta table that includes the table's schema. Use the GENERATED BY DEFAULT AS IDENTITY feature to leverage Delta table capabilities to index the newly arriving data automatically. Also, add a table property to set the Change Data Feed to true.

```
%sql
--Note that we need to enable Change Data Feed on the table to create the index
CREATE TABLE IF NOT EXISTS pdf_documentation_text (
  id BIGINT GENERATED BY DEFAULT AS IDENTITY,
  pdf_name STRING,
  content STRING,
  embedding ARRAY <FLOAT>
  ) TBLPROPERTIES (delta.enableChangeDataFeed = true);
```

Figure 3.19 – Create an empty Delta table with the name pdf_documentation_text

3. For the next step, read the raw PDFs from the `volume` folder and save them to a table named `pdf_raw` (*Figure 3.20*). We will come back to the `pdf_documentation_text` table.

```
df = (
    spark.read.format("binaryfile")
    .option("recursiveFileLookup", "true")
    .load('dbfs:'+ documents_folder)
    )

df.write.mode("overwrite").saveAsTable(f"{catalog}.{database_name}.{table_name}")
```

Figure 3.20 – Read the PDF file in the binary format and write it into a Bronze layer table

4. Store the PDFs in the binary format in the `content` column to extract the text later. Let's see how it looks in a Delta table view. The binary format of each PDF is in the `content` column:

Figure 3.21 – Displaying ingested content in the Delta table

5. Next, we write a helper function using the `unstructured` library to extract the text from the PDF bytes. The function is in the `mlia_utils.rag_funcs` script.

```
1   from unstructured.partition.auto import partition
2   import io
3
4   def extract_doc_text(x : bytes) -> str:
5       # Read files and extract the values with unstructured
6       sections = partition(file=io.BytesIO(x))
7       def clean_section(txt):
8           txt = re.sub(r'\n', '', txt)
9           return re.sub(r' ?\.', '.', txt)
10      # Default split is by section of document, concatenate them all together because we want to split by sentence instead.
11      return "\n".join([clean_section(s.text) for s in sections])
```

Figure 3.22 – Creating a helper function to extract document text

6.   Let's apply this function to one of the PDF files we have and check the content of our document:

```
with open(f"{documents_folder}2303.10130.pdf", mode="rb") as pdf:
    doc = extract_doc_text(pdf.read())
    print(doc)
```

GPTs are GPTs: An Early Look at the Labor Market Impact Potential of Large Language Models
Tyna Eloundou1, Sam Manning1,2, Pamela Mishkin*1, and Daniel Rock3
1OpenAI 2OpenResearch 3University of Pennsylvania
August 22, 2023
Abstract
We investigate the potential implications of large language models (LLMs), such as Generative Pre- trained Transformers (GPTs), on the U.S. labor market, focusing on the increased capabilities arising from LLM-powered software compared to LLMs on their own. Using a new rubric, we assess occupations based on their alignment with LLM capabilities, integrating both human expertise and GPT-4 classifications. Our findings reveal that aro und 80% of the U.S. workforce could have at least 10% of their work tasks affected by the introduction of LLMs, while approximately 19% of workers may see at least 50% of their tasks impacted. We do not make prediction s about the development or adoption timeline of such LLMs. The projected effects span all wage levels, with higher-income jobs potentially facing greater exposure to LLM capabilities and LLM-powered software. Significa ntly, these impacts are not restricted to industries with higher recent productivity growth. Our analysis suggests that, with access to an LLM, about 15% of all worker tasks in the US could be completed significantly f aster at the same level of quality. When incorporating software and tooling built on top of LLMs, this share increases to between 47 and 56% of all tasks. This finding implies that LLM-powered software will have a subs tantial effect on scaling the economic impacts of the underlying models. We conclude that LLMs such as GPTs exhibit traits of general-purpose technologies, indicating that they could have considerable economic, social, and policy implications.

Figure 3.23 – Applying a helper function to extract information from the PDF

Great! *Figure 3.23* gives us a glimpse into one of the ingested documents. You may have many PDFs, which can be very long. Long documents can potentially be a problem for our future chatbot because they can easily exceed most LLMs maximum context lengths (check out *Further reading* for more information on context lengths). Additionally, we likely don't need an entire document's worth of text to answer a specific question. Instead, we need a section or "chunk" of this text. For this project, we create chunks of no more than 500 tokens with a chunk overlap of 50, using the SentenceSplitter module of the LlamaIndex library. You could also use the LangChain library or any library you choose to split the content into chunks. We will use the open source Llama-tokenizer, as this will be our main family of models across our project. Note that tokenizers may play a crucial role in your RAG quality. We have leveraged a Pandas **User Defined Function** (UDF) to scale across all pages of all documents.

```
@pandas_udf("array<string>")
def read_as_chunk(batch_iter: Iterator[pd.Series]) -> Iterator[pd.Series]:
    #set llama2 as tokenizer
    set_global_tokenizer(
        AutoTokenizer.from_pretrained("hf-internal-testing/llama-tokenizer")
    )
    #Sentence splitter from llama_index to split on sentences
    splitter = SentenceSplitter(chunk_size=500, chunk_overlap=50)
    def extract_and_split(b):
        txt = extract_doc_text(b)
        nodes = splitter.get_nodes_from_documents([Document(text=txt)])
        return [n.text for n in nodes]

    for x in batch_iter:
        yield x.apply(extract_and_split)
```

Figure 3.24 – Creating a pandas UDF for our extractor function

7. Now, let's apply this function to our Delta table:

Figure 3.25 – Applying a helper function to extract information from the PDF using PySpark

Once our chunks are ready, we need to convert them into embeddings. Embeddings are the format required to perform a semantic search when ingesting into our Silver layer later.

Databricks Model Serving now supports **Foundation Model APIs** (**FMAPIs**), which allow you to access and query state-of-the-art open models from a serving endpoint. With FMAPIs, you can quickly and easily build applications that leverage a high-quality GenAI model without maintaining your own model deployment (for more information, see *Deploy provisioned throughput Foundation Model APIs* in the *Further reading* section).

FMAPIs are provided in two access modes:

*   **Pay-per-token**: This is the easiest way to start accessing foundation models on Databricks and is recommended for beginning your journey with them.

*   **Provisioned throughput**: This model is recommended for workloads that require performance guarantees, fine-tuned models, or have additional security requirements:

Figure 3.26 – Available models for access via the FMAPIs of Databricks

> **Important note**
>
> At the time of writing, the FMAPI is available only to US regions. If your workspace is not yet in a supported region, you can use any model of your choice (OpenAI, BERT, a LlaMA tokenizer, etc.) to convert your content into embeddings.
>
> You may also need to fine-tune your model embedding to learn from your own content for better retrieval results.

Next, we leverage the DI Platform's pay-per-token capability from the FMAPI that provides you with access to the BGE_large_En endpoint, through the new functionality recently added to the mlflow >=2.9 - mlflow deployments (previously known as AI Gateway). This functionality unifies the model serving endpoint management on Databricks.

```python
from mlflow.deployments import get_deploy_client

# bge-large-en Foundation models are available using the /serving-endpoints/databricks-bge-large-en/invocations api.
deploy_client = get_deploy_client("databricks")

## NOTE: if you change your embedding model here, make sure you change it in the query step too
embeddings = deploy_client.predict(endpoint="databricks-bge-large-en", inputs={"input": ["What is ChatGPT?"]})
pprint(embeddings)
```

```
                          -0.033355712890625, -0.0207366943359375, -0.030029296875, 0.06976318359375,
                          -0.0264892578125, -0.026458740234375, -0.0474853515625, 0.04815673828125,
                          -0.036590576171875, -0.004947662353515625, 0.05316162109375,
                          0.0292816162109375, 0.027740478515625, -0.0068511962890625,
                          -0.031707763671875, -0.0158538818359375, 0.0306609130859375,
                          0.024078369140625, 0.0234527587890625, -0.034210205078125,
                          0.033782958984375, -0.007549285888671875, -0.007053375244140625,
                          0.0054779052734375, -0.07965087890625, 0.009918212890625,
                          0.022796630859375, 0.02301025390625, 0.02178955078125,
                          -0.0011930465698242188, -0.01041412353515625, -0.0175933837890625,
                          0.0255279541015625, -0.006103515625, -0.005084991455078125,
                          0.00148868560791015625, 0.064697265625, -0.046356201171875,
                          0.000837707519531252, -0.023193359375, 0.087890625, 0.015838623046875,
                          -0.0022525787353515625, -0.01235198974609375, 0.0036296844482421875,
                          0.00536346435546875],
              'index': 0,
              'object': 'embedding'}],
   'id': '457a4c4d-d6c5-4b9d-8b86-66f2844a6ddf',
   'model': 'bge-large-en-v1.5',
   'object': 'list',
   'usage': {'prompt_tokens': 8, 'total_tokens': 8}}
```

Figure 3.27 – Applying the FMAPI with the BGE endpoint to convert "What is ChatGPT?" into an embedding

Now, we apply this embedding conversion across all our chunks, and we again make pandasUDF for scalability purposes.

```python
@pandas_udf("array<float>")
def get_embedding(contents: pd.Series) -> pd.Series:
    import mlflow.deployments
    deploy_client = mlflow.deployments.get_deploy_client("databricks")
    def get_embeddings(batch):
        #Note: this will gracefully fail if an exception is thrown during embedding creation (add try/except if needed)
        response = deploy_client.predict(endpoint="databricks-bge-large-en", inputs={"input": batch})
        return [e['embedding'] for e in response.data]

    # Splitting the contents into batches of 150 items each, since the embedding model takes at most 150 inputs per request.
    max_batch_size = 150
    batches = [contents.iloc[i:i + max_batch_size] for i in range(0, len(contents), max_batch_size)]

    # Process each batch and collect the results
    all_embeddings = []
    for batch in batches:
        all_embeddings += get_embeddings(batch.tolist())

    return pd.Series(all_embeddings)
```

Figure 3.28 – pandasUDF to apply embedding conversion across all chunks

Applying our UDF will append our `raw_table` chunks with the corresponding embeddings:

Figure 3.29 – pandasUDF to apply embedding conversion across all chunks

Once the final step of our data preparation process is completed, we save our table in the initially pre-created Delta table `pdf_documentation_text` using append mode.

> **Note**
>
> We've ingested our PDFs for this project in one big batch, which works perfectly fine as an example. However, it also means that anytime you want to add a new PDF to your chatbot's knowledge base, you must manually rerun all of the preceding steps. We recommend a workflow for production-grade solutions to automate the preceding steps and incrementally ingest PDFs as they arrive in storage.

We now have a dataset ready for a vector search index, which we'll cover in *Chapter 4*.

Project – multilabel image classification

In *Chapter 2*, we extracted and stored our raw image data in our volume. In this chapter, we prepare our image dataset and save training and validation sets into Delta tables. To follow along in your workspace, open the `Ch3-01-Loading_Images_2_DeltaTables` notebook:

1. We start by creating variables and removing existing data if the `Reset` widget value is `True`.

```
delta_train_name = "train_imgs_main.delta"
delta_val_name = "valid_imgs_main.delta"

if bool(dbutils.widgets.get('Reset')):
  !rm -rf {main_dir_2write}{delta_train_name}
  !rm -rf {main_dir_2write}{delta_val_name}
```

Figure 3.30 – Cleaning up existing data if Reset = True

2. Next, we create a function to ingest all our images in one table. Initially, each label is in its own `folder_label_name`. We extract `image_name`, `image_id`, and `label_id`, as well as create `label_name` using append mode.

```python
from pyspark.sql import functions as f
def prep_data2delta(dir_name,outcomes,name2write,path2write="YOUR_PATH",write2delta=True,returnDF=None,):
    mapping_dict = {"buildings": 0,"sea": 1,"glacier": 2,"forest": 3,"street": 4,"mountain": 5,}
    # As we have multi label problem we will loop over labels to save them all under 1 main training set
    for label_name in outcomes:
        df = (
            spark.read.format("binaryfile")
            .option("recursiveFileLookup", "true")
            .load(f"{dir_name}/{lable_name}")
            .withColumn("label_name", f.lit(f"{label_name}"))
            .withColumn("label_id", f.lit(f"{mapping_dict[label_name]}").astype("int"))
            .withColumn("image_name", f.split(f.col("path"), "/").getItem(10))
            .withColumn("id", f.split(f.col("image_name"), ".jpg").getItem(0).astype("int"))
        )
        if write2delta:
            df.write.format("delta").mode("append").save(f"{path2write}{name2write}")
        if returnDF:
            return df
```

Figure 3.31 – Creating the prep_data2delta function

We use the `prep_data2delta` function to load and prepare our training and validation datasets (*Figure 3.32*). Note that the function will save a Delta table if the `write2delta` flag is `True` and will return a DataFrame if the value for the `returnDF` flag is `True`. Next, in the notebook, we call `prep_data2delta` for the training and validation sets.

Let's talk about data loaders

We load data in a fixed-size batch when fine-tuning or training our deep learning models. Each framework natively supports specific data types; some expand their native formats to other open source formats. Data scientists sometimes prefer to keep their data (images, in our case) in blob storage and read it directly from storage rather than using Delta tables, as they think this avoids additional work. However, we recommend storing images in a Delta table unless you are working with large images greater than one GB per image. Storing your images in a Delta table allows you to take advantage of Delta and Unity Catalog's additional benefits, such as lineage of data and models, data version control, duplicate data checks, and quality assurance.

At the time of writing, you have a few options to read your data while working with a PyTorch or PyTorch Lightning framework:

*   `DeltaTorchLoader` (recommended)
*   Petastorm
*   Reading images directly from blob/disk/volumes

Our recommendation is to use DeltaTorchLoader. It handles data batching, sampling, and multiprocessing while training PyTorch pipelines without requiring a temporary copy of files, like with Petastorm. See *Further reading* for more information.

At the time of writing, DeltaTorchLoader, which we are going to use to load and transform our data from Delta into the PyTorch/Lightning dataloader framework to train our model in *Chapter 6*, requires you to have tables in the unmanaged Delta format in volumes when using UC. Don't worry; the lineage is associated with the same path to the volume as your main dataset. We'll talk more about lineage in *Chapter 6*. This requirement is due to UC's read/write security permissions with blob storage. The blob storage maintainers do not support these security settings yet. If you are not using UC, you should be able to read Delta tables directly from the managed tables.

There is also an option to read your data using the Petastorm library. We don't recommend Petastorm because it requires a deeper understanding of certain pitfalls. The most common are memory usage issues due to data caching and the fact that it uses Apache `Parquet` files rather than Delta files, so it consumes all versions of your parquet files.

The creators of the DeltaTorchLoader performed a few benchmarks with Petastorm. The benchmark was shared at the **Data and AI Summit** (**DAIS**) and is featured in *Figure 3.33*. In this project, we will compare Petastorm to the classic Torch loader in *Chapter 6* to show the performance gain. The comparison demonstrates an incredible speed increase when reading the batch of data. We've also included a great video on *TorchDeltaLoader* in *Further reading* if you want to learn more.

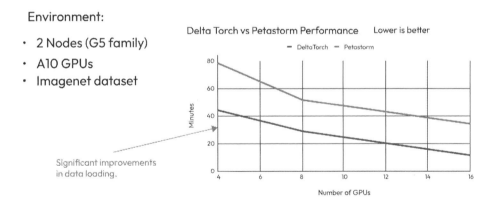

Figure 3.32 – The DeltaTorchLoader benchmark – a performance comparison between the DeltaTorch and Petastorm loaders

You can keep filenames in your Delta table instead of the images and collect them while passing them to the main PyTorch Loader with the `trainer` function. Keeping files in Delta is essential to avoid duplicates and control the list used during training and validation, as you can pass the Delta version to MLflow during tracking for full replication purposes.

Optimizing our data

Once our tables are created and written to the storage, we use a few functions to improve read performance on the Delta tables. First, we use OPTIMIZE to keep an ideal number of files (*Figure 3.34*). Second, we disable deletion vectors because the DeltaTorchReader does not support them yet (*Figure 3.35*). We use the SQL magic command, %sql, to perform these operations, using SQL in the Python notebook.

```
1   %sql
2   -- you can set up a widget to a notebook and consume widgets via $ variables with SQL
3   --OPTIMIZE delta.`/Volumes/$catalog/$database_name/files/intel_image_clf/valid_imgs_main.delta`
4   OPTIMIZE delta.`/Volumes/ml_in_action/cv_clf/files/intel_image_clf/train_imgs_main.delta`
```

Figure 3.33 – Optimizing the file size and count of the training table

Note that the variables we saved in Python are inaccessible in SQL, so we hardcode them in this example. You could include SQL variables in the global-setup notebook to avoid this.

```
1   %sql
2   ALTER TABLE delta.`/Volumes/ml_in_action/cv_clf/files/intel_image_clf/train_imgs_main.delta` SET TBLPROPERTIES ('delta.enableDeletionVectors' = false);
3   ALTER TABLE delta.`/Volumes/ml_in_action/cv_clf/files/intel_image_clf/valid_imgs_main.delta` SET TBLPROPERTIES ('delta.enableDeletionVectors' = false);
```

Figure 3.34 – Optimizing the training table

Now, we have the training and validation tables loaded and optimized to efficiently work with this image data to fine-tune our multi-class computer vision models.

Summary

In this chapter, we focused on the essentials of building out the Bronze data layer within the Databricks Data Intelligence Platform. We emphasized the importance of schema evolution, DLT, and the conversion of data into the Delta format and applied these principles in our example projects. This chapter highlighted the significance of tools such as Auto Loader and DLT in this process. Auto Loader, with its proficiency in handling file tracking and automating schema management, alongside DLT's robust capabilities in pipeline development and data quality assurance, are pivotal in our data management strategy. These tools facilitate an efficient and streamlined approach to data pipeline management, enabling us as data scientists to focus more on valuable tasks, such as feature engineering and experimentation.

With our Bronze layer created, we now move on from this foundational work to a more advanced layer of data – the Silver layer. *Chapter 4, Transformations toward Our Silver Layer*, will take us deeper into our data and demonstrate various Databricks tools that will aid us in the exploration and transformations of our data.

Questions

The following questions solidify key points to remember and tie the content back to your experience:

1. What are the names of the layers in the Medallion architecture design?

2. If you wanted to build a managed pipeline with streaming data, which product would you use – Structured Streaming or DLT?

3. What feature did we use to add the `product` column to our streaming transaction data without manual intervention?

4. Do you have projects from your current position, experience, or on your roadmap that would benefit from one or more of the topics covered in this chapter?

5. What is a possible way to lessen the number of partitions when partitioning on a high cardinality column?

Answers

After putting thought into the questions, compare your answers to ours:

1. The layers of the Medallion architecture are Bronze, Silver, and Gold.

2. We recommend DLT build managed pipelines.

3. In the streaming transactions project example, we used Auto Loader's schema evolution feature to add a column without manual intervention.

4. We hope so! One example is a managed streaming data pipeline that could benefit from the built-in data quality monitoring that comes with DLT.

5. Bucketing is an optimal method specifically designed to provide an additional layer of organization in your data. It can reduce the number of output files and organize the data better for subsequent reading, and it can be especially useful when the partitioning column has high cardinality.

Further reading

This chapter covered different methods of ingesting data into your Bronze layer. Take a look at these resources to read more about the areas that interest you most:

*   *Use liquid clustering for Delta tables*: `https://docs.databricks.com/en/delta/clustering.html`

*   *Spark Structured Streaming*: `https://spark.apache.org/docs/latest/structured-streaming-programming-guide.html`

*   *Delta Live Tables*: `https://docs.databricks.com/en/delta-live-tables/index.html`

- *DLT Databricks Demo*: https://www.databricks.com/resources/demos/tutorials/lakehouse-platform/full-delta-live-table-pipeline

- *Auto Loader options*: https://docs.databricks.com/ingestion/auto-loader/options.html

- *Schema evolution with Auto Loader*: https://docs.databricks.com/ingestion/auto-loader/schema.html#configure-schema-inference-and-evolution-in-auto-loader

- *Common loading patterns with Auto Loader*: https://docs.databricks.com/ingestion/auto-loader/patterns.html

- *Stream processing with Apache Kafka and Databricks*: https://docs.databricks.com/structured-streaming/kafka.html

- *How We Performed ETL on One Billion Records For Under $1 With Delta Live Tables*: https://www.databricks.com/blog/2023/04/14/how-we-performed-etl-one-billion-records-under-1-delta-live-tables.html

- *Create tables – Managed vs External*: https://docs.databricks.com/en/data-governance/unity-catalog/create-tables.html#create-tables

- *Take full advantage of the auto-tuning available*: https://docs.databricks.com/delta/tune-file-size.html#configure-delta-lake-to-control-data-file-size

- Import Python modules from Databricks repos: https://docs.databricks.com/en/delta-live-tables/import-workspace-files.html

- Deletion Vectors: https://docs.databricks.com/en/delta/deletion-vectors.html

- *Databricks ML Runtime*: https://docs.databricks.com/runtime/mlruntime.html#introduction-to-databricks-runtime-for-machine-learning

- *Cluster advanced options*: https://docs.databricks.com/en/clusters/configure.html#spark-configuration

- *Deploy provisioned throughput Foundation Model APIs*: https://docs.databricks.com/en/machine-learning/foundation-models/deploy-prov-throughput-foundation-model-apis.html

- *Scaling Deep Learning Using Delta Lake Storage Format on Databricks*: https://www.databricks.com/dataaisummit/session/scaling-deep-learning-using-delta-lake-storage-format-databricks/

- *DeltaTorchLoader*: https://github.com/delta-incubator/deltatorch

Part 2:
Heavily Use Case-Focused

This part introduces you to taking a set of data sources and working with them throughout the platform, from one end to another. The goal of this part is simply to demonstrate how to thoughtfully use all the bells and whistles of the platform. This part provides stories, code, lakehouse features, and best practices.

This part has the following chapters:

4

Getting to Know Your Data

"Truth, like gold, is to be obtained not by its growth, but by washing away from it all that is not gold."

—*Leo Tolstoy*

In this chapter, we explore features within the Databricks DI Platform that help improve and monitor data quality and facilitate data exploration. There are numerous approaches to getting to know your data better with Databricks. First, we cover how to oversee data quality with **Delta Live Tables** (**DLT**) to catch quality issues early and prevent the contamination of entire pipelines. We'll take our first close look at Lakehouse Monitoring, which helps us analyze data changes over time and can alert us to changes that concern us. Lakehouse Monitoring is a big time-saver, allowing you to focus on mitigating or responding to data changes rather than creating notebooks that calculate standard metrics.

Moving on to data exploration, we will look at a couple of low-code approaches: Databricks Assistant and **AutoML**. Finally, we will touch on embeddings. We created embeddings from chunks of text in *Chapter 3*, and you'll learn how to use Databricks **Vector Search** (**VS**) to explore your embeddings.

Here is what you will learn as part of this chapter:

- Improving data integrity with DLT

- Monitoring data quality with Databricks Lakehouse Monitoring

- Exploring data with Databricks Assistant

- Generating data profiles with AutoML

- Preparing data for vector search and database indexing

- Enhancing data retrieval with Databricks Vector Search

- Applying our learning

Improving data integrity with DLT

In the last chapter, we introduced DLT as a helpful tool for streaming data and pipeline development. Here, we focus on how to use DLT as your go-to tool for actively tracking data quality. Generally, datasets are dynamic, not neat, and tidy like they often are in school and training. You can use code to clean data, of course, but there is a feature that makes the cleaning process even easier: DLT's expectations. DLT's expectations catch incoming data quality issues and automatically validate that incoming data passes specified rules and quality checks. For example, you might expect your customer data to have positive values for age or that dates follow a specific format. When data does not meet these expectations, it can negatively impact downstream data pipelines. With expectations implemented, you ensure that your pipelines won't suffer.

Implementing expectations gives us more control over data quality, alerting us to unusual data requiring attention and action. There are several options when dealing with erroneous data in DLT:

1. First, we can set a warning, which will report the number of records that failed an expectation as a metric but still write those invalid records to the destination dataset; see `@dlt.expect()` in *Figure 4.1* for an example.

2. Second, we can drop invalid records so that the final dataset only contains records that meet our expectations; see `@dlt.expect_or_drop()` in *Figure 4.1*.

3. Third, we can fail the operation entirely, so nothing new is written (note that this option requires manual re-triggering of the pipeline).

4. Finally, we can quarantine the invalid data to another table to investigate it further. The following code should look familiar to the DLT code in *Chapter 3*, but now with the addition of expectations.

```
1   def generate_table():
2     table_name = spark.conf.get('table_name')
3     @dlt.table(name=f'{table_name}',table_properties={"quality":"bronze"})
4     @dlt.expect_or_drop("valid_CustomerID", "CustomerID IS NOT NULL")
5     @dlt.expect("valid_Product", "Product IS NOT NULL")
6     def create_table():
7       return build_autoloader_stream()
```

Figure 4.1 – Using DLT expectations to enforce data quality

Let's look at our streaming transactions project as an example. In the *Applying our learning* section in *Chapter 3*, we used DLT to write the transaction data to a table. Utilizing the same DLT code, we will save ourselves the manual effort of cleaning the CustomerID column by adding an expectation to the original code to drop any records with a null CustomerID. We will set another expectation to warn us if the Product field is null.

Now, when we call `generate_table()`, the DLT pipeline will automatically clean up our table by dropping any null `CustomerID` values and flagging records without a `Product` value. Moreover, DLT will automatically build helpful visualizations to immediately investigate the data's quality.

To try this yourself, update the DLT code from *Chapter 3* (here's the path to the notebook as a reminder: `Chapter 3: Building Out Our Bronze Layer/Project: Streaming Transactions/delta_live_tables/`) to match *Figure 4.1*, and then rerun the DLT pipeline as you did before. Once the pipeline is complete, it generates the DAG. Click on the `synthetic_transactions_silver` table, then click the **Data Quality** tab from the table details. This will display information about the records processed, such as how many were written versus dropped for failing a given expectation, as shown in *Figure 4.2*.

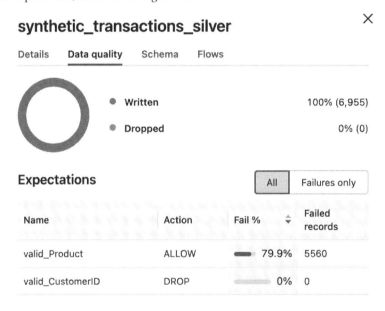

Figure 4.2 – The DLT data quality visualizations

These insights illustrate how expectations help automatically clean up our tables and flag information that might be useful for data scientists using this table downstream. In this example, we see that all records passed the `valid_CustomerID` expectation, so now we know we don't have to worry about null customer IDs in the table. Additionally, almost 80% of records are missing a `Product` value, which may be relevant for data science and **machine learning** (**ML**) projects that use this data.

Just as we've considered the correctness and consistency of incoming data, we also want to consider how we can expand our data quality oversight to include data drift, for example, when your data's distribution changes over time. Observing data drift is where Databricks Lakehouse Monitoring emerges as a vital complement to DLT, offering a configurable framework to consistently observe and verify the statistical properties and quality of input data.

Monitoring data quality with Databricks Lakehouse Monitoring

Use Databricks Lakehouse Monitoring to proactively detect and respond to any deviations in your data distribution. Over time, your data may undergo changes in its underlying patterns. This could be feature drift, where the distribution of feature data changes over time, or concept drift, where the relationship between inputs and outputs of your model changes. Both types of drift can cause model quality to suffer. These changes can occur slowly or rapidly in your production environment, which is why monitoring your data even before it becomes an input into your ML models and data products is essential.

Mechanics of Lakehouse Monitoring

To monitor a table in Databricks, you create a monitor attached to that table. To monitor the performance of a ML model, you attach the monitor to an inference table that holds the model's inputs and corresponding predictions. Databricks Lakehouse Monitoring provides the following profile types of analysis: snapshot, time series, and inference.

In addition to selecting the table to be monitored, called the **primary table**, you can optionally specify a baseline table to reference for measuring drift or the change in values over time. A baseline table is useful when you have a sample of what you expect your data to look like, such as the data with which your model was trained. Lakehouse Monitoring automatically computes drift relative to expected data values and distributions of the baseline table.

Creating a table monitor automatically creates two metric tables, `profile_metrics` and `drift_metrics`. Lakehouse Monitoring computes metric values on the table for the time windows and data subsets or "slices" you specify when you create the monitor. You can also add your own custom metrics; see *Further reading* for details.

Visualization and alerting

Lakehouse Monitoring generates an SQL dashboard automatically for every monitor. These dashboards provide a crucial platform for examining metrics and acting on results. Databricks' alert system serves as a vigilant guardian, promptly notifying you of the significant shifts in data quality or distributions you subscribe to. *Figure 4.3* shows how all the Lakehouse Monitoring components work together, using the data from the primary table and optional baseline table to generate a profile metrics table and drift table, which then populate the dashboard and power alerts.

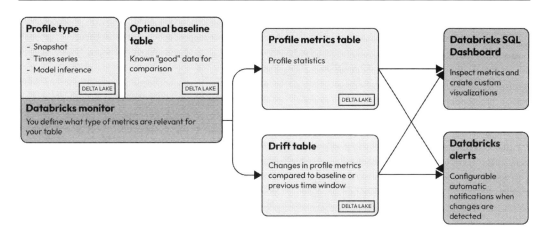

Figure 4.3 – Relationship between the input tables, the metric tables, the monitor, and the dashboard

Creating a monitor

You can create a Databricks Lakehouse Monitor using the **user interface** (**UI**) or, for a more flexible and programmable approach, you can use the API. The API method is particularly advantageous when you want to script the creation of monitors to integrate them into your automated data pipelines. The following is a high-level summary of the steps to create a Lakehouse Monitor using the API:

1. **Choose the profile type**: Decide on the profile type parameter that best suits your monitoring needs. The available types are `Snapshot`, `TimeSeries`, and `Inference`. Each type is suitable for different monitoring scenarios, with the `TimeSeries` and `Inference` types requiring a timestamp column. The inference profile also requires `prediction_col` and `model_id_col`.

2. **Create the monitor**: Use the `lakehouse_monitoring` module to call the `create_monitor` function, providing your table's catalog schema, table name, the chosen profile type, and the output schema for the monitor's results.

3. **Set the schedule**: If you wish to run the monitor at regular intervals, you can specify a schedule using the `MonitorCronSchedule` object, which takes a cron expression and a time zone ID.

4. **Control access**: After you create the monitor, you can manage access to the resulting metrics tables and dashboard using Unity Catalog privileges.

5. **Refresh and review results**: Use the `run_refresh` function to refresh and update the metric tables. You can also check the status of specific runs with the `get_refresh` function and list all refreshes associated with a monitor using `list_refreshes`.

6. **Review monitor settings**: The `get_monitor` function allows you to retrieve your monitor's current settings for review.

Figure 4.4 shows an example of how to use the Lakehouse Monitoring API to create a `TimeSeries` profile monitor:

```
1    from databricks import lakehouse_monitoring as lm
2
3    # Create a TimeSeries monitor
4    lm.create_monitor(
5        table_name=f"{catalog}.{schema}.{table_name}",
6        profile_type=lm.TimeSeries(
7            timestamp_col="ts",
8            granularities=["30 minutes"]
9        ),
10       output_schema_name=f"{catalog}.{schema}",
11       schedule=lm.MonitorCronSchedule(
12           quartz_cron_expression="0 0 12 * * ?",  # Refresh every day at noon PST
13           timezone_id="PST",
14       )
15   )
```

Figure 4.4 – Creating a simple TimeSeries table monitor

After establishing a robust framework for data quality monitoring with Databricks Lakehouse Monitoring, we can focus on enhancing our data exploration. This leads us to Databricks Assistant, a feature dedicated to helping developers be more productive in Databricks.

Exploring data with Databricks Assistant

Databricks Assistant is a feature designed to boost your productivity in Databricks. It has many capabilities, including generating SQL from English, explaining code, helping troubleshoot errors, and optimizing code. Databricks Assistant is an exciting feature to watch as more capabilities emerge, and we want to give you a taste of the possibilities. Since this chapter is about exploring and monitoring data, let's see how you can use Databricks Assistant as a low-code solution to explore your data. Suppose you are analyzing the Favorita Sales Forecasting data. You are looking to uncover insights into retail store distributions across various regions. You have a specific query in mind: you want to understand the store landscape in the Guayas region. However, SQL queries aren't your strong suit, and maybe crafting the perfect query seems daunting. In order to explore your data regardless, you can use Databricks Assistant. There is no notebook in the project repo for this section, but we encourage you to try Databricks Assistant on the Favorita Forecasting project tables. Any of the *Chapter 4* Favorita notebooks would be a great place to access Databricks Assistant. To access it, click on the icon shown in *Figure 4.5*, found in the left-hand sidebar of a notebook. Clicking on the icon will open the chat interface to the left of the notebook, where we will type in our questions.

Figure 4.5 – The Databricks Assistant icon

First, we ask Databricks Assistant how many stores and store types are in the state of Guayas in the favorita_stores table (*Figure 4.6*). Note that Databricks Assistant does not require Unity Catalog, but using Unity Catalog provides table information. The additional information makes Databricks Assistant's responses more helpful and specific to the table you're working with. This should sound similar to the **Retrieval Augmented Generation** (**RAG**) project. We are augmenting the generation of answers by providing relevant information. Now, let's see whether it can help us write the SQL query we need. Keep in mind that Databricks Assistant is powered by **generative AI**, so you may see different outputs when using it yourself.

mandy.baker@databricks.com

How many stores and types of stores are in the state of Guaya in the favorita_stores table

Assistant

You can run the following SQL query to get the number of stores and types of stores in the state of Guaya in the favorita_stores table:

```
1  %sql
2  SELECT COUNT(DISTINCT store_nbr) AS num_stores, COUNT(DISTINCT
   type) AS num_store_types
3  FROM lakehouse_in_action.favorita_forecasting.favorita_stores
4  WHERE state='Guayas'
```

This query counts the distinct store_nbr and type values in the favorita_stores table for the state of Guayas. The WHERE clause filters the query by state.

Figure 4.6 – Question and response interaction with Databricks Assistant

Nice! Databricks Assistant gave us some SQL code to paste into a notebook and run directly. However, a quick scan of the query shows us that we will only get a distinct count of stores and types rather than looking at the store type distribution we want. Let's refine our question and try again (*Figure 4.7*).

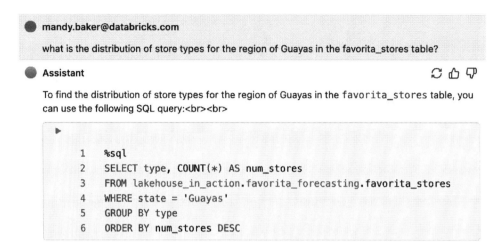

Figure 4.7 – The updated question submitted to Databricks Assistant and the results

After submitting the second question in *Figure 4.7*, Databricks Assistant provides a new query that accurately captures what we want to know. To make sure, let's copy the SQL code provided, paste it into a notebook, and run it.

Figure 4.8 – Results from Databricks Assistant-generated SQL query

Now we see the distribution of stores by type in the Guayas region, just as we wanted. Databricks Assistant is a handy tool, and we can confirm that playing with it is also fun! We encourage you to try it out on your own to see how you can use English to explore your data.

Databricks Assistant also generates comment suggestions for your tables and fields. From the **Unity Catalog Explorer** page, navigate to the same `favorita_stores` table we explored previously. We see in *Figure 4.9* that Databricks Assistant has a suggestion for a table comment to help others understand the table's contents.

Catalogs › lakehouse_in_action › favorita_forecasting ›

▦ lakehouse_in_action.favorita_forecasting.favorita_stores ⚠

Owner: stephanie.rivera@databricks.com ✎   Popularity: ⫑   Size: 2.6KiB, 1 file Last Updated: 3 months ago

Tags: [Add tags]

✦ **AI Suggested Comment** [Preview]   ✕

The 'favorita_stores' table contains data related to our chain of stores. It includes information such as the store's location, its type, and a unique identifier for each store. This data can be used for various purposes such as analyzing store performance, planning logistics, or forecasting sales trends based on location and store type.

[✓ Accept]   [✎ Edit]   ☺ Send feedback

Figure 4.9 – Databricks Assistant suggests a descriptive table comment

Databricks Assistant can also generate descriptive comments for each field in the table by selecting the **AI Generate** button on the right-hand side of the table's **Columns** tab page. You can accept or edit the suggested comments. You can toggle off the suggestions by selecting the **Hide AI suggestions** button, as shown in *Figure 4.10*.

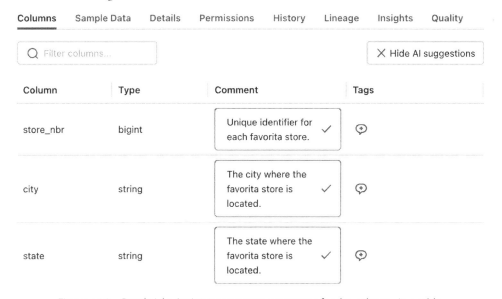

Column	Type	Comment	Tags
store_nbr	bigint	Unique identifier for each favorita store. ✓	⊕
city	string	The city where the favorita store is located. ✓	⊕
state	string	The state where the favorita store is located. ✓	⊕

Figure 4.10 – Databricks Assistant suggests comments for the columns in a table

The generated comments might seem like they fall outside the scope of getting to know your data, but documentation is vital to making your data more easily discoverable for everyone else (and let's hope others use generated comments so you can explore their datasets more easily too). The faster you understand a dataset, the easier it is to further explore that data.

Databricks Assistant is a great way to analyze your data when you prefer to work in English rather than code directly, and when you have specific questions in mind. Now let's discuss another method for broader **exploratory data analysis** (**EDA**): autogenerated notebooks using AutoML.

Generating data profiles with AutoML

We introduced Databricks AutoML in *Chapter 1*. This tool automates ML development and augments data science workflows. AutoML is best known for generating models, but we'll get to modeling in *Chapter 6*. Since we're talking about getting to know your data, we first want to focus on one extremely useful feature built into AutoML that often flies under the radar: autogenerated Python notebooks. AutoML provides a notebook for data exploration in addition to the notebook code for every experiment it runs. We will jump right into creating an AutoML experiment, view the data exploration code, and then return to explore the modeling portion later.

We'll cover how to create an AutoML experiment via an API in the Favorita project notebooks. We encourage you to follow the instructions here to set up a simple regression experiment with the AutoML UI, so that we can take a look at the data profile created. Before you begin, make sure you have a DBR ML 9.1+ cluster running (you can use the **DBR ML 14.2** cluster set up in *Chapter 2*):

1. **Start the experiment**: Navigate to the **Experiments** tab on the platform's left-hand navigation bar. Click the **AutoML Experiment** button to initiate a new experiment.

2. **Configure the AutoML experiment**:

   - **Compute configuration**:

     i.   **Cluster**: Select the **DBR ML 14.2** cluster set up in *Chapter 2*, or any other cluster with an ML runtime with a version greater than 9.1. Note that the cluster won't appear in the drop-down menu unless it's running.

   - **Experiment configuration**:

     i.   **ML problem type**: Select the type of ML problem you're addressing. Select **Regression**, which is suitable for predicting continuous outcomes such as sales figures or temperature.

     ii. **Input training dataset**: Specify the dataset you will use to train the model. You can use the Favorita project's `ml_in_action.favorita_forecasting.favorite_train_set` table, or your own data (just make sure to update the problem type if `Regression` does not apply).

iii. **Prediction target**: Choose the specific column in your dataset that you want to predict. The AutoML process will use the other columns in your dataset to try and predict the values in this target column. If you're following along with the Favorita scenario, select **sales**.

Figure 4.11 shows the configuration of an AutoML experiment using the `favorite_train_set` training table. It illustrates how you can customize the AutoML process to fit the specific requirements of your ML task. By selecting the appropriate problem type, dataset, and prediction target, you're instructing the AutoML system on how to approach the model-building process.

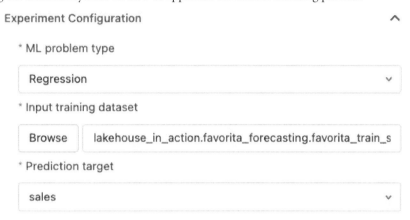

Figure 4.11 – Configuration of an AutoML experiment using the Favorita train_set table

Once you've filled out the UI and specified the Favorita table (or another table of your choice) as your input training dataset, click **Start AutoML** at the bottom of the screen. AutoML experiments may run for up to several hours as improvements in the evaluation metric continue, although you can set a shorter time limit for the experiment by changing the **Timeout** value (found under **Advanced Configuration**). As the experiment begins, a new page will open with progress updates. Once the experiment is complete, you will see links to two data artifacts: the notebook containing the code for the best model, labeled **View notebook for best model**, and the data exploration notebook, labeled **View data exploration notebook**, as shown in *Figure 4.12*.

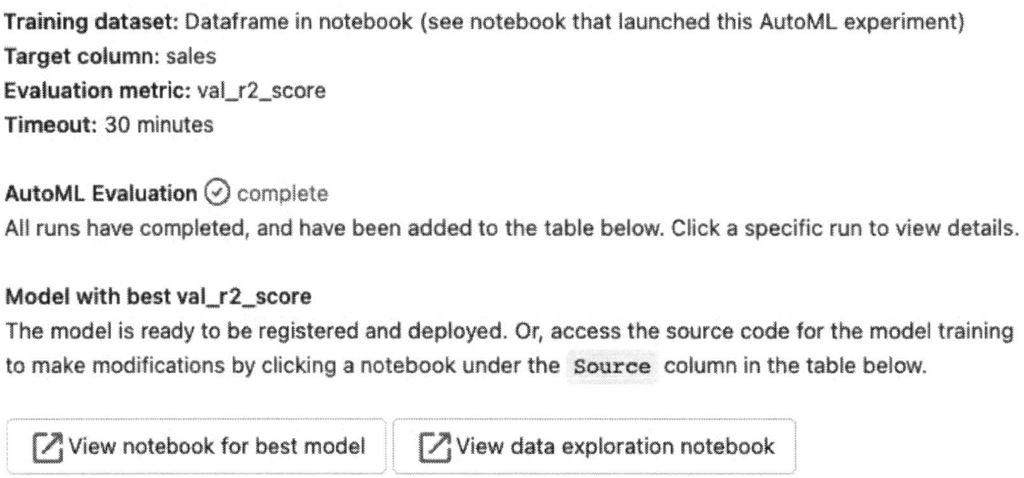

Training dataset: Dataframe in notebook (see notebook that launched this AutoML experiment)
Target column: sales
Evaluation metric: val_r2_score
Timeout: 30 minutes

AutoML Evaluation ⊘ complete
All runs have completed, and have been added to the table below. Click a specific run to view details.

Model with best val_r2_score
The model is ready to be registered and deployed. Or, access the source code for the model training to make modifications by clicking a notebook under the `Source` column in the table below.

[↗ View notebook for best model]   [↗ View data exploration notebook]

Figure 4.12 – The AutoML experiment page with the links to view the
notebook for the best model and the data exploration notebook

The exploration notebook uses `ydata-profiling`, formerly referred to as pandas' profiler library, to generate statistics and summarize data for all the fields in the table. It also provides alerts on fields with high correlation issues, which could negatively impact models. These warnings are also available in the MLflow experiment UI, as shown in *Figure 4.13*.

Severity	Type	Affected Data	Action
Low	Data exploration notebook ran on a subset of rows because dataset is too big		Modify the data exploration notebook and rerun it to profile the entire dataset.
Low	High correlation columns	**onpromotion id data sales family +1 more**	Correlations found. Refer to data exploration notebook for more details.
Low	Unique values in categorical columns	id	

Figure 4.13 – AutoML warnings called out during the experiment run

Look through the data exploration notebook for an overview of your data, from summary statistics to thorough profiles for each variable.

We have now explored two tools for data exploration: Databricks Assistant and the `ydata-profiling` library. These are great places to start for many classical ML projects. Next, we'll discuss a more advanced data format and how you can use the DI Platform to explore it: data embeddings and vector search. Embeddings are advanced transformations that translate complex, unstructured data into a numerical format conducive to ML algorithms, capturing intricate relationships within the data that are pivotal for sophisticated models.

Using embeddings to understand unstructured data

So far, we've focused on how to explore your structured data. What about unstructured data, such as images or text? Recall that we converted PDF text chunks into a specific format called embeddings in *Chapter 3*'s RAG chatbot project work. We require embeddings, meaning numerical vector representations of the data, to perform a similarity (or hybrid) search between chunks of text. That way, when someone asks our chatbot a question, such as "What are the economic impacts of automation technologies using LLMs?" the chatbot will be able to search through the stored chunks of text from the arXiv articles, retrieve the most relevant chunks, and use those to better answer the question. For more visual readers, see the data preparation workflow in *Figure 4.14*. We completed the **Data Preparation** step in *Chapter 3*. We'll run through the remaining setup steps in the workflow now.

Vector Database Preparation

Data Preparation	Embedding Model	Databricks VS	Vector Database
1. Download the PDFs 2. Extract the text 3. Create chunks of text	1. Tokenize chunks (Llama) 2. Covert chunks to embeddings (Out-of-the-box BG Embedding Model)	1. Create a Vector Search endpoint	1. Create an index on the VS endpoint

Figure 4.14 – Vector database setup is the prerequisite process supporting RAG's retrieval step

Embeddings are an essential part of building any chatbot. Pay attention to your embedding model to ensure it is relevant to the task. You wouldn't want to build a chatbot designed to answer questions in French but use an embedding model that only knows English – your chatbot's response quality will definitely suffer!

Embeddings that capture the nuances of language are essential for the chatbot to understand and generate contextually relevant responses. Equally important are the searching and filtering techniques you apply to the **vector database** itself. A vector database is similar to a SQL database, but instead of storing tabular data, it stores vector embeddings. A search algorithm can then search the embeddings. In the final flow of a RAG project, a user's question is also converted into embeddings, and the search algorithm uses those embeddings to find similar embeddings stored in the vector database. The chatbot receives the most similar embeddings from the vector database to help it craft a response to the user's question.

Let's consider the requirements of a good vector database solution:

- **Quality of the retrievals**: The correctness and completeness of embeddings returned as relevant by the search algorithm
- **Scalability of the solution**: The ability to scale per the number of requests coming to the application with dynamic traffic

- **Accessibility**: The ability to easily access, read, write to, and use the application in real time

- **Governance**: The ability to govern vector storage with the same access controls as the original sources used to create the vector embeddings and models

- **Integration**: The ability to easily integrate with current market technologies and eliminate time spent stitching technologies and solutions together

Using embeddings and vector search is a powerful way to improve a variety of ML projects. There are many uses for vector databases, the most common of which are as follows:

- **RAG systems**: Vector search facilitates efficient data retrieval, which is then used to augment a **Large Language Model** (**LLM**)'s response. Augmenting an LLM with results from vector search leads to more accurate chatbot responses and minimizes errors such as hallucinations in LLM outputs.

- **Recommendation systems**: E-commerce and streaming platforms use vector search for efficient nearest-neighbor searches, matching user behavior with relevant suggestions.

- **Image and video recognition**: Vector search facilitates quick searches for similar features in images and videos.

- **Bioinformatics**: Vector search can be applied to tasks such as DNA sequence alignment and protein structure similarity search to improve clinical research.

Enhancing data retrieval with Databricks Vector Search

Databricks VS is transforming how we refine and retrieve data for LLMs. Functioning as a serverless similarity search engine, VS enables the storage of vector embeddings and metadata in a dedicated vector database. Through VS, you can generate dynamic vector search indices from **Delta** tables overseen by Unity Catalog. Using a straightforward API, you can retrieve the most similar vectors through queries.

Here are some of Databricks VS's key benefits:

- **Seamless integration**: VS works harmoniously within Databricks' ecosystem, particularly Delta tables. This integration ensures that your data is always up to date, making it model-ready for ML applications. With VS, you can create a vector search index from a source Delta table and set the index to sync when the source table is updated.

- **Streamlined operations**: VS significantly simplifies operational complexity by eliminating the need to manage third-party vector databases. VS runs on serverless compute, meaning Databricks handles the infrastructure management for you.

- **Enhanced scalability**: Unlike standalone vector libraries, VS offers unparalleled scalability. VS handles large-scale data effortlessly, scaling automatically to meet the demands of your data and query load. This scalability is crucial for organizations with vast amounts of data and complex search requirements.

- **Unified data asset governance**: VS integrates with Unity Catalog; Unity Catalog handles data governance and access control lists. To prevent productional data leakage, you can manage access to the Databricks VS API and the underlying databases with Unity Catalog.

- **Model Serving integration**: Model Serving automates querying of the model serving endpoint for embedding generation without any overhead from users.

Flexibility in embedding model support

One of VS's major strengths is its support for any of the embedding models of your choice. VS supports hosted or fully managed embeddings. Hosted embeddings are self-managed. You create the embeddings and save them on a Delta table. For fully managed embeddings, the prepared text is saved in a Delta table, and embeddings are created by Databricks Model Serving. Model Serving will convert your incoming data into embeddings with the model of your choice. Databricks VS can support any model through the Databricks Model Serving endpoints, the Foundation Model API (as mentioned in *Chapter 3*), or external models. External models include SaaS models, for example, OpenAI's ChatGPT and Anthropic's PaLM. You can connect external models through the Databricks unified model serving gateway. See *External models in Databricks Model Serving* in *Further reading* for more information.

Setting up a vector search

As mentioned, VS is a serverless product. Hence, we require a real-time connection with our chatbot application to the relevant content stored in the vector database. We'll cover this again in the *Applying our learning, Project – RAG chatbot* section, but if you're ready to set up your own endpoint, you just need a few lines of code, as shown in *Figure 4.15*.

```
1    from databricks.vector_search.client import VectorSearchClient
2
3    vsc = VectorSearchClient()
4    vsc.create_endpoint(name="my_vector_search_endpoint", endpoint_type="STANDARD")
```

Figure 4.15 – Creating a Databricks VS endpoint

Once you create an endpoint, you can host multiple vector search indices under one endpoint. The endpoint will scale according to the demand. The code to host your first index is presented in the *Apply our learning* section).

There are limitations on the number of endpoints you can create indices per endpoint, and the embedding dimensions. Please review the documentation linked in *Further reading*, as Databricks may remove or update limits as the product evolves.

Technology moves fast, especially in the world of generative AI. Databricks VS was built even as we wrote this book, and we expect it to continue evolving to search not only through text but also images and audio with a more robust hybrid search engine in the future.

We've walked through various Databricks products and features geared toward helping you understand your data. Get ready to follow along in your own Databricks workspace as we work through the *Chapter 4* code by project and put these concepts into practice.

Applying our learning

It's time to apply these concepts to our example projects. We will use what we have learned to explore each project dataset, from using Databricks Assistant to AutoML, to creating a vector search index and exploring image data.

Technical requirements

Before you begin, review, and prepare the technical requirements necessary for the hands-on work in this chapter:

- We use the `missingno` library to address missing numbers in our synthetic transactions project data: `https://pypi.org/project/missingno/`

- For the RAG project, you will need to install the following either on your cluster or in the `CH4-01-Creating_VectorDB` notebook. If you choose to install them in the notebook, the code is included for you:

  - `typing_extensions==4.7.1`

  - `transformers==4.30.2`

  - `llama-index==0.9.3`

  - `langchain==0.0.319`

  - `unstructured[pdf,docx]==0.10.30`

Project – Favorita Store Sales – time-series forecasting

For the Favorita Store Sales project, we use many simple DBSQL queries for data exploration and to understand the relationships between datasets. Additionally, we use the `ydata_profiling` library to produce data profiles in HTML format, as shown in *Figure 4.19*. To follow along in your own workspace, please refer to the following notebooks:

- `CH4-01-Exploring_Favorita_Sales_Data`

- `CH4-02-Exploring_Autogenerated_Notebook`

- `CH4-03-Imputing_Oil_Data`

In the last chapter, we created tables of the Favorita Sales Forecasting dataset from Kaggle. Now it's time to explore! Open up the first notebook, CH4-01-Exploring_Favorita_Sales_Data, to do some initial data exploration in SQL:

1. The first cell is a simple select * SQL command. After running the cell, focus on the in-cell **Data Profile** and **Visualization** options.

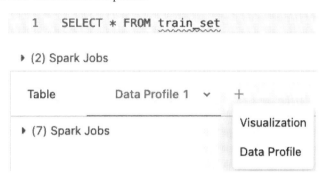

Figure 4.16 – You can create visualizations and a data profile of a SQL query result in a notebook

2. Choose **Data Profile** and investigate the information autogenerated about the data.

3. Choose **Visualization**. You can create a line chart with the date (month) versus the sum of sales and grouped by family. Notice that not all data is used to produce the visualization; we only see January at first. Once you save the visualization, the chart will display in the cell. The **Truncated data** message should be present at the bottom of the visualization. To increase the number of records in the chart, select **Aggregate over more data**.

4. Continue to play with the options. In the next cell, we filter to the top-performing product families. Investigate how different or similar the charts appear.

Now that we've done some initial exploration of the Favorita data, we can run a Databricks AutoML experiment to generate a baseline model. AutoML can be launched in the UI, which we demonstrated earlier in this chapter in the *Generating data profiles with AutoML* section (*Figure 4.11*), or you can create an experiment via an API as shown in *Figure 4.17*. For this project, we will launch both a regression experiment and a forecasting experiment. Let's start with the regression run.

Notice that at the top of the notebook, the default language is SQL rather than Python. Therefore, when we want to execute Python code, we need to include %python at the top of the cell. We use Python for AutoML in the last cell of the first notebook. We've set the timeout_minutes variable to 30, so the experiment will run for up to 30 minutes. However, AutoML stops training models if the validation metric is no longer improving. In that case, the experiment will finish in less time. Once the run is complete, the notebook UI will display links to the MLflow experiment where the model versions are accessible, the best trial notebook with the best model's code, and the data exploration notebook. Since this chapter focuses on exploring data, we will only open the data exploration notebook for now.

```
1    from databricks import automl
2    summary = automl.regress(df, target_col="sales", timeout_minutes=30)
```

▸ (1) Spark Jobs

▾ (1) MLflow run

    Logged 1 run to an experiment in MLflow. Learn more

```
2023/08/20 22:46:13 INFO databricks.automl.client.manager: AutoML will optimize for R
2 metric, which is tracked as val_r2_score in the MLflow experiment.
2023/08/20 22:46:14 INFO databricks.automl.client.manager: MLflow Experiment ID: 1570
387049089135
2023/08/20 22:46:14 INFO databricks.automl.client.manager: MLflow Experiment: http
s://e2-demo-field-eng.cloud.databricks.com/?o=1444828305810485#mlflow/experiments/157
0387049089135
2023/08/20 22:47:30 INFO databricks.automl.client.manager: Data exploration notebook:
https://e2-demo-field-eng.cloud.databricks.com/?o=1444828305810485#notebook/157038704
9089154
2023/08/20 23:16:56 INFO databricks.automl.client.manager: AutoML experiment complete
d successfully.
```

For exploratory data analysis, open the data exploration notebook

To view the best performing model, open the best trial notebook

To view details about all trials, navigate to the MLflow experiment

Figure 4.17 – Creating an AutoML experiment from a notebook

AutoML for data exploration

When you executed the final cell in CH4-01-Exploring_Favorita_Sales_Data, you received several links in the results, as shown in *Figure 4.17*. Click on the link to the data exploration notebook (you can also open CH4-02-Exploring_Autogenerated_Notebook for a version that was autogenerated when we ran the AutoML experiment ourselves). Let's look at this notebook.

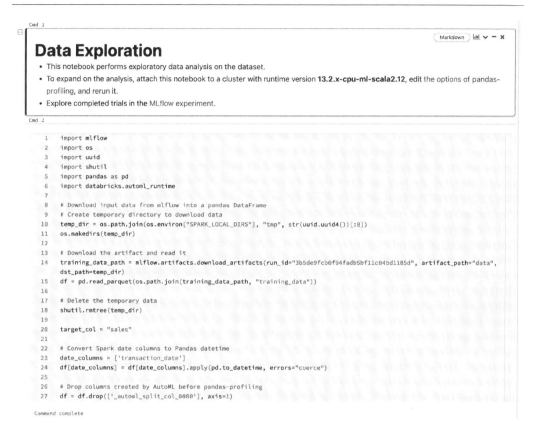

```
Cmd 1

                                                                    Markdown ⌄ — ✕

# Data Exploration
• This notebook performs exploratory data analysis on the dataset.
• To expand on the analysis, attach this notebook to a cluster with runtime version 13.2.x-cpu-ml-scala2.12, edit the options of pandas-
  profiling, and rerun it.
• Explore completed trials in the MLflow experiment.

Cmd 2

1   import mlflow
2   import os
3   import uuid
4   import shutil
5   import pandas as pd
6   import databricks.automl_runtime
7
8   # Download input data from mlflow into a pandas DataFrame
9   # Create temporary directory to download data
10  temp_dir = os.path.join(os.environ["SPARK_LOCAL_DIRS"], "tmp", str(uuid.uuid4())[:8])
11  os.makedirs(temp_dir)
12
13  # Download the artifact and read it
14  training_data_path = mlflow.artifacts.download_artifacts(run_id="3b5de9fcb0f94fadb5bf11c04bd1185d", artifact_path="data",
    dst_path=temp_dir)
15  df = pd.read_parquet(os.path.join(training_data_path, "training_data"))
16
17  # Delete the temporary data
18  shutil.rmtree(temp_dir)
19
20  target_col = "sales"
21
22  # Convert Spark date columns to Pandas datetime
23  date_columns = ['transaction_date']
24  df[date_columns] = df[date_columns].apply(pd.to_datetime, errors="coerce")
25
26  # Drop columns created by AutoML before pandas-profiling
27  df = df.drop(['_automl_split_col_0000'], axis=1)

Command complete
```

Figure 4.18 – EDA notebook created with AutoML

Figure 4.18 shows a portion of the automatically generated data exploration notebook. This notebook imports libraries and points to the training data. It also automatically converts the datetime columns to pandas datetime.

The notebook uses a pandas-based library, so the notebook limits the data to 10,000 rows.

Next, the notebook imports the ydata_profiling library, along with three additional correlation calculations added in this case. The ydata_profiling library provides similar data to what we would get using summary() functions, such as details about missing and correlated data. The library is easily imported into a notebook for exploring data. Once finished, you can export the details to HTML or PDF for easy sharing. It's a great timesaver when exploring new datasets.

```
1    from ydata_profiling import ProfileReport
2    df_profile = ProfileReport(df,
3                               correlations={
4                                   "auto": {"calculate": True},
5                                   "pearson": {"calculate": True},
6                                   "spearman": {"calculate": True},
7                                   "kendall": {"calculate": True},
8                                   "phi_k": {"calculate": True},
9                                   "cramers": {"calculate": True},
10                              }, title="Profiling Report", progress_bar=False, infer_dtypes=False)
11   profile_html = df_profile.to_html()
12
13   displayHTML(profile_html)
```

Figure 4.19 – ydata_profiling in the AutoML-created notebook

As shown in *Figure 4.17*, we launched a regression experiment via the API by calling `automl.regress()`. Now, we create another experiment with a forecasting problem type using the UI.

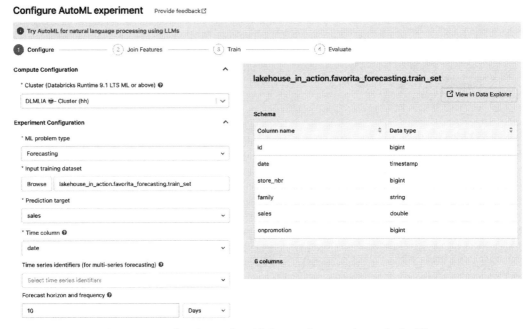

Figure 4.20 – Creating an AutoML forecasting experiment in the UI

When we create an AutoML forecasting experiment, we can incorporate a country's holidays into the model under the **Country Holidays** option in the **Advanced Configuration** section. We will choose **NONE** for this project, because although many countries are present in the drop-down menu, Ecuador is not among them. **NONE** will ensure holidays are not included as a feature in the model.

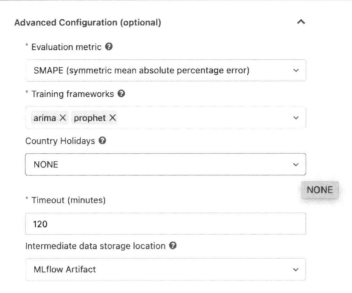

Figure 4.21 – AutoML forecasting experiment advanced configurations

Once all the fields are completed, click **Start AutoML** at the bottom of the screen to run the experiment (adjust the **Timeout** variable down if you want to ensure the run finishes within a given amount of time). When the experiment has finished running, you will see a new screen with a list of generated models.

We have now created an AutoML experiment in a notebook, used AutoML to generate a notebook for EDA, and used AutoML for time-series analysis. Databricks AutoML does a lot of the heavy lifting with minimal code for ML and EDA.

The Favorita sales dataset contains oil prices, which we think could impact sales, so let's augment the autogenerated data exploration with some of our own to explore the oil price data and see how we can use it.

Exploring and cleaning oil price data

To get started with the oil data, open the CH4-03-Imputing_Oil_Data notebook. We use the pandas API on Spark to view the data (*Figure 4.22*). We reindex the data because it's out of order and data for some dates is missing. Notice that initially, the data starts in May 2015 rather than January 2013. Also, the dates May 9th and May 10th appear to be missing.

```
1  import pyspark.pandas as ps
2
3  df = ps.read_table("oil_prices")
4  df.head(10)
```

▸ (2) Spark Jobs

	date	dcoilwtico
0	2015-05-04	58.92
1	2015-05-05	60.38
2	2015-05-06	60.93
3	2015-05-07	58.99
4	2015-05-08	59.41
5	2015-05-11	59.23
6	2015-05-12	60.72

Figure 4.22 – View the oil price data provided by Kaggle in the Favorita Sales dataset

If we add the `date` column as the index column, as shown in the notebook, you'll see that the rows are then in order. However, January 5th and January 6th are missing. This occurs because stock prices are not given for holidays or weekends.

```
1  df = (
2      df.reindex(ps.date_range(df.index.min(), df.index.max()))
3      .reset_index()
4      .rename(columns={"index": "date"})
5      .ffill()
6  )
7  df.to_table("oil_prices_silver")
8  df.head(10)
```

Figure 4.23 – Reindex to include all dates and fill forward missing prices

We use the `reindex()` command to create an updated index based on the minimum and maximum dates in the oil price data. The reindex creates rows for all missing dates. When new rows are created for the missing dates, the prices are NaNs. We use the `ffill()` function, or forward fill, to update the DataFrame by filling in dates without prices with the price from the day before. January 1st, 2013, doesn't have a previous day to fill from, so it remains NaN.

Now, we have a clean and consistent silver table of oil prices that we can pull into our Favorita time-series models. In the next chapter, we will do feature engineering with the Favorita sales data.

Project – streaming transactions

The synthetic dataset does not need cleaning (since we created it), but we can still explore the data to understand it better. To follow along in your own workspace, please refer to the following notebook:

- `CH4-01-Exploring_Synthetic_Transactions_Data`

Open the notebook to generate visualizations with the `seaborn` library, as shown in *Figure 4.24*.

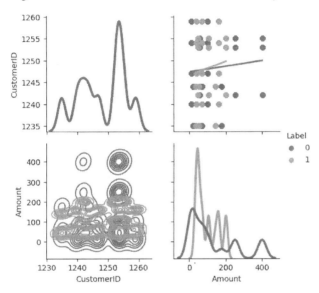

Figure 4.24 – Data visualizations of the synthetic transactions data

Feel free to explore the transaction data further. Next, we'll move on to the RAG chatbot.

Project – RAG chatbot

In the last chapter, we extracted chunks of text from our PDF documents. We converted those chunks into embeddings using the BGE embedding model. As a result, we are now ready to take the next step in preparing our data for retrieval. To follow along in your own workspace, please refer to the following notebook:

- `CH4-01-Creating_VectorDB`

We explained in the *Enhancing data retrieval with Databricks Vector Search* section that Databricks VS is a serverless managed solution. In other words, we need to create the VS endpoint to host our indices.

```
from databricks.vector_search.client import VectorSearchClient

vsc_endpoint_name = "ml_action_vs"
vsc = VectorSearchClient()

if vsc_endpoint_name not in [e['name'] for e in vsc.list_endpoints()['endpoints']]:
  vsc.create_endpoint(name=vsc_endpoint_name, endpoint_type="STANDARD")
  print(f"Endpoint named {vsc_endpoint_name} is in creation, wait a moment.")

print(f"Endpoint named {vsc_endpoint_name} is ready.")
```

Figure 4.25 – Creating the Databricks VS endpoint for the RAG chatbot

As a reminder, we will ingest the source table we prepared in *Chapter 3* into the index for retrieval search within the chatbot application.

```
display(spark.read.table(f"{catalog}.{database_name}.pdf_documentation_text"))
```

Figure 4.26 – Reading our source table containing text from the documentation

We import functions from the project's `utils` folder, `mlia_utils.rag_funcs`. The index only needs to be created once. Going forward, we will only write into it or read from it. We use an `if/else` clause to check whether an index with the name `catalog.database.docs_vsc_idx_cont` exists or not. If it exists, we just synchronize our `catalog.database.pdf_documentation_text` source table to it.

```
from databricks.sdk import WorkspaceClient
from mlia_utils.rag_funcs import *
# import databricks.sdk.service.catalog as c

# The table we'd like to index
source_table_fullname = f"{catalog}.{database_name}.pdf_documentation_text"
# Where we want to store our index
vs_index_fullname = f"{catalog}.{database_name}.docs_vsc_idx_cont"

if not index_exists(vsc, vsc_endpoint_name, vs_index_fullname):
  print(f"Creating index {vs_index_fullname} on endpoint {vsc_endpoint_name}...")
  vsc.create_delta_sync_index(
    endpoint_name=vsc_endpoint_name,
    index_name=vs_index_fullname,
    source_table_name=source_table_fullname,
    pipeline_type="TRIGGERED", # TRIGGERED or CONTINUOUS
    primary_key="id",
    embedding_dimension=1024, # Match your model embedding size (bge)
    embedding_vector_column="embedding"
  )
else:
  # Trigger a sync to update our vs content with the new data saved in the table
  vsc.get_index(vsc_endpoint_name, vs_index_fullname).sync()
```

Figure 4.27 – Check whether the index exists and create it if needed

There are a few key pieces we must make sure are in place before proceeding with the rest of our chatbot project:

- **Source data preparation**: `catalog.database.pdf_documentation_text` is the Delta table you have prepared with your self-managed embedding functions as the primary data repository for their vector search index.

- **Vector search index creation**: An index named `catalog.database.docs_vsc_idx_cont` using Databricks VS. This index is linked to the source Delta table. The index is set on a trigger base update (`pipeline_type="TRIGGERED"`), which means that any modifications or new additions to the historical texts should be synced manually to your vector search index. If you wish to have changes reflected in the vector search index automatically, choose the `CONTINUOUS` mode instead. This continuous update mechanism ensures the data is always current and ready for analysis.

- **Embedding model integration**: To transform the text data into a vector format, we are using self-managed embeddings. This means no model for embedding conversion is provided. However, you may want to choose managed embeddings, where `text_chunks` is automatically converted into embeddings with a model that is served through Databricks Model Serving. This can be specified in the setup under the `embedding_model_endpoint_name` parameter. This integration guarantees that the textual data is efficiently converted into vectors, making it suitable for advanced similarity searches.

We import the `wait_for_index_to_be_ready()` function from the `utils` folder. We run the code in *Figure 4.28* to repeatedly check the index's status until it is in an "online" state. As the VS index only needs to be created once, this function can take some time before the embeddings reach your VS index. Proceed once your index is in a "ready" state.

```
wait_for_index_to_be_ready(vsc, vsc_endpoint_name, vs_index_fullname)
```

Figure 4.28 – The wait for index function checks for the index status until it is online and ready

Once the index is online, we call `get_index()` to perform a similarity search. We also call a `describe()` method to show you the broader API options you have.

```
# Checking the information about the VS
vsc.get_index(vsc_endpoint_name, vs_index_fullname).describe()
```

```
{'name': 'ml_in_action.rag_chatbot.docs_vsc_idx_cont',
 'endpoint_name': 'ml_action_vs',
 'primary_key': 'id',
 'index_type': 'DELTA_SYNC',
 'delta_sync_index_spec': {'source_table': 'ml_in_action.rag_chatbot.pdf_documentation_text',
   'embedding_vector_columns': [{'name': 'embedding',
     'embedding_dimension': 1024}],
   'pipeline_type': 'TRIGGERED',
   'pipeline_id': 'aa31e35b-7af3-4823-ad83-2c803b59cca4'},
 'status': {'detailed_state': 'ONLINE_NO_PENDING_UPDATE',
   'message': 'Index creation succeeded using Delta Live Tables: https://adb-984752964297111.11.azuredatabricks.net#joblist/pipelines/aa31e35b-7af
3-4823-ad83-2c803b59cca4/updates/5a93e1c5-dbfc-4035-a4af-6875819cd5c6',
   'indexed_row_count': 327,
   'triggered_update_status': {'last_processed_commit_version': 1,
     'last_processed_commit_timestamp': '2024-01-03T16:20:14Z'},
   'ready': True,
   'index_url': 'adb-984752964297111.11.azuredatabricks.net/api/2.0/vector-search/endpoints/ml_action_vs/indexes/ml_in_action.rag_chatbot.docs_vsc
_idx_cont'},
 'creator': 'anastasia.prokaieva@databricks.com'}
```

Figure 4.29 – Using get_index with the describe method shows the index configuration

Because we use self-managed embeddings, our VS index is not connected to any model that can convert our input text query into embeddings to be mapped to the one under a database, so we need to convert them first! Here we are again leveraging the BGE embedding model from the Foundational Model Serving API and then passing embedded text to our index for similarity search:

```
import mlflow.deployments
deploy_client = mlflow.deployments.get_deploy_client("databricks")

question = "What are the economic impacts of automation technologies using LLMs?"

response = deploy_client.predict(endpoint="databricks-bge-large-en", inputs={"input": [question]})
embeddings = [e['embedding'] for e in response.data]

results = vsc.get_index(vsc_endpoint_name, vs_index_fullname).similarity_search(
    query_vector=embeddings[0],
    columns=["pdf_name", "content"],
    num_results=3)
docs = results.get('result', {}).get('data_array', [])
pprint(docs)
```

Figure 4.30 – Converting our query text into embeddings and passing to the index for similarity search

Here is the result of the retrieved queries (only the first found one with two columns pdf_name and content):

```
[['dbfs:/Volumes/ml_in_action/rag_chatbot/files/raw_documents/2303.10130.pdf',
  '7 Conclusion\n'
  'In conclusion, this study offers an examination of the potential impact of LLMs on various '
  'occupations and industries within the U.S. economy. By applying a new rubric for understanding '
  'LLM capabilities and their potential effects on jobs, we have observed that most occupations '
  'exhibit some degree of exposure to LLMs, with higher-wage occupations generally presenting more '
  'tasks with high exposure. Our analysis indicates that approximately 19% of jobs have at least '
  '50% of their tasks exposed to LLMs when considering both current model capabilities and '
  'anticipated LLM-powered software.\n'
  'Our research aims to highlight the general-purpose potential of LLMs and their possible '
  'implications for US workers. Previous literature demonstrates the impressive improvements of '
  'LLMs to date (see 2.1). Our findings confirm the hypothesis that these technologies can have '
  'pervasive impacts across a wide swath of occupations in the US, and that additional '
  'advancements supported by LLMs, mainly through software and digital tools, can have significant '
  'effects on a range of economic activities. However, while the technical capacity for LLMs to '
  'make human labor more efficient appears evident, it is important to recognize that social, '
  'economic, regulatory, and other factors will influence actual labor productivity outcomes. As '
  'capabilities continue to evolve, the impact of LLMs on the economy will likely persist and '
  'increase, posing challenges for policymakers in predicting and regulating their trajectory.\n'
  'Further research is necessary to explore the broader implications of LLM advancements, '
```

Figure 4.31– Sample of result of the retrieved query

Now, our VS index is ready to be used in our chatbot. We will explore how to connect all the tools together to generate a proper human-readable answer in *Chapter 6*!

Project – multilabel image classification

In the last chapter, we saved our image data into volumes. Next, we will explore our data. To follow along in your own workspace, please refer to the following notebook:

- `CH4-01-Exploring_Dataset`

We create our training dataset of images. Print the labels and a sample of the training data for a look at what we want our model to classify.

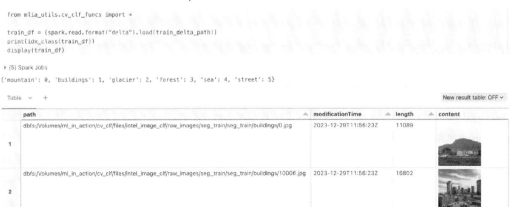

Figure 4.32 – Load and view the training dataset

We can use `display_image` to view a few pictures from our volumes.

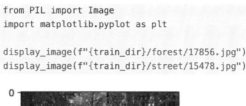

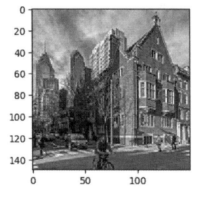

Figure 4.33 – Display images within the notebook

It's good to have an idea of the proportion of the different labels of our data. This is how you can view the proportion of data in our training dataset. Wherever you perform a multilabel classification, make sure you have a good distribution of labels. Otherwise, consider training individual models that might be combined or augment missing labels!

proportion_labels(labels_dict_train)

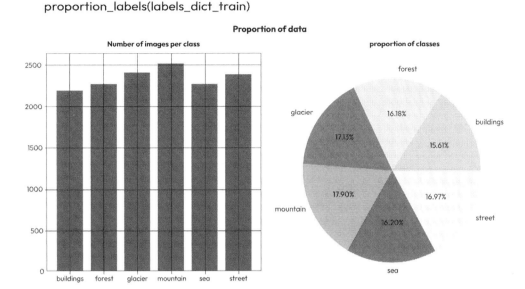

Figure 4.34 – View the proportion of labels in the training dataset

Now we have done some high-level exploration of our image classification dataset. For this project, no transformations are needed, so our next step with this data will be in *Chapter 6*.

Summary

It is critical to understand your data before using it. This chapter highlighted a variety of methods to explore and analyze our data within the Databricks ecosystem.

We began by revisiting DLT, this time focusing on how we use a feature called **expectations** to monitor and improve our data quality. We also introduced Databricks Lakehouse Monitoring as another tool for observing data quality. Among its many capabilities, Lakehouse Monitoring detects shifts in data distribution and alerts users to anomalies, thus preserving data integrity throughout its life cycle. We used Databricks Assistant to explore data with ad hoc queries written in English and showed why AutoML is an extremely useful tool for data exploration by automatically creating comprehensive data exploration notebooks. Together, all of these tools create a strong foundation to understand and explore your data. Finally, the chapter delved into Databricks VS and how using it to find similar documents can improve chatbot responses.

We have now set the foundation for the next phase of our data journey. *Chapter 5* will focus on how to build upon our bronze-layer data to create rich sets of features for data science and ML projects.

Questions

The following questions are meant to solidify key points to remember as well as tie the content back to your own experience:

1. What are some low-code options for data exploration that we discussed in this chapter?

2. When might you use Databricks Assistant for data exploration, and when might you use AutoML's data profile notebook?

3. How and why would you set expectations on your data?

4. When would you use a regular database versus a vector database? What are some common use cases for vector databases?

Answers

After putting thought into the questions, compare your answers to ours:

1. Some low-code data exploration options include using the `ydata` library, in-cell data profile, Databricks Assistant, and AutoML.

2. Databricks Assistant is useful for data exploration when you have a good idea of the analyses you want to build and you want code assistance. Databricks Assistant is a great way to speed up the coding process or augment your SQL knowledge. On the other hand, AutoML is very useful for automatically creating a profile notebook that broadly covers your dataset.

3. We would use Delta Live Tables to set expectations. Expectations are a way to flexibly handle data abnormalities and give the options to report bad data, drop that data, or fail the pipeline entirely.

4. Regular databases, or relational databases, are designed for data in tabular form, typically organized in rows or columns. A vector database is designed to store vector data, such as embeddings and high-dimensional data. Vector databases are optimized for operations based on vector space models, similarity searches, image and video analysis, and other ML problems. Some common use cases include **Retrieval Augmented Generation** (**RAG**) systems, recommendation systems, and image and video recognition.

Further reading

In this chapter, we pointed out specific technologies, technical features, and options. Please take a look at these resources to get deeper into the areas that interest you most:

- *Enabling visualizations with Aggregations in DBSQL*: `https://docs.databricks.com/sql/user/visualizations/index.html#enable-aggregation-in-a-visualization`

- Using the ydata profiler to explore data: `https://ydata-profiling.ydata.ai/docs/master/index.html`

- *Advancing Spark - Meet the new Databricks Assistant*: `https://youtu.be/Tv8D72oI0xM`

- *Introducing Databricks Assistant, a context-aware AI assistant*: `https://www.databricks.com/blog/introducing-databricks-assistant`

- *Model monitoring custom metrics creation*: `https://docs.databricks.com/en/lakehouse-monitoring/custom-metrics.html`

- Databricks Vector Search: `https://docs.databricks.com/en/generative-ai/vector-search.html`

- External models in Databricks Model Serving: `https://learn.microsoft.com/en-us/azure/databricks/generative-ai/external-models/`

5

Feature Engineering on Databricks

"Applied machine learning is basically feature engineering."

– Andrew Ng

As we progress from *Chapter 4*, where we harnessed the power of Databricks to explore and refine our datasets, we are now ready to delve into the components of Databricks that enable the next step: feature engineering. We will start by covering **Databricks Feature Engineering** (**DFE**) in Unity Catalog to show you how you can efficiently manage engineered features using **Unity Catalog** (**UC**). Understanding how to leverage DFE in UC is crucial for creating reusable and consistent features across training and inference. Next, you will learn how to leverage Sparka Structured Streaming for calculating features on a stream, which allows you to create stateful features needed for models to perform quick decision-making. Feature engineering is a broad topic. We will focus on how the DI Platform facilitates the development of certain feature categories, such as **point-in-time lookups** and **on-demand features**. You will also learn how to calculate features in real time during model inference, which is vital for scenarios requiring immediate data processing. The last product feature we will cover is the **Databricks online store**. You will understand how to make features available for real-time access and enhance the responsiveness of machine learning models in low-latency applications.

Here is what you will learn about as part of this chapter:

- Databricks Feature Engineering in Unity Catalog
- Feature engineering on a stream
- Employing point-in-time lookups
- Computing on-demand features
- Publishing features to the Databricks Online Store
- Applying our learning

Databricks Feature Engineering in Unity Catalog

In this chapter, we will focus on several types of features. Feature types can be roughly grouped based on when they are calculated relative to the time of model prediction. The three types we cover in this chapter are batch, streaming, and on-demand:

- **Batch features**: These are features that are generated hours, days, or even further ahead of when the feature will be used as a model input. There are several reasons for this; the model may be offline and run in a batch prediction fashion, or perhaps the feature values change slowly relative to the model inference timeline. In these cases, it is not necessary to recompute the values more frequently. An example of a batch feature is the `holidays` field in our *Favorita Sales Forecasting* project, as we can compute it before we need it and don't expect the values to change frequently.

- **Streaming features**: These are features processed in real or near-real time as the source data is ingested in the data pipeline, allowing for continuous and incremental feature creation. To demonstrate this, we will calculate a streaming feature for our *Streaming Transactions* project with Spark Structured Streaming.

- **On-demand features**: Unlike batch or streaming features, on-demand features are only computed when needed, which is to say, at the time of inference. These features are crucial for scenarios where feature values are unknown beforehand and must be calculated in real time. We will delve into the mechanics of computing and storing these features, demonstrating their implementation and integration into predictive models.

Any Unity Catalog table with a defined primary key constraint can be a centralized repository for materialized, pre-computed (e.g., batch or streaming) features. These types of tables, whose explicit purpose is to centrally store features to be used throughout an organization's analytics, data science, and machine learning projects, are commonly called **feature tables**. Feature tables allow data scientists to share their engineered features and find features that other team members have built.

They are a wonderful way to ensure business logic is centrally stored, save team members from recreating already-created features, and prevent duplicate work. Plus, Unity Catalog manages all data's discoverability, lineage, and governance, so your feature tables are easily managed just like any other table. In Databricks, any table with a non-nullable primary key can be a feature table. While there is no specific API call to list all tables eligible to be a feature table or to list those officially created as a feature table, we recommend using tags or naming conventions to identify feature tables. This book's example projects will follow the convention of appending `_ft` at the end of feature table names. Feature Engineering in Unity Catalog provides the `FeatureEngineeringClient` Python client (commonly imported under the alias of `fe`) for creating and updating feature tables (*Figure 5.1*):

```
1   fe.create_table(
2       name="lakehouse_in_action.database_name.
        feature_table_name_ft",
3       primary_keys=["sequence_id","sequence_step"],
4       df=feature_dataframe,
5       description="This feature table was created by
        x,y,z and would be great for augmenting w for
        modeling or business use case q.")
```

Figure 5.1 – Example of creating a feature table with FeatureEngineeringClient

As we mentioned, the combination of Delta, UC, and the Feature Engineering client provides considerable benefits. Features can be shared and reused across teams, reducing the need to recreate them from scratch. Reusability can save time and resources, and it can also help to ensure that features are consistent across different teams. Centralized feature tables ensure the same code computes feature values for training and inference. This is especially important to avoid online/offline skew – that is, the discrepancy that can occur when the data transformations used during the model training phase (offline) are different from those used when the model is deployed and making predictions (online). *Figure 5.2* shows a data science project workflow and highlights the offline and online transformations that must match.

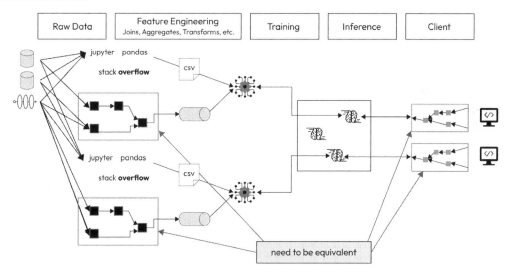

Figure 5.2 – You can avoid accuracy issues by guaranteeing that the transformations
performed on training data are the same as those performed on inference data

We will prevent online/offline skew in the *Streaming Transactions* project by wrapping the data transformation processes into a packaged model in *Chapter 6*. Consistency can improve the accuracy of models, as it ensures the same input generates the same output in production as in training.

> **Note**
>
> For those who are familiar with the Databricks Feature Store, you may wonder why we do not utilize it in this chapter. Before Unity Catalog, the Databricks Feature Store provided incredible value with added lineage and metadata details. With the advancement of UC, instead of having a separate Feature Store product, every table utilizing UC automatically has these added benefits. The original Databricks Feature Store has been absorbed into UC.

In the *Applying our learning* section ahead, we will save our features to a feature table using both SQL and `FeatureEngineeringClient`. Once stored, Unity Catalog makes it easy to track the data sources used to create your features and the downstream artifacts (such as models and notebooks) that use each feature. Even better, when you log a model using a training set of features from a feature table, feature metadata is packaged with the resulting model. Watch for this when we are working on the *Streaming Transactions* project.

Feature engineering on a stream

Before diving into feature engineering on a stream, we want to clarify the difference between **streaming pipelines** and **streaming data**. If you have not used Spark Structured Streaming before, it is a stream processing engine built on the Spark SQL engine. It makes it easy to write streaming calculations or transformations like you would write expressions for static data. Structured Streaming pipelines can process batch or streaming data. Streaming pipelines have elements such as checkpoints to automate the data flow. Streaming pipelines, however, are not necessarily always running; rather, they only run when the developer chooses it. In contrast, streaming data (also known as **real-time data**) refers to continuously generated data that can be processed in real time or batch. To simplify, think of streaming pipelines as a series of automated conveyor belts in a factory set up to process items (data) as they come. These conveyor belts can be turned on or off as needed. On the other hand, streaming data is like a never-ending flow of items piling up at the beginning of the line. Depending on the volume of the stream, immediate handling may be necessary. In the context of our *Streaming Transactions* example in the *Applying our learning* section, we are using these automated conveyor belts (streaming pipelines) to efficiently manage and transform this continuous flow of items (streaming data) into a useful form.

Streaming data has several benefits:

- **Immediate insights**: Streaming data allows you to receive quick insights and make real-time decisions based on the data. Speed is essential for applications where timing is critical, such as financial trading or the real-time monitoring of industrial equipment.

- **Up-to-date analysis**: Processing streaming data in real time allows for more current data analysis. Real-time analysis can help you find patterns and trends as they occur and take proactive steps to address potential data quality issues.

- **Improved efficiency**: Streaming data can help organizations become more efficient by enabling them to respond to events quickly and proactively. Short response times can improve customer satisfaction, reduce downtime, and increase productivity.

Streaming data can provide significant benefits for organizations that need to process large volumes of data quickly and make real-time decisions based on that data. However, there are transformations that require a more complex type of streaming, specifically, **stateful streaming**. Stateful streaming refers to stream processing that consumes a continuous data stream and persists the state of past events. Persisting the state allows for the stream to "know" information from previous transactions. This is particularly helpful when calculating aggregates over a time window since the aggregate would need values from the previous window in the stream. To make this clearer, we provide an example of this in the *Streaming Transactions* project. There is also an informative video linked in the *Further reading* section that explains stateful streaming in detail.

> **Note**
>
> Streaming feature tables should be altered before you begin writing to them. Running an ALTER TABLE command causes the stream to quit. However, you can restart the stream if you must alter the table. Be prepared and plan ahead as much as possible!

The DFE client supports intelligent handling and lookups for time-based features, such as our timestamped streaming features. Let's go over this time-saving product feature next.

Employing point-in-time lookups for time series feature tables

Time series feature tables are any table in Unity Catalog with a TIMESERIES primary key. These tables are eligible for point-in-time lookups, which is a mechanism for looking up the correct feature values. Before training_sets, coming in *Chapter 6*, we often joined tables to connect training rows with their feature values. However, a fine-grained event timestamp is not ideal for joining. This led to rounding the timestamps to minutes, hours, or even days. Depending on the use case, this method may or may not work. For example, joining on TransactionTimestamp in *Figure 5.3* is not realistic in a standard join so one might create TransactionMinute or TransactionHour.

TransactionTimestamp	TransactionMinute	TransactionHour
2023-09-03 19:23:09.765676	2023-09-03 19:23:00	2023-09-03 19:00:00
2023-09-03 19:23:09.765821	2023-09-03 19:23:00	2023-09-03 19:00:00
2023-09-03 19:23:09.765899	2023-09-03 19:23:00	2023-09-03 19:00:00

Figure 5.3 – Example of timestamp rounding for easy joining

Employing point-in-time lookups fixes this problem by handling the time matching for you. For those familiar with *The Price Is Right*, it's the closest feature value without going over. More specifically, it will match with the latest feature value as of the event timestamp without ever providing a feature value calculated after the event. You don't worry about data leakage during training. Without a `Timeseries` primary key, the latest value for a feature is matched.

> **Note**
>
> It's recommended to apply Z-ordering on time series tables for better performance in point-in-time lookups. Z-ordering is covered in *Chapter 7*.

Looking up features is great and often the best choice for your use case. However, in some data science and machine learning tasks, we need feature values calculated quickly on data that we do not have ahead of time. For those projects, we need on-demand features.

Computing on-demand features

Calculating the number of transactions per customer in a brief time window works in a streaming fashion because we only need to use historical data. When we want to use a feature that requires data available only at inference time, we use on-demand features, with unknown values until inference time. In Databricks, you can create on-demand features with Python **user-defined functions** (**UDFs**). These Python UDFs can then be invoked via `training_set` configurations to create training datasets, as you will see in *Chapter 6*.

Let's consider the *Streaming Transactions* project again. We want to add a feature for the amount a product sold at, compared to its historical maximum price, and use this as part of the training data to predict the generated classification label. In this scenario, we don't know the purchase price until the transaction has been received. We'll cover how to build a Python UDF for calculating an on-demand feature for the *Streaming Transactions* project in the *Applying our learning* section.

Additionally, we recommend checking out the *How Databricks AI improves model accuracy with real-time computations* and *Best Practices for Realtime Feature Computation on Databricks* articles for in-depth advice from the on-demand experts at Databricks; see the *Further reading* section for the links.

We have discussed saving features to feature tables in Unity Catalog, the standard "offline" pattern for applications that do not have low-latency requirements. If your business problem requires low latency or fast results, you'll need your data in an online table or implement Databricks Feature Serving. Feature Serving can serve functions as well as precomputed features. For low-latency projects, we recommend Databricks Model Serving because it removes any need for Feature Serving. We don't cover Feature Serving in this book, but if you are going to serve your models externally to Databricks, Feature Serving may be of interest to you.

Next, we learn about how to leverage the Databricks Online Store.

Publishing features to the Databricks Online Store

If you want to use your features with real-time serving, you can publish the features to a low-latency database, also known as an online store. Publishing feature tables to a low-latency database allows for automatic feature lookup during model inference. There are a variety of options to choose from when choosing an online store. A typical data-serving solution requires expert engineers to select an appropriate database for online access, build data publishing pipelines, and orchestrate deployment. After deployment, someone has to monitor, manage, and optimize the pipelines feeding the online store. This is why we recommend Databricks' own fully managed serverless online store built right into the platform. It automatically syncs your Delta feature table with the online store, making it amazingly easy to use. Databricks Online Store is integrated with Databricks Model Serving, so it's easy to set up your online store without ever leaving Databricks. To create an online store, go to the **Compute** tab, select **Online stores**, and then **Create store**. The next step is to enter your online store's name and you can select a size for your store, based on how many lookups per second, as shown in *Figure 5.4*.

Figure 5.4 – Creating an online store from the Compute screen

To sync data to your online store, go to the table with the data you want in the store, and from the hotdog menu to the left of the **Create** button, select **Sync to online store**.

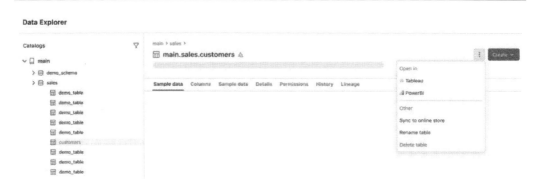

Figure 5.5 – Syncing data from a table to your online store

You will need to specify the primary key for lookup, and a timestamp column if needed, then confirm to sync your data.

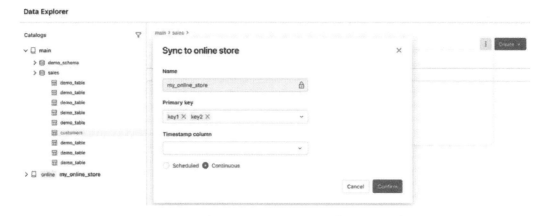

Figure 5.6 – Confirming the online store with its primary keys

You can check the sync status on your online store on the **Details** tab.

Figure 5.7 – The in-notebook UI for viewing the experiment runs

Syncing your tables is simple. No additional engineering is required! Once your feature tables are established and ready for Databricks Online Store, simply sync the table by providing the primary keys, a timestamp column (if appropriate), and how often to sync (*Figure 5.8*).

Sync to online store   ✕

Name

| us-west-online-store | 🔒 |

Primary Key

| Product,TransactionHour | 🔒 |

Timeseries Key ⓘ

| | ⌄ |

| TransactionHour |

◉ **Snapshot**   ◯ Incremental – continuous   ◯ Incremental – triggered

Cancel   Confirm

Figure 5.8 – UI for syncing a feature table to Databricks Online Store

Online stores are ideal for storing only a record's most recent feature values when accessing the values at low latency speeds. Common use cases include models that require fast feature lookups and serving data to applications. You can use the Delta Lake **change data feed** (**CDF**) to make the most of Databricks Online Store, which tracks row-level changes in a Delta table. Using CDF, you can update feature tables with just the changed values instead of overwriting the entire table or keeping track of timestamps. As a result, there is less data you need to sync with Databricks Online Store learned about declaring feature tables by saving them with a primary key as a Delta table in Unity Catalog. Additionally, we can create an online feature store and sync our tables to make the features available for low-latency use cases or serving data to applications. Next, we must consider how to use features in our training datasets.

We've gone through ways to save feature tables, build streaming features, implement point-in-time lookups, create on-demand features, and publish to the Databricks Online Store. It's time to get ready to follow along in your own Databricks workspace as we work through the *Chapter 5* project code.

Applying our learning

Now that we have learned about the feature engineering components of the DI platform, let's put these topics into action and build on the example project datasets with new features that will enhance the data science projects.

Technical requirements

Here are the technical requirements needed to complete the hands-on examples in this chapter:

- The *Streaming Transactions* project requires more compute power than is available in the single node cluster. We created a multi-node cluster to address this. See *Figure 5.9* for the multi-node CPU configuration we used.

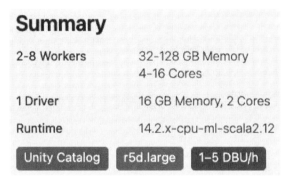

Figure 5.9 – Multi-node CPU cluster configuration (on AWS) used for this book

- We will use managed volumes to store cleaned, featurized data.

Project – Streaming Transactions

If you've been following the code in the previous chapters, at this point, you have the streaming data you need. In this chapter, we will augment that data with some of the feature engineering techniques discussed earlier. First, we will create a streaming feature to count the number of transactions that have arrived in the last two minutes for each customer.

Before we jump in, let's remember where we are and where we are going.

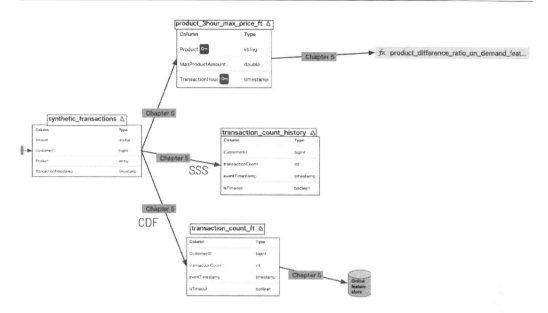

Figure 5.10 – The project pipeline for the Streaming Transactions project

We are building a streaming pipeline to process the incoming transactions into a feature. We will use stateful streaming to count the number of transactions per customer over a two-minute timeframe. Stateful streaming is required because the calculations in the stream need to know how many transactions have already occurred and when a transaction falls outside the two-minute window. This information is known as the state of a customer.

The streaming feature and the on-demand feature are created in two different notebooks. In the code repository, you have the following four notebooks:

- CH5-01-Generating Records: This notebook is nearly identical to the data generator used in the previous chapters. The two key differences are that there is now always a product present in the records, and the total (meaning the number of time steps) has been increased to provide a stream for a longer period of time.

- CH5-02-Auto Loader: The only change to the Auto Loader notebook is the location the data is being written to.

- CH5-03-FE Using Spark Structured Streaming: This notebook is explained in detail in the *Building a streaming feature with Spark Structured Streaming* subsection of this project. The code is written in Scala. Stateful streaming is now also available with PySpark. See the *Further reading* section at the end of this chapter for more details.

- CH5-04-Building Maximum Price Feature Table: This notebook calculates the maximum price for a product over a time window. The calculated price will be used at inference time by the Python UDF also created in this notebook.

The first two notebooks are nearly identical to their counterparts from the last chapter, so we won't cover them again. We start from the CH5-03-FE_Using_Spark_Structured_Streaming notebook.

Building a streaming feature with Spark Structured Streaming

We calculate the number of transactions per customer in the last two minutes and call this new feature transactionCount, which is a case class in the code.

CustomerID	transactionTimestamp	...	...
1	2023-09-03 19:23:09.765676		
4	2023-09-03 19:23:09.765821		
2	2023-09-03 19:23:09.765899		

Figure 5.11 – The table contains example data corresponding to readStream – namely, inputDf

We need to aggregate the transactions from the incoming stream, the InputRow case class, by the CustomerID field. *Figure 5.11* shows an example table of the incoming stream. Additionally, we must remove transactions once they have fallen outside the specified window; we will call these "expired transactions." This means we must create and maintain a state for each customer, the TransactionCountState case class. Each customer state consists of CustomerID, transactionCount, and transactionList containing the times that the transactions occurred for each transaction accounted for in the transaction count. *Figure 5.12* is a visual representation of the customer state. As a customer transaction arrives, it is added to a list of transactions with a timestamp as part of the customer state.

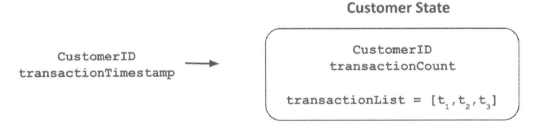

Figure 5.12 – Each transaction updates the customer state

The state is created by applying the stateful streaming logic to the input data. The customer state is then used to write the feature table, transaction_count_ft, shown in *Figure 5.13*:

CustomerID	transactionCount	eventTimestamp	isTimeout
5	3	2023-09-03T19:24:14.388	false
2	4	2023-09-03T19:24:16.721	true
3	0	2023-09-03T19:24:16.720	true

Figure 5.13 – This table is the result after applying the stateful streaming transformation

The feature table shown in *Figure 5.13* includes the CustomerID reference, transactionCount for that customer, eventTimestamp, and a Boolean variable, isTimeout. The eventTimestamp is the time the feature record was written. We call it eventTimestamp because a new transaction or a timeout could have triggered the update to the customer state/event. To know which type of event it is, we include isTimeout. A timeout occurs when no new transactions for a customer have occurred but the value of transactionCount has changed – an indication that the count has decreased.

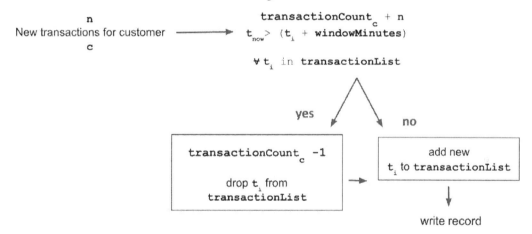

Figure 5.14 – Logic flow for the stateful streaming transformation

Figure 5.14 visually represents the update logic applied to the customer state. The logical path can be broken into steps:

1. For n new transactions coming in for customer c, transactionCount is incremented n times.

2. Then, for each transactionTimestamp, ti, in transactionList, we compare the current time with expirationTimestamp (ti+windowMinutes) to determine whether the transaction accounted for in transactionCount has expired:

   I. If any transactions have expired, we decrement transactionCount by one for each and drop the corresponding transactionTimestamp from transactionList.

II.   If no transaction has expired or `transactionTimestamp` for the expired transactions has been dropped, then we add the new `transactionTimestamp` to `transactionList` and write out the customer record.

Now that we have outlined the goal of our transformation, let's look at the code. To follow along in your own workspace, please refer to the following notebooks:

- `CH5-01-Generating Records`
- `CH5-02-Auto Loader`
- `CH5-03-FE Using Spark Structured Streaming`
- `CH5-04-Building Maximum Price Feature Table`

Before you begin executing *notebook 3*, please open *notebooks 1* and *2* and click **Run All** for both. These two notebooks relaunch the data streams that we need running in order to run *notebook 3*. However, you do not need all streams running in order to run *notebook 4*.

The code we are jumping into is in the `CH5-03-FE Using Spark Structured Streaming` notebook. We start with the basics – imports and delta configurations – as shown in the following screenshot:

```scala
import java.time.Instant
import java.util.concurrent.TimeUnit
import scala.collection.mutable.ListBuffer
import org.apache.spark.sql.streaming.{GroupStateTimeout, OutputMode, GroupState}

spark.conf.set("spark.databricks.delta.optimizeWrite.enabled", "true")
spark.conf.set("spark.databricks.delta.autoCompact.enabled", "true")
```

Figure 5.15 – Setting delta configurations for optimized writes and compaction

These configurations can also be set in the cluster configurations, but we call them out explicitly in *Figure 5.15*. These settings will automatically compact sets of small files into larger files as it writes for optimal read performance. *Figure 5.16* primarily shows the reset commands that enable starting fresh when needed:

```python
%python
table_name = "transaction_count_ft"
history_table_name = "transaction_count_history"
if bool(dbutils.widgets.get('Reset')):
  dbutils.fs.rm(f"{volume_file_path}/{table_name}/streaming_outputs/", True)
  dbutils.fs.rm(f"{volume_file_path}/{history_table_name}/streaming_outputs/", True)
  sql(f"DROP TABLE IF EXISTS {table_name}")
  sql(f"DROP TABLE IF EXISTS {history_table_name}")
```

Figure 5.16 – Setting the widget value to True runs the commands in this cell, removing the output data, including the checkpoint, and dropping the table

We define the necessary variables in this next code snippet and create our table. Notice that variables passed from the setup file are in Python and SQL, meaning they are unavailable in Scala. Although all three languages can be used in a notebook, they do not share constants or variable values between them. As a result, we define the variables we need in Scala for access in the Scala notebook. We set the volume location for files, output paths, and the `inputTable` name:

```scala
// variables passed from the setup file are in python
val table_name = "transaction_count_ft"
val history_table_name = "transaction_count_history"
val volumePath = "/Volumes/ml_in_action/synthetic_transactions/files/"
val outputPath = f"$volumePath/$table_name/streaming_outputs/"
val outputPath2 = f"$volumePath/$history_table_name/streaming_outputs/"
val inputTable = "ml_in_action.synthetic_transactions.raw_transactions"
```

Figure 5.17 – Setting variables, constants, and paths in Scala

Notice that we enable the CDF on our streaming feature table, `transaction_count_ft`, in *Figure 5.18*. We could publish this table to an online store if desired. Additionally, we set the table name we want to write all transactions, `transaction_count_history`:

```
sql(f"""CREATE OR REPLACE TABLE $table_name (CustomerID Int, transactionCount Int,
eventTimestamp Timestamp, isTimeout Boolean)""")
sql(f"""ALTER TABLE $table_name ALTER COLUMN CustomerID SET NOT NULL""")
sql(f"""ALTER TABLE $table_name ADD PRIMARY KEY(CustomerID)""")
sql(f"ALTER TABLE $table_name SET TBLPROPERTIES (delta.enableChangeDataFeed=true)")
```

Figure 5.18 – Creating a table and enabling CDF

Next, the `windowMinutes` constant is the number of minutes we want to aggregate transactions for each customer, whereas `maxWaitMinutes` is exactly what it sounds like. It is the minutes the stream waits for a transaction before writing out the state without new transactions. The value of `maxWaitMinutes` should always be less than the value of `windowMinutes`:

```scala
// aggregate transactions for windowMinutes
val windowMinutes = 2
// wait at most max_wait_minutes before writing a record
val maxWaitMinutes = 1
```

Figure 5.19 – Setting windowMinutes and maxWaitMinutes for our stream

We will initiate `FeatureEngineeringClient` and set feature table tags so we can easily see which project these tables are associated with:

```python
%python
from databricks.feature_engineering import FeatureEngineeringClient
fe = FeatureEngineeringClient()

fe.set_feature_table_tag(name=f"{table_name}", key="Project", value="MLIA")
fe.set_feature_table_tag(name=f"{history_table_name}", key="Project", value="MLIA")
```

Figure 5.20 – Setting feature table tags on our table

Next, we define the case class structures. *Figure 5.21* shows that our case classes define our data structures. This is because Scala is a typed language.

```
1    case class InputRow(CustomerID: Long,
2                        TransactionTimestamp: java.time.Instant)
3
4    case class TransactionCountState(latestTimestamp: java.time.Instant,
5                        currentTransactions: List[InputRow])
6
7    case class TransactionCount(CustomerID: Long,
8                        transactionCount: Integer,
9                        eventTimestamp: java.time.Instant,
10                       isTimeout: Boolean)
```

Figure 5.21 – Defining class structures to support aggregations for each customer ID

In *Figure 5.22*, we see the addNewRecords function. latestTimestamp is calculated by comparing the latest timestamp in transactionCountState with the latest timestamp from the new records. This is in case we've received data out of order. Finally, we create and return the new TransactionCountState object with the newly calculated latestTimestamp and combine the two record lists:

```
13   def addNewRecords(newRecords: List[InputRow],
14                     transactionCountState: TransactionCountState):
                       TransactionCountState =
15   {
16     val recordWithLatestTimestamp =
17       newRecords.maxBy(record => record.TransactionTimestamp)
18     val latestNewTimestamp = recordWithLatestTimestamp.TransactionTimestamp
19     val latestTimestamp =
20       if (latestNewTimestamp.toEpochMilli() > transactionCountState.
         latestTimestamp.toEpochMilli()
21       ) latestNewTimestamp else transactionCountState.latestTimestamp
22
23     new TransactionCountState(latestTimestamp,
24       transactionCountState.currentTransactions ::: newRecords)
25   }
```

Figure 5.22 – Defining the addNewRecords function

The next function, *Figure 5.23*, drops the records that are more than `windowMinutes` old from `TransactionCountState` by calculating the state expiration timestamp (the latest timestamp minus the transaction count minutes). Then, it loops through the list of current transactions and keeps any that occur before the expiration timestamp. This is shown in the following screenshot:

```
28    def dropExpiredRecords(newLatestTimestamp: java.time.Instant,
29        currentTransactions: List[InputRow]): TransactionCountState = {
30        val newTransactionList = ListBuffer[InputRow]()
31        val expirationTimestamp = Instant.ofEpochMilli(newLatestTimestamp.
          toEpochMilli() - TimeUnit.MINUTES.toMillis(windowMinutes))
32
33        if (currentTransactions.size > 0) {
34          currentTransactions.foreach { value =>
35            if (value.TransactionTimestamp.toEpochMilli() >=
              expirationTimestamp.toEpochMilli())
36              newTransactionList.append(value)
37          }
38        }
39
40        new TransactionCountState(newLatestTimestamp,
41                                  newTransactionList.toList)
42    }
```

Figure 5.23 – Defining a function to drop stale records

The `updateState` function uses our helper functions to – you guessed it – update the customer state. This is the function called `flatMapGroupsWithState`. The `updateState` function receives the customer ID, values, and the current state. `CustomerID` is the key we are grouping on. `values` is an iterator of `InputRow`. In *Figure 5.11*, we see that `InputRow` is a transaction record consisting of a `CustomerID` reference and the time the transaction occurred. The `updateState` function behaves in two ways. Suppose one or more `InputRow` records for a given `CustomerID` are received. In that case, it will add those records to the state, drop any records that are older than `windowMinutes` from the state, and calculate the transaction count. See *Figure 5.18* for the notebook code.

```
if (!state.hasTimedOut) {
  val transactionList = new ListBuffer[InputRow]()
  values.foreach { value =>
    transactionList.append(value)}

  var prevState = state.getOption.getOrElse {
    val firstTransactionTimestamp = transactionList.head.
    TransactionTimestamp
    new TransactionCountState(firstTransactionTimestamp, List
    [InputRow]())}

  val stateWithNewRecords = addNewRecords(transactionList.toList,
    prevState)

  val stateWithRecordsDropped =
    dropExpiredRecords(stateWithNewRecords.latestTimestamp,
    stateWithNewRecords.currentTransactions)

  val output = new TransactionCount(CustomerID,
    stateWithRecordsDropped.currentTransactions.size,
    stateWithRecordsDropped.latestTimestamp, false)

  transactionCounts.append(output)
  state.update(stateWithRecordsDropped)
  state.setTimeoutTimestamp(
    stateWithRecordsDropped.latestTimestamp.toEpochMilli(),
    "30 seconds")
} else {
```

Figure 5.24 – If the state has not timed out, the updateState function receives and processes records

On the other hand, as shown in *Figure 5.25*, if no records are received for a given CustomerID within a minute since the last time this function was called, it will drop any records that are older than windowMinutes from the state and adjust the count:

```
} else {
  val prevState = state.get
  val newTimestamp = Instant.now
  val stateWithRecordsDropped = dropExpiredRecords(newTimestamp,
    prevState.currentTransactions)
  val output = new TransactionCount(CustomerID,
    stateWithRecordsDropped.currentTransactions.size,
    stateWithRecordsDropped.latestTimestamp, true)

  transactionCounts.append(output)
  state.update(stateWithRecordsDropped)
  state.setTimeoutTimestamp(
    stateWithRecordsDropped.latestTimestamp.toEpochMilli(),
    "30 seconds")
}
```

Figure 5.25 – If the state has timed out, the updateState function receives no
records and only updates the state after dropping expired records

Note that the `transactionCounts` list buffer created at the beginning of the `updateState` function is returned as an iterator. In this case, the output will contain one record: the transaction count record for the specific customer.

Next, as we prepare to create a read stream, we define the input schema we need for our read stream; see *Figure 5.26*:

```
import org.apache.spark.sql.types.{StringType,
        StructField, StructType, IntegerType,
        FloatType, TimestampType}

// The schema for the incoming records
val schema = StructType(Array(
        StructField("Source", StringType, true),
        StructField("TransactionTimestamp", StringType, true),
        StructField("CustomerID", IntegerType, true),
        StructField("Amount", FloatType, true),
        StructField("Product", StringType, true),
        StructField("Label", IntegerType, true),
                ))
```

Figure 5.26 – Read stream input schema

We now must create the read and write components of the stream. The read stream reads in the Delta table we created in *Chapter 3*. Recall we created the Bronze layer by streaming in JSON files and writing them to our `inputTable`. The `readStream` and `writeStream` code is long so we will break it up into smaller sections in the following steps:

1. You should recognize this from earlier chapters. The difference is we are using `selectExpr` to isolate `CustomerID` and `TransactionTimestamp`. Additionally, we specifically set the type of output dataframe to the case class that `flatMapGroupsWithState` is expecting:

```
val inputDf =
  spark.readStream
    .format("delta")
    .schema(schema)
    .table(inputTable)
    .selectExpr("CustomerID", "cast(TransactionTimestamp as timestamp) TransactionTimestamp")
    .as[InputRow]
```

Figure 5.27 – InputDF is a read stream reading the table we created in Chapter 3

2. We apply the watermark and `flatMapGroupsWithState` function to `inputDf`. In Spark Streaming, a watermark is a time threshold determining the maximum allowable delay for late events. We're allowing data to be 30 seconds late before it is dropped (*Watermarking in Spark Structured Streaming*, by Thomas Treml: https://towardsdatascience.com/watermarking-in-spark-structured-streaming-9e164f373e9). The `flatMapGroupsWithState` function is an arbitrary stateful streaming aggregation operator. It applies our `updateState` function to each micro-batch of transactions while maintaining the state for each customer ID:

```
val flatMapGroupsWithStateResultDf =
  inputDf
    .withWatermark("TransactionTimestamp", "30 seconds")
    .groupByKey(_.CustomerID)
    .flatMapGroupsWithState(OutputMode.Append,
      GroupStateTimeout.EventTimeTimeout)(updateState)
```

Figure 5.28 – Applying the watermark and flatMapGroupsWithState function to inputDf

3. We define the `updateCounts` function for `foreachBatch` to update the counts in the write stream. It performs upserts of the new transaction counts into the `transaction_count_ft` table; this is the CDC component:

```
21   def updateCounts(newCountsDs: Dataset[TransactionCount], epoch_id: Long): Unit = {
22     val newCountsDf = newCountsDs.toDF
23     val aggregationTable = DeltaTable.forName(table_name)
24     aggregationTable.alias("t")
25       .merge(newCountsDf.alias("m"), "m.CustomerID = t.CustomerID")
26       .whenMatched().updateAll()
27       .whenNotMatched().insertAll()
28       .execute()
29   }
```

Figure 5.29 – The updateCounts function upserts the new transaction
counts into the transaction_count_ft table

4. The last piece of the stream is the write, or, more clearly, the update. The write stream applies the `updateCounts` function. Delta tables do not support streaming updates directly, so we need to use a `foreachBatch` function. The `foreachBatch` function is like a streaming `for` loop applying the function to each micro-batch of data in the stream. This write stream is similar to `flatMapGroupsWithState` without grouping the data or maintaining the state. We are simply updating the CDC result table. Notice the checkpointing is handled for us, and our stream is triggered every 10 seconds, meaning every 10 seconds is a new micro-batch of the data. The query name is optional. It shows up in the SparkUI.

```
32   flatMapGroupsWithStateResultDf.writeStream
33     .foreachBatch(updateCounts _)
34     .option("checkpointLocation", f"$outputPath/checkpoint")
35     .trigger(Trigger.ProcessingTime("10 seconds"))
36     .queryName("flatMapGroups")
37     .start()
```

Figure 5.30 – The write stream applies the updateCounts function using foreachBatch

5. In addition to the writing out to the CDC table, we also want a historical record of the transaction values:

```
flatMapGroupsWithStateResultDf.writeStream
  .option("checkpointLocation", f"$outputPath2/checkpoint")
  .trigger(Trigger.ProcessingTime("10 seconds"))
  .queryName("flatMapGroupsHistoryTable")
  .table(history_table_name)
```

Figure 5.31 – The write stream records all of the transactionCounts values to the Delta table

6. While the stream runs, we can observe the output table, `transaction_count_ft`. While your streams are running, refresh the table view so you can follow along with the output changes as the input data changes:

```sql
%sql
select * from lakehouse_in_action.synthetic_streaming_features order by eventTimestamp desc;
```

▸ (2) Spark Jobs

Table ∨   Visualization 1   +

#	CustomerID	transactionCount	eventTimestamp	isTimeout
2	1	49	2023-10-08 18:54:47.686	false
3	8	58	2023-10-08 18:54:47.686	false
4	9	64	2023-10-08 18:54:47.686	false
5	4	49	2023-10-08 18:54:47.686	false
6	7	63	2023-10-08 18:54:47.686	false
7	11	50	2023-10-08 18:54:47.686	false

Figure 5.32 – A snapshot of the transaction_count_ft table

7. Another thing you can observe while the stream runs is the stream statistics. This view is found by expanding the results section.

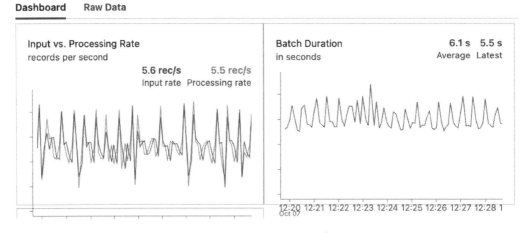

Figure 5.33 – Stream real-time statistics for writeStream

Navigate to the Catalog view to see that the two new tables have appeared. This wraps up our streaming feature. Next, we will build a Python UDF.

Building an on-demand feature with a Python UDF

Let's also create a second feature table using on-demand feature engineering. Focus on the CH5-04-Building_Maximum_Price_Feature_Table notebook. We briefly introduced a scenario in an early section of this chapter requiring us to calculate a transaction's difference from the maximum price on the fly. This could be useful for modeling. To get the difference as an on-demand feature, we do the following:

1. Calculate the maximum price per product over a rolling window. We begin with creating time_window. We want the maximum price in the last three minutes:

```
fe = FeatureEngineeringClient()

time_window = F.window(
    F.col("TransactionTimestamp"),
    windowDuration="3 minutes",
    slideDuration="1 minute",
).alias("time_window")
```

Figure 5.34 – Creating a time window to calculate the rolling maximum prices by product

2. Now that we have a window, we can calculate and save that maximum price to a DataFrame. Usually, the value of a maximum price doesn't drastically change, so hourly is an appropriate timeframe. We add a new time column called LookupTimestamp for joining on.

```
max_price_df = (
  raw_transactions_df
    .groupBy(F.col("Product"),time_window)
    .agg(F.max(F.col("Amount")).cast("float").alias("MaxProductAmount"))
    .withColumn("LookupTimestamp",
                F.date_trunc('minute',
                    F.col("time_window.end") + F.expr('INTERVAL 1 MINUTE')))
    .drop("time_window")
)
```

Figure 5.35 – Creating a DataFrame feature table of product maximum prices

3.   Next, let's create a new feature table from our DataFrame. We will assume that the maximum price for a specific product does not vary enough to calculate this value more than hourly, so we can set this table to update on a set schedule. In the GitHub code, we'll instantiate `FeatureEngineeringClient`. In *Figure 5.36*, we use it to write the new feature table as a Delta table in Unity Catalog:

```
fe.create_table(
  df=max_price_df,
  name='product_3minute_max_price_ft',
  primary_keys=['Product','LookupTimestamp'],
  timeseries_columns='LookupTimestamp',
  schema=max_price_df.schema,
  description="Maximum price per product over the last 3 minutes for Synthetic
Transactions. Join on TransactionTimestamp to get the max product price from last
minute's 3 minute rolling max"
)
```

Figure 5.36 – Writing our table to a Delta table in Unity Catalog

4.   Next, we need a Python UDF to calculate the discount or the difference between the transaction amount and the product's maximum price. We'll name it `product_difference_ratio_on_demand_feature`. We can use the same notebook to build and save this simple function under the same catalog and schema as our tables in Unity Catalog.

```
1   %sql
2   CREATE FUNCTION IF NOT EXISTS product_difference_ratio_on_demand_feature(max_price FLOAT, transaction_amount FLOAT)
3   RETURNS float
4   LANGUAGE PYTHON
5   COMMENT 'Calculate the difference ratio for a product at time of transaction (maximum price - transaction amount)/maximum price.'
6   AS $$
7   def calc_ratio_difference(n1: float, n2: float) -> float:
8     return round(((n1 - n2)/n1),2)
9
10    return calc_ratio_difference(max_price, transaction_amount)
11  $$
```

Figure 5.37 – Building an on-demand function to calculate product discounts

5. Once we run this code, we can navigate to Unity Catalog and see `product_difference_ratio_on_demand_feature` listed. It's ready to use in a training set! We'll refer to this function in *Chapter 6*.

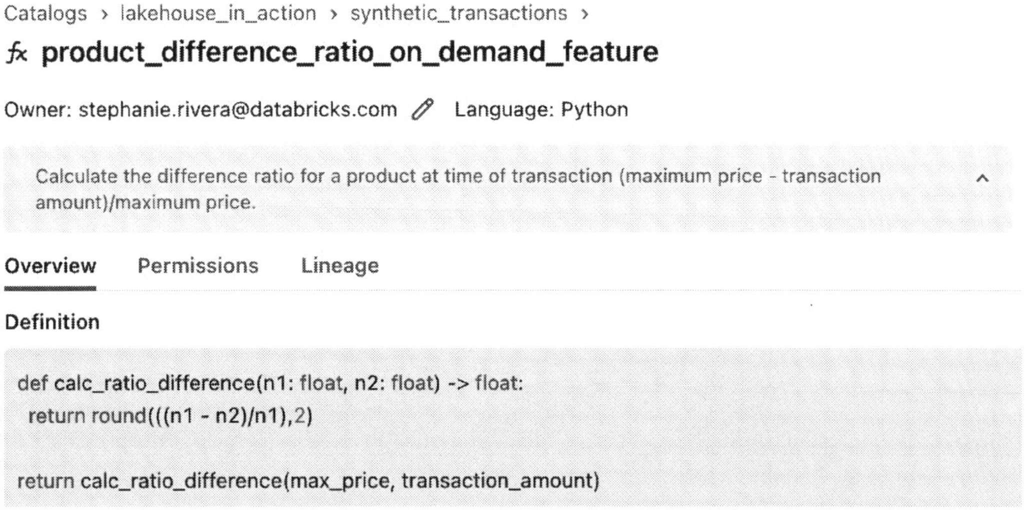

Catalogs › lakehouse_in_action › synthetic_transactions ›

ƒx **product_difference_ratio_on_demand_feature**

Owner: stephanie.rivera@databricks.com *✎* Language: Python

> Calculate the difference ratio for a product at time of transaction (maximum price - transaction amount)/maximum price.

Overview   Permissions   Lineage

Definition

```python
def calc_ratio_difference(n1: float, n2: float) -> float:
  return round(((n1 - n2)/n1),2)


return calc_ratio_difference(max_price, transaction_amount)
```

Figure 5.38 – Viewing the on-demand feature we created in Unity Catalog

And with that, we have engineered features for our *Streaming Transactions* dataset. We enriched the original data with a streaming feature called `transactionCount` and an on-demand feature function that we will use to build the training dataset in the next chapter.

In the next section, we will aggregate store sales data and save it to a feature table.

Project – Favorita Store Sales – time series forecasting

In *Chapter 4,* we used AutoML to explore the *Favorita Sales* dataset and create a baseline model predicting sales. To follow along in your own workspace, please refer to the following notebook: `CH5-01-Building -Favorita -Feature Tables`.

To create a Databricks feature table, we can use either Python (via `FeatureEngineeringClient`) or SQL. This chapter primarily uses Python, but we start by creating a `stores_ft` feature table using SQL:

```
CREATE
OR REPLACE TABLE stores_ft AS(
  SELECT
    store_nbr,
    city,
    state,
    `type` as store_type,
    `cluster` as store_cluster
  FROM
    favorita_stores
  );
ALTER TABLE stores_ft ALTER COLUMN store_nbr SET NOT NULL;
ALTER TABLE stores_ft ADD PRIMARY KEY(store_nbr);
COMMENT ON TABLE stores_ft IS 'Favorita Store features include geography, store
cluster, and store_type.';
```

Figure 5.39 – Creating the stores_ft feature table from the favorita_stores table using SQL

Executing the code in *Figure 5.39* creates a feature table called stores_ft that we will use as a central repository for important store details. store_nbr is set to NOT NULL because it is the primary key. The table does not contain a date column, so this feature table is not a time series feature table. If it did, we could include an additional TIMESERIES primary key. Note that when adding the primary key to the table, you can name the constraint for the primary key with a unique name, as shown in the documentation. We prefer to let the DFE client name the constraint automatically. You can use DESCRIBE TABLE EXTENDED to see the name of your primary key constraint.

The remaining two feature tables are time series tables. After some transformations, we will create the feature tables using Python and the DFE client. Let's focus on the holidays first.

📅 date	A⃝c type	A⃝c locale	A⃝c locale_name	A⃝c description	≔ transferred
2012-03-02 00:00:00.000	Holiday	Local	Manta	Fundacion de Manta	false
2012-04-01 00:00:00.000	Holiday	Regional	Cotopaxi	Provincializacion de Cotopaxi	false
2012-04-12 00:00:00.000	Holiday	Local	Cuenca	Fundacion de Cuenca	false
2012-04-14 00:00:00.000	Holiday	Local	Libertad	Cantonizacion de Libertad	false
2012-04-21 00:00:00.000	Holiday	Local	Riobamba	Cantonizacion de Riobamba	false

Figure 5.40 – The holiday events table

The features we create are their respective store's local, regional, and national holidays. We can look at *Figure 5.40* to recall what the holiday data looked like.

One thing to note about our data is that there are days when multiple holidays occur for the same store. We process the three types of holidays very similarly. The transformations for national holidays are slightly different, given that there is no need to match on locale. All holiday transformations are present in the GitHub code. However, we do not cover each in detail in the book.

The following steps take you through the transformations for the local holiday type we use for the holiday feature table:

1. We begin the ETL for the local holidays by singling out the local locale and renaming the type to holiday_type:

```
sql("""
  CREATE OR REPLACE TABLE local_holidays_bronze AS (
    SELECT
      `date`,
      `type` as holiday_type,
      locale_name
    FROM
      holiday_events
    WHERE
      locale == "Local"
    GROUP BY
      ALL
    ORDER BY
      `date`)
""")
```

Figure 5.41 – Isolating the local holidays

Using the bronze table created in *Step 1*, we construct a silver table consisting of the date, store number, and local holiday type. We must account for the issue of multiple local holidays happening on the same day for the same stores. We do so by grouping with a MIN function to select a holiday type. The local holiday type is changed to Multiple using a case statement and num_holidays accounts for these instances:

```
sql(
"""
CREATE OR REPLACE TABLE local_holidays_silver AS
SELECT
  `date`, store_nbr,
  CASE
    WHEN num_holidays >= 2 THEN "Multiple"
    ELSE local_holiday_type
  END as local_holiday_type
FROM
  (
    SELECT
      h.`date`, s.store_nbr,
      MIN(h.holiday_type) as local_holiday_type,
      count(1) as num_holidays
    FROM
      favorita_stores s
      INNER JOIN local_holidays_bronze h ON (
        s.city == h.locale_name
        OR s.state == h.locale_name
      )
    GROUP BY
      ALL
    ORDER BY
      h.`date`
  )
)
""")
```

Figure 5.42 – SQL checking for multiple holiday instances and identifying
them with a new holiday type for the local holidays

The resulting silver table is shown in *Figure 5.43*:

date	store_nbr	local_holiday_type
2012-03-02 00:00:00.000	52	Holiday
2012-03-02 00:00:00.000	53	Holiday
2012-04-12 00:00:00.000	37	Holiday
2012-04-12 00:00:00.000	39	Holiday
2012-04-12 00:00:00.000	42	Holiday

Figure 5.43 – The first five rows of the local_holidays_silver table

2. After completing the same process in the previous steps for regional and national holidays, we combine the silver tables into a single DataFrame. We use full joins to include all holidays. To avoid `null` dates and store numbers, we chain two `ifnull()` functions:

```
df = sql("""
    SELECT
        ifnull(n.`date`,ifnull(r.`date`, l.`date`)) as `date`,
        ifnull(n.store_nbr,ifnull(r.store_nbr, l.store_nbr)) as store_nbr,
        n.national_holiday_type,
        r.regional_holiday_type,
        l.local_holiday_type
    FROM
        national_holidays_silver n
    FULL JOIN regional_holidays_silver r ON n.`date`=r.`date` AND n.store_nbr = r.store_nbr
    FULL JOIN local_holidays_silver l ON n.`date`=l.`date` AND n.store_nbr = l.store_nbr
    ORDER BY
        `date`
    """)
```

Figure 5.44 – Combining all three silver tables into a single DataFrame

3. Now that we have prepared our DataFrame with the features we want to save, we use the DFE `create_table` method to save the DataFrame as a feature table. We specify `primary_keys`. Be sure to note that we are *not* including a time series column. This is because we want the feature table lookup only to match exact dates. Holidays would not function well with the point-in-time logic. The primary keys will also be our lookup keys when we create the training set in the next chapter. A best practice is to include a thoughtful description as well.

```
fe.create_table(
    name = f"store_holidays_ft",
    primary_keys=["date", "store_nbr"],
    df=df,
    description="Holidays in Ecuador by date and store number. Table includes
    holiday types for national, regional, and local. Days where a store has more
    than one holiday is indicated by holiday type being 'Multiple'. Nulls indicate
    non-holiday days.",
)
```

Figure 5.45 – Creating the store holidays feature table using the DFE client

4. Notice that in our feature table, *Figure 5.46*, there are `null` values when there is not a holiday of a specific holiday of such type. When we create the training set, the feature lookup functionality will have `null` for the values of dates not in the table. We do not need to create `null` rows for each date that is not a holiday, thus saving us the preprocessing time.

📅 date	🔢 store_nbr	ᴬᵇ꜀ national_holiday_type	ᴬᵇ꜀ regional_holiday_type	ᴬᵇ꜀ local_holiday_type
2012-03-02 00:00:00.000	52	null	null	Holiday
2012-03-02 00:00:00.000	53	null	null	Holiday
2012-04-01 00:00:00.000	13	null	Holiday	null
2012-04-01 00:00:00.000	12	null	Holiday	null
2012-04-12 00:00:00.000	37	null	null	Holiday

Figure 5.46 – The store_holidays_ft feature table

5. In addition to the holiday and store data, we were provided with oil prices data. We can use this data as a proxy for the economy. Let's create one more feature table using the `oil_price_silver` table. Unlike `store_holidays_ft`, having the previous value of a stock price in the place of `null` would be helpful. This is a fitting example of when to use the point-in-time lookup functionality. To do so, a second primary key is required. Therefore, we include the date as the primary key but not as `timeseries_column`, as shown in *Figure 5.47*:

```
df = sql(
    """
    SELECT
        timestamp(`date`) as price_date,
        timestamp(date(`date`) -10) as date,
        dcoilwtico as lag10_oil_price
    FROM
        oil_prices_silver
    """
)


fe.create_table(
    name=f"oil_10d_lag_ft",
    primary_keys=["date"],
    df=df,
    description="The lag10_oil_price is the price of oil 10 days after
    date. The price date is the actual date of the oil price. The oil
    prices were imputed to replace nulls with the previous day's price.
    The stock market is not open on weekends and holidays.",
)
```

Figure 5.47 – Creating a feature table from the oil prices

We have multiple feature tables that we can use with the specific training data provided on Kaggle or any other related training data. For example, `oil_10d_lag_ft` can be used as a proxy for the economy for any dataset based in Ecuador.

For future modeling, saving the features in feature tables using the DFE client will be helpful. Doing so makes it seamless to look up the features with the model at inference time. In the next chapter, using the DFE client, we will combine our feature tables to create a training set for our model.

Summary

As we conclude *Chapter 5*, we have successfully navigated the multifaceted realm of feature engineering on Databricks. We have learned how to organize our features into feature tables, in both SQL and Python, by ensuring there is a non-nullable primary key. Unity Catalog provides lineage and discoverability, which makes features reusable. Continuing with the streaming project, we also highlighted creating a streaming feature using stateful streaming. We touched on the latest feature engineering products from Databricks, such as point-in-time lookups, on-demand feature functions, and publishing tables to the Databricks Online Store. These product features will reduce time to production and simplify production pipelines.

You are now ready to tackle feature engineering for a variety of scenarios! Next up, we take what we've learned to build training sets and machine learning models in *Chapter 6*.

Questions

The following questions solidify key points to remember and tie the content back to your experience:

1. What element of the Delta format helps with reproducibility?

2. What are some of the reasons why you would choose to publish a feature to an online store?

3. How would you create a training set using the Feature Engineering API?

4. What distinguishes a feature table from any other table in Unity Catalog?

5. In the *Streaming Transactions dataset* section of *Applying our learning,* we created a stream with a transformation. What could be the business drivers for creating this pipeline? We did the *how*; what is the *why*?

Answers

After putting thought into the questions, compare your answers to ours:

1. Delta's ability to time travel helps with reproducibility. Delta has versioning that allows us a point-in-time lookup to see what data our model was trained on. For long-term versioning, deep clones or snapshots are appropriate.

2. Writing data to an online store provides real-time feature lookup for real-time inference models.

3. Create `FeatureLookups` for each feature table you wish to include. Then, use `create_training_set`.

4. A feature table has a unique primary key, which indicates the object or entity the features describe.

5. The possibilities are vast. An example is behavior modeling or customer segmentation to support flagging fraud.

Further reading

In this chapter, we identified specific technologies, technical features, and options. Please take a look at these resources to get deeper into the areas that interest you most:

- *How Databricks AI improves model accuracy with real-time computations*: https://www.databricks.com/blog/how-lakehouse-ai-improves-model-accuracy-real-time-computations

- *Use time series feature tables with point-in-time support*: https://docs.databricks.com/en/machine-learning/feature-store/time-series.html

- *Python Arbitrary Stateful Processing in Structured Streaming* – Databricks blog: https://www.databricks.com/blog/2022/10/18/python-arbitrary-stateful-processing-structured-streaming.html

- *Databricks Volumes*: https://docs.databricks.com/en/sql/language-manual/sql-ref-volumes.html

- *Experimenting with Databricks Volumes*: https://medium.com/@tsiciliani/experimenting-with-databricks-volumes-5666cecb166

- *Optimize stateful Structured Streaming queries*: https://docs.databricks.com/en/structured-streaming/stateful-streaming.html

- Databricks blog – *Introducing Delta Time Travel for Large Scale Data Lakes*: https://www.databricks.com/blog/2019/02/04/introducing-delta-time-travel-for-large-scale-data-lakes.html

- YouTube video – *Arbitrary Stateful Aggregations in Structured Streaming in Apache Spark by Burak Yavuz*: https://youtu.be/JAb4FIheP28?si=BjoeKkxP_OUxT7-K

- Databricks documentation – *Compute features on demand using Python user-defined functions*: https://docs.databricks.com/en/machine-learning/feature-store/on-demand-features.html

- *Delta Lake change data feed (CDF)*: https://docs.databricks.com/en/delta/delta-change-data-feed.html

6

Searching for a Signal

In this chapter, we'll cover how to use data science to search for a signal hidden in the noise of data.

We will leverage the features we created within the Databricks platform during the previous chapter. We start by using **automated machine learning** (**AutoML**) for a basic modeling approach, which provides autogenerated code and quickly enables data scientists to establish a baseline model to beat. When searching for a signal, we experiment with different features, hyperparameters, and models. Historically, tracking these configurations and their corresponding evaluation metrics is a time-consuming project in and of itself. A low-overhead tracking mechanism, such as the tracking provided by MLflow, an open source platform for managing data science projects and supporting **ML operations** (**MLOps**) will reduce the burden of manually capturing configurations. More specifically, we'll introduce MLflow Tracking, an MLflow component that significantly improves tracking each permutation's many outputs. However, that is only the beginning. As data science teams are being pressed to leverage **generative artificial intelligence** (**GenAI**), we will also showcase how to leverage a **large language model** (**LLM**) to create a SQL bot and a **deep learning** (**DL**) model utilizing PyTorch. These examples demonstrate that in addition to building our own solutions, we can integrate external innovative solutions into our workflows. This openness allows us to pick from the best of both worlds.

Here is what you will learn as part of this chapter:

- Baselining with AutoML
- Classifying beyond the basic
- Applying our learning

Technical requirements

Here are the technical requirements needed to complete the hands-on examples in this chapter:

- Databricks ML Runtime:

  - AutoML

  - MLflow

  - Pandas

  - Sklearn

  - Torch

- For our LLM model, we will integrate with the **ChatGPT** model from **OpenAI** (`https://openai.com/`)

- We will use the **PyTorch Lightning AI** Python package (`https://www.pytorchlightning.ai/index.html`) and **TorchMetrics** (`https://torchmetrics.readthedocs.io/en/stable/`) while building the classification model for the Parkinson's **Freezing of Gait** (**FOG**) problem

Baselining with AutoML

A baseline model is a simple model used as a starting point for ML. Data scientists often use a baseline model to compare the performance of more complex models. Baseline models are typically simple or common algorithms, such as the majority class classifier or a random forest.

Baseline models are valuable for several reasons, some of which are listed here:

- They can help you understand the difficulty of finding a signal given your current dataset. If even the best baseline model performs poorly, it may indicate that more complex models will also struggle to find useful patterns (that is, garbage data in, garbage models out).

- Baseline models can help you to identify features that are most important for the ML task. If a baseline model performs well, it may be because it can learn from the most salient features.

- Baseline models can help you avoid overfitting. Overfitting is a frequent problem with more complex models. It occurs when a model learns the training data too well and cannot generalize to new data. You can determine whether the more complex model is overfitting by comparing its performance to the baseline model. If the complex model performs better than the baseline on training data but worse on unseen test data, you know you've overfit.

There are multiple ways to create a baseline model. One straightforward approach is to use a random model. A random model is created by randomly assigning labels to the data. This type of model helps you evaluate how other models perform compared to random guessing. Another common approach is to use the majority class classifier. The majority class classifier always predicts the most common class in the training data and gives you another simplistic algorithm against which you can compare more complex models.

In the lakehouse, we have AutoML, which is another straightforward way to get a baseline. This is our personal favorite way to start an ML task because it gives us a head start on model selection compared to the simpler baseline options. Recall that we used AutoML in *Chapter 4* to explore the *Favorita sales* data. While generating that exploration notebook, AutoML also generated model experiments, which is what we are focusing on now.

AutoML rapidly explores many model/hyperparameter permutations to find the best baseline model for your data, along with evaluation metrics and actual code. Once you have created a baseline model, you can evaluate its performance using accuracy, precision, recall, confusion matrices, **receiver operating characteristic** (**ROC**) curves, and more to choose the best experiment. However, it is essential to remember that AutoML is not a magic bullet. It can remove some of the overhead of coding multiple algorithms for experimentation, but you are still in charge of where to go next. Luckily, AutoML automatically tracks these model artifacts in MLflow, which is where MLflow shines. Tracking the many features, models, hyperparameters, and evaluation metrics is a real headache. Using MLflow to track everything natively is a lifesaver, so let's explore that next.

Tracking experiments with MLflow

MLflow is an open source platform developed by Databricks for managing data science projects through the entire ML life cycle, from the experimentation phase to packaging code to model deployment in production. We'll cover deployment in a later chapter. For now, let's focus on the **Tracking** component of MLflow (`https://mlflow.org/docs/latest/tracking.html#tracking`). Before we had MLflow Tracking, ML experiments required a lot of work outside of actual experimentation. MLflow Tracking handles the overhead of capturing configurations of features, algorithms, and hyperparameters during testing. Additionally, using MLflow in the lakehouse gives you access to Managed MLflow, which is built on top of MLflow. Databricks notebooks have built-in integrations that make it easy to manage and compare experiment results both programmatically via Mlflow's lightweight APIs or through **user interfaces** (**UIs**). For example, *Figure 6.1* shows how we can view our experiment runs while still in our notebook:

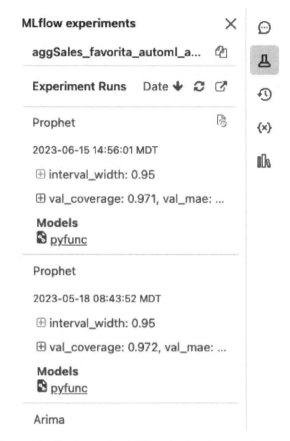

Figure 6.1 – The in-notebook UI for viewing the experiment runs

In MLflow Tracking lingo, the execution of data science code is called a **run**. Each run can record the following:

- **Parameters**: Key-value pairs of input parameters, such as the features used for a given run or the number of trees in a random forest.

- **Metrics**: Evaluation metrics such as **Root Mean Squared Error** (**RMSE**) or **Area Under the ROC Curve** (**AUC**).

- **Artifacts**: Arbitrary output files in any format. This can include images, pickled models, and data files.

- **Source**: The code that originally ran the experiment and a reference to the exact version of the data used for training.

When you train models in the notebook, model training information is automatically tracked with MLflow Tracking. To customize the auto-logging configuration, call `mlflow.autolog()` before your training code. Please note that although many common libraries have auto-logging support (such as Scikit-learn, XGBoost, and Keras), check the documentation for a full list: `https://mlflow.org/docs/latest/models.html#built-in-model-flavors`.

When working on a particular ML task, it's helpful to group your runs into "experiments." This is an easy way to compare runs, either programmatically or via the Databricks Experiments UI.

In *Chapter 4* and *Chapter 5*, we used AutoML for traditional regression and classification models. In the next session, we will lean into more advanced classification techniques for more complex business problems.

Classifying beyond the basic

The Databricks AutoML product is a solid starting point for classification, regression, and forecasting models. There are more advanced classification techniques beyond tree-based models, gradient boost models, and logistic regression that you can use with the lakehouse, as it is designed to work with virtually any open source ML model.

The Databricks ML runtimes include pre-built DL infrastructure and libraries such as PyTorch, TensorFlow, and Hugging Face transformers. DL models are computationally intensive, and **distributed DL** (**DDL**) frameworks such as Horovod also work in conjunction with these DL libraries for more efficient DDL. Be sure to check out the new PyTorch on Databricks! There is a *PyTorch on Databricks – Introducing the Spark PyTorch Distributor* blog that is useful if you are working with PyTorch (`https://www.databricks.com/blog/2023/04/20/pytorch-databricks-introducing-spark-pytorch-distributor.html`).

Another exciting type of ML is **generative adversarial networks** (**GANs**). A quick introduction for those not familiar: GANs are a type of generative model that consists of two **neural networks** (**NNs**) – a generator and a discriminator. The generator network learns to generate synthetic data, such as images or text, that is similar to the real data, while the discriminator network tries to distinguish between the real and synthetic data. GANs have been used for image synthesis, data augmentation, and generating realistic deepfake videos. We used GANs in the past to thwart image classification algorithms. The goal was to alter an image just enough to confuse the DL algorithms but not so much that the human eye would recognize the image was altered. To see other applications of GANs, watch this awesome talk from *Data + AI Summit 2023*: *Generative AI at Scale Using GAN and Stable Diffusion* (`https://www.youtube.com/watch?v=YsWZDCsM9aE`).

Integrating innovation

The world of data science and ML moves very fast. You will likely come across projects that will benefit from innovations outside the standard ML libraries. For example, if you want to work on a project using text data, you will want to explore LLMs. LLMs are a type of advanced language model trained using DL techniques on massive amounts of text data. Fortunately, the Databricks platform makes it easy to integrate with projects such as OpenAI's ChatGPT and other available options from Hugging Face.

Next, let's look at an example of using an LLM to help business users or analysts get information from their tables without knowing SQL. We will build a chatbot using OpenAI's **Generative Pre-trained Transformer 4** (**GPT-4**) as a data analyst. In this example, you create instructions on how it can ask for a list of tables, get information from those tables, and sample data from the tables. The chatbot is able to build a SQL query and then interpret the results. To run these notebooks in the example, you will need an account with OpenAI at the OpenAI developer site (`https://platform.openai.com`) and must request a key for the OpenAI API.

In the first notebook, `sql_resource`, we will create instructions and references for the chatbot.

The notebook starts with commented text with tips on responses and response format, as shown here:

```
1   SQL_INSTRUCTION = """You are a Data Analyst and SQL expert, here to build a SQL
    Query in response to a business user's prompt. Please do not make assumptions if
    the user has given you an ambiguous request. Getting the SQL Query correct is
    extremely important. If you do not have the information you need to write the
    correct SQL Statement, request additional information.
2
3   Your responses are very limited and must be returned in a strict format of "
    [response-type]|[response]".
4
5   Table of Allowed Responses:
6   response-type|response-value|description
7   list|tables|This will request a list of tables
8   define|[table-name]|This will retrieve the table definition for the provided table
    names. Replace [table-name] with a comma separated list of table names
9   sample|[table-name]|This will retrieve sample records for the provided table names.
    Replace [table-name] with a comma separated list of table names
10  Q|[question]|Allows you to ask the user a clarifying question. Replace [question]
    with your clarifying question. Only use this response as a last resort if you need
    information beyond the other responses.
11  SQL|[SQL]|Use this to return the final SQL Statement that answers the user's
    original prompt. [SQL] should be replaced with the generated SQL. This response
    will end the chat conversation.
```

Figure 6.2 – Instruction text for response and response format for this chatbot

The next lines are where you create text for invalid responses and the response format for your chatbot to share its output:

```
37  INVALID_RESPONSE = 'I did not understand your response. Please make sure you are
    replying in the form of [response-type]|[response] per your instructions.'
38
39  FINAL_INSTRUCTION = """
40  Given this data below:
41
42  {data}
43
44  And the context provided below:
45
46  {context}
47
48  Provide an answer to the following prompt:
49
50  {prompt}
51
52  """
```

Figure 6.3 – Text for invalid responses and the chatbot response format

For your chatbot to understand the landscape of data, you will need to create a catalog and define functions to identify your list of tables, table definitions, and schemas as follows:

```
71  def setDataLocation(catalog, schema):
72    global CATALOG
73    global SCHEMA
74    CATALOG = catalog
75    SCHEMA = schema
76    spark.sql(f'use catalog {CATALOG};')
77    spark.sql(f'use schema {SCHEMA};')
78
79  def getTableList():
80    sql = f"""
81        select table_name, comment
82        from system.information_schema.tables
83        where table_catalog = '{CATALOG}' and table_schema = '{SCHEMA}'
84        """
85    #print(sql)
86    tables = spark.sql(sql)
87    return f'List of tables: \ntable_index' + tables.toPandas().to_csv(sep='|')
88
89  def table_def(df, table):
90    table_schema = df.drop('table_catalog', 'table_schema', 'table_name',
      'ordinal_position', 'character_octet_length', 'numeric_precision',
      'numeric_precision_radix', 'numeric_scale', 'datetime_precision', 'interval_type',
      'interval_precision', 'identity_start', 'identity_increment', 'identity_maximum',
      'identity_minimum', 'identity_cycle', 'is_system_time_period_start',
      'is_system_time_period_end', 'system_time_period_timestamp_generation',
      'is_updatable').where(f'table_name = "{table}"')
91
92    return f'Table Schema for {table}: \ncolumn_index' + table_schema.toPandas().to_csv
      (sep='|')
```

Figure 6.4 – Defining tables and table locations for the chatbot

Now, your chatbot knows where to get information. To communicate with your chatbot, we need to teach it how to have a conversation. To do this, we define a log for a conversation and conversation function and the function to send the conversation to the OpenAI GPT-4 model. This is also where you can change which model your chatbot uses:

```
132    def submit_conversation(convo_array):
133        #print(convo_array)
134        completion = openai.ChatCompletion.create(
135            model="gpt-4",#model="gpt-3.5-turbo",
136            messages=convo_array
137        )
138
139        return completion.choices[0].message.content
140
141
142    def log_conversation(convo_type, convo_array):
143        row = 1
144        convo = copy.deepcopy(convo_array)
145        for line in convo:
146            line['conversation_id'] = conversation_id
147            line['conversation_type'] = convo_type
148            line['ordinal_position'] = row
149            row += 1
```

Figure 6.5 – Defining function to submit conversation to OpenAI API

We want our chatbot to build SQL queries to get data from our tables, so we create a function to teach it how to build a Spark SQL query:

```
155    def processSQL(sql):
156        df = spark.sql(sql)
157        ret = []
158        ret.append(buildPromptItem('system', "You are a Data Analyst. Use Data and additional
           Context (if provided) to respond to the prompt."))
159        ret.append(buildPromptItem('user', FINAL_INSTRUCTION.format(data=df.toPandas().to_csv
           (sep='|'), context="", prompt=original_prompt)))
160        resp = submit_conversation(ret)
161        ret.append(buildPromptItem('assistant', resp))
162        log_conversation('SQL_RESPONSE_INTERPRETATION', ret)
163        return resp
```

Figure 6.6 – Function to process SQL

The function we created in *Figure 6.6* is just a few lines of code, but it enables the chatbot to effectively build SQL queries against the tables defined in *Figure 6.4*. Now, we need to tie it all together by defining how to process the conversation and create a response:

```
171  def process_conversation():
172    #print(f'process: {conversation}, original prompt {original_prompt}')
173    while 1==1:
174      resp = submit_conversation(conversation)
175      conversation.append(buildPromptItem('assistant', resp))
176
177      resp_type = resp.split('|')[0]
178      resp_value = resp.split('|')[1]
179
180      if resp_type == 'list': #list tables
181        print('LLM Requesting List of Tables...')
182        conversation.append(buildPromptItem('user', getTableList()))
183        continue
184      elif resp_type == 'define': #define table schema
185        print('LLM Requesting Table Definitions...')
186        conversation.append(buildPromptItem('user', getTableDefinition(resp_value)))
187        continue
188      elif resp_type == 'sample': #get sample records for table
189        print('LLM Requesting Data Samples...')
190        conversation.append(buildPromptItem('user', getTableSampleRecords(resp_value)))
191        continue
192      elif resp_type == 'Q': #Question for User
193        print(resp_value)
194        return resp_value
195      elif resp_type == 'SQL': #SQL for getting the final answer
196        print('LLM Querying Data...')
197        log_conversation('SQL_ANALYST', conversation)
198        answer = processSQL(resp_value)
199        print(answer)
200        return answer
201      else:
202        print('LLM Gave an Invalid Response...')
203        conversation.append(buildPromptItem('user', INVALID_RESPONSE))
```

Figure 6.7 – Function to process request and response

We have now constructed the chatbot, created the initial language for the chatbot to interact with prompts, designated the data and tables available, and showed it how to assemble queries and respond to prompts. In the next section, we start working with the chatbot.

Our next notebook is where we interact with the chatbot, and it starts by installing the OpenAI library:

```
1    %pip install openai
```

Figure 6.8 – Installing OpenAI library

Next, we will pull in the functions that we defined in our `sql_resource` file:

```
1    from sql_resource import startConversation, continueConversation, setDataLocation
2    from sql_resource import CATALOG, SCHEMA
3
4    setDataLocation('us_stores', 'sales_dw')
```

Figure 6.9 – Importing functions from sql_resources

With the library installed and the functions loaded, we have all of the parts assembled that are needed to interact. We start by using the `startConversation()` function to initiate a conversation with our chatbot:

```
1    startConversation("Who ordered the most?")
```

```
LLM Requesting List of Tables...
LLM Requesting Table Definitions...
LLM Querying Data...
Christopher Cooper ordered the most with a total sales amount of $139.
```

Figure 6.10 – Starting a conversation with the chatbot

One thing that we have all experienced when interacting with chatbots is they don't always give you the information you want the first time, so with our chatbot, we can have a back-and-forth conversation. In the preceding conversation, we wanted to know which customer ordered the most, but we don't know how many orders the customer ordered, so in *Figure 6.11*, we ask the question in a different way:

```
1    continueConversation("I was looking for the customer that ordered the most products.")
```

```
LLM Querying Data...
Based on the data provided, Christopher Cooper with customer_id 2 has the most orders, with a total
of 2 orders.
```

Figure 6.11 – Continuing the conversation with the chatbot

As new versions of OpenAI's GPT model are released, the results and behavior of your chatbot may change. In this case, GPT-3.5 asked more questions than the GPT-4 version, but the GPT-4 version was better at using the commands to list tables and request table definitions. As new models and approaches become available, it is good practice to test them and see how the changes impact your work and the results of your chatbot. Leveraging MLflow with your chatbot experiment will help you track and compare different features and configurations and assist in your production process.

In this next section, we will combine the features created in *Chapter 5* to create models for our different datasets.

Applying our learning

In this chapter, we have learned how to create baseline models using AutoML, tracking our MLOps with MLflow, and even using more advanced language models in order to extract more information and ultimately business value from our data. Now, let's take what we have learned and apply it to our datasets that we cleaned in *Chapter 4* and featurized in *Chapter 5*.

We will start with creating and training a classification model for our Parkinson's data so that, ultimately, we can classify hesitation using the patients' tracking data.

Parkinson's FOG

As mentioned in the *Technical requirements* section, we are using PyTorch. To use this, either install the packages in your notebook using `pip` or add it to your cluster configuration under `libraries`:

```
1    %pip install torchmetrics pytorch_lightning
```

Figure 6.12 – Installing the PyTorch library

Once you have your libraries loaded, we import all the libraries we use:

```
1    import pandas as pd
2    import numpy as np
3    from enum import Enum
4    from sklearn import preprocessing
5    from sklearn.model_selection import StratifiedGroupKFold
6    import torch
7    from torch import nn
8    from torch.nn import functional as F
9    from torch.utils.data import Dataset
10   from torch.utils.data import DataLoader
11   from torchmetrics.classification import BinaryF1Score
12   from pytorch_lightning import LightningModule, Trainer
13   import mlflow
14
15   mlflow.pytorch.autolog()
```

Figure 6.13 – Importing libraries

For simplicity, we create a model focused on one target label, namely `StartHesitation`. For ease of reuse, define feature and target variables:

```
1    measures = ["AccV", "AccML", "AccAP"]
2    target_col = "StartHesitation"
```

Figure 6.14 – Defining measures and target variable

Next, we create a custom `FogDataset` class. The class is used by PyTorch and requires three specific class methods: `__init__`, `__len__`, `__getitem__`.

For the `LightningModel` class, as earlier, the `__init__` class method sets the labels and converts the features to tensors. The `__len__` class method returns the total amount of samples in your dataset. The `__getitem__` class method returns, given an index, the i-th sample and label:

```python
 5 ∨ class FogDataset(Dataset):
 6 ∨     def __init__(self, df, feature_cols, target_col):
 7           self.df = df
 8           # set label
 9           self.df_label = self.df[[target_col]].astype(float)
10           self.df_features = self.df[feature_cols].astype(float)
11           # convert to tensors
12           self.dataset = torch.tensor(self.df_features.to_numpy().reshape
             (-1, 3), dtype=torch.float32)
13           self.label = torch.tensor(self.df_label.to_numpy(), dtype=torch.
             float32).reshape(-1)
14
15       # This returns the total amount of samples in your Dataset
16 ∨     def __len__(self):
17           return len(self.dataset)
18
19       # This returns given an index the i-th sample and label
20 ∨     def __getitem__(self, idx):
21           return self.dataset[idx], self.label[idx]
```

Figure 6.15 – Creating custom FogDataset class

Next, we are going to define the PyTorch model with functions. In the PyTorch model definitions, we call `self.log`, defining a `forward` and `test set()` function to surface scalars in TensorBoard. This will then be directly usable with PyTorch Lightning to make a lightning-fast model:

```
1    # Pytorch Lightning Model
2    class FogModel(LightningModule):
3      def __init__(self,train,test,val):
4        super().__init__()
5        self.train_ds=train
6        self.val_ds=val
7        self.test_ds=test
8        # Define PyTorch model
9        noutputs=1
10       nfeatures=3
11       self.model = nn.Sequential(
12         nn.Flatten(),
13         nn.Linear(nfeatures, 32),
14         nn.ReLU(),
15         nn.Dropout(0.1),
16         nn.Linear(32, 32),
17         nn.ReLU(),
18         nn.Dropout(0.1),
19         nn.Linear(32, noutputs),
20         nn.Sigmoid()
21         )
22       self.F1 = BinaryF1Score()
23       self.criterion = nn.BCELoss()
24
25     def forward(self, x):
26       x = self.model(x)
27       return F.log_softmax(x, dim=1)
28
29     def training_step(self, batch, batch_idx):
30       x, y = batch
31       target = y.unsqueeze(1)
32       logits = self.model(x)
33       logits = F.log_softmax(logits, dim=1)
34       loss = self.criterion(logits, target)
35       self.log("train_loss", loss, on_epoch=True)
36       f1 = self.F1(logits, target)
37       self.log(f"train_f1", f1, on_epoch=True)
38       return loss
```

Figure 6.16 – Defining the PyTorch model up to the training step definition

Figure 6.16 defines the PyTorch model, the forward feed, and the training step details. In the second half of the model code, we define test and validation steps, as shown here:

```
39
40    def test_step(self, batch, batch_idx, print_str='test'):
41      x, y = batch
42      target = y.unsqueeze(1)
43      logits = self.model(x)
44      loss = self.criterion(logits, target)
45      f1 = self.F1(logits, target)
46      # Calling self.log will surface up scalars for you in TensorBoard
47      self.log(f"{print_str}_loss", loss, on_epoch=True)
48      self.log(f"{print_str}_f1", f1, on_epoch=True)
49      return loss
50
51    def validation_step(self, batch, batch_idx):
52      # Here we just reuse the test_step for testing
53      return self.test_step(batch, batch_idx,print_str='val')
54
55    def configure_optimizers(self):
56      return torch.optim.Adam(self.parameters(), lr=0.001)
57
58    # This will then directly be usable with Pytorch Lightning to make a super quick model
59    def train_dataloader(self):
60      return DataLoader(self.train_ds, batch_size=2048, num_workers=4,shuffle=False)
61
62    def test_dataloader(self):
63      return DataLoader(self.test_ds, batch_size=512, num_workers=4,shuffle=False)
64
65    def val_dataloader(self):
66      return DataLoader(self.val_ds, batch_size=512, num_workers=4,shuffle=False)
```

Figure 6.17 – The second half of the PyTorch model definition

We are creating training data using SQL to join the `tdcsfog` data and `tdcsfog_metadata`. We check the label count and then convert the training data to Pandas to prepare it for the Sklearn library:

```
1    traindata = sql("SELECT t.*, m.Subject FROM hive_metastore.lakehouse_in_action.
     parkinsons_train_tdcsfog t INNER JOIN hive_metastore.lakehouse_in_action.
     parkinsons_tdcsfog_metadata m ON t.id = m.Id")
2
3    traindata = traindata.toPandas()
```

Figure 6.18 – Creating Parkinson's training dataset

We will stratify the training data by subject, printing the label distribution to look for the most representative train/test split:

```
1   sgkf = StratifiedGroupKFold(n_splits=8, random_state=416, shuffle=True)
2
3   splits = sgkf.split(X=traindata['id'], y=traindata[target_col], groups=traindata['Subject'])
4   for fold, (train_index_0, test_index) in enumerate(splits):
5       print(f"--- Fold = {fold} ---")
6       print(f"Training label distribution {traindata.loc[train_index_0].groupby([target_col]).size
        ()/(1.0*len(train_index_0))*100}")
7       print(f"Testing label distribution {traindata.loc[test_index].groupby([target_col]).size()/(1.
        0*len(test_index))*100}")
```

Figure 6.19 – Stratifying the training dataset

The following is a snippet of the output to illustrate why examining the folds is a necessary step in the process. There are some folds where there is a notable difference between the label distribution in the test and training data:

```
--- Fold = 0 ---
Training label distribution StartHesitation
0 95.713681 1 4.286319
Testing label distribution StartHesitation
0 94.87899 1 5.12101

--- Fold = 1 ---
Training label distribution StartHesitation
0 95.403613 1 4.596387
Testing label distribution StartHesitation
0 97.745471 1 2.254529

--- Fold = 2 ---
Training label distribution StartHesitation
0 94.968068 1 5.031932
Testing label distribution StartHesitation
0 99.912157 1 0.087843
```

Figure 6.20 – Reviewing the test and train labels of the folds

We now implement our splits with fold 0:

```
1   valsplits = sgkf.split(X=model_traindata['id'], y=model_traindata[target_col],
    groups=model_traindata['Subject'])
2   for fold, (train_index, val_index) in enumerate(valsplits):
3       if fold == 3:
4           break
```

Figure 6.21 – Implementing the splits at fold 3

Now that we have train test indices, we can clean our DataFrames by resetting the indices:

```
10    model_valdata = model_traindata.loc[val_index].reset_index(drop=True)
11    new_model_traindata = model_traindata.loc[train_index].reset_index(drop=True)
```

Figure 6.22 – Resetting the indices after training

Improperly indexed DataFrames cause issues with the __getitem__ method in our FogDataset class. Now, we create custom datasets:

```
1    model_traindataset = FogDataset(new_model_traindata,feature_cols=measures,target_col=target_col)
2    model_valdataset = FogDataset(model_valdata,feature_cols=measures,target_col=target_col)
3    model_testdataset = FogDataset(model_testdata,feature_cols=measures,target_col=target_col)
```

Figure 6.23 – Creating customer train, test, and validation datasets

Now, we build the model with the custom datasets we created and train using PyTorch's Trainer:

```
2    trainer = Trainer(max_epochs=10,)
3
4    model = FogModel(model_traindataset, model_testdataset, model_valdataset)
5
6    trainer.fit(model)
```

Figure 6.24 – Building and training the model

We have now used our Parkinson's FOG data to build and train a classification PyTorch model to predict hesitation in our dataset.

Forecasting Favorita sales

In *Chapter 4*, we used AutoML to jump-start our **exploratory data analysis** (**EDA**). Now, we'll use AutoML to create a baseline model.

To get started, we create an aggregated table to feed into AutoML. This is not required but is an easy way to get started:

```
1   df = sql(
2       """ SELECT
3       `date`,
4       store_nbr,
5       sum(sales) as aggSales
6   FROM
7       favorita_train_set
8   GROUP BY
9       `date`,
10      store_nbr
11  ORDER BY
12      `date`
13      """)
14  df.createOrReplaceTempView("aggView")
15
16  aggAutoML = sql(
17      """SELECT t.*, o.dcoilwtico as oil_ten_day_lag, s.city,
18          s.state,s.`cluster` as store_cluster,s.type as store_type FROM aggView t
19  LEFT JOIN favorita_stores s ON t.store_nbr == s.store_nbr
20  RIGHT JOIN favorita_oil o ON date(t.`date`) == (date(o.`date`)+10)
21      """
22  )
23
24  aggAutoML = aggAutoML.where(aggAutoML.date >= "2016-01-01")
25  print(aggAutoML.columns)
26  aggAutoML.write.option("overwriteSchema", "true").mode("overwrite").saveAsTable(
27      "favorita_autoML_agg"
28  )
```

Figure 6.25 – Creating a table of aggregated sales data

Note that the code creates a `favorita_autoML_agg` table, which includes the lag features we created in *Chapter 5*.

We create our AutoML experiment similarly to our previous one. See the experiment configurations in *Figure 6.1*:

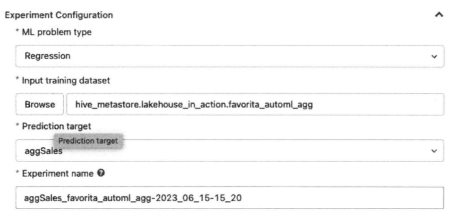

Figure 6.26 – AutoML experiment configuration for the Favorita forecasting sales example

Notice that during this experiment, we are treating the forecasting problem like a regression problem by selecting the ML problem type as **Regression**. As a result, we also must include the date variable in the **Advanced Configuration** section as the time column; see *Figure 6.27*:

Figure 6.27 – AutoML advanced configuration for the Favorita forecasting sales example

The experiment created about 100 runs before reaching the point where it was no longer making progress against the metric of choice – in our case, **R-squared**, as shown in *Figure 6.27*:

		Run Name	Created	Dataset	Duration	Source	Models	val_r2_score	model_type
☐	◉	● useful-grouse-161	⊘ 11 minutes ago	-	8.2s	📓 Noteb...	🔹 sklearn	0.854	lightgbm_r...
☐	◉	● salty-shad-332	⊘ 10 minutes ago	-	9.6s	📓 Noteb...	🔹 sklearn	0.852	lightgbm_r...
☐	◉	● adventurous-deer-223	⊘ 10 minutes ago	-	9.9s	📓 Noteb...	🔹 sklearn	0.851	lightgbm_r...
☐	◉	● casual-carp-736	⊘ 10 minutes ago	-	8.2s	📓 Noteb...	🔹 sklearn	0.851	lightgbm_r...
☐	◉	● sassy-dove-915	⊘ 9 minutes ago	-	6.5s	📓 Noteb...	🔹 sklearn	0.85	lightgbm_r...
☐	◉	● defiant-swan-537	⊘ 12 minutes ago	-	8.4s	📓 Noteb...	🔹 sklearn	0.85	lightgbm_r...
☐	◉	● abundant-fly-694	⊘ 10 minutes ago	-	9.9s	📓 Noteb...	🔹 sklearn	0.849	lightgbm_r...
☐	◉	● rambunctious-kit-989	⊘ 9 minutes ago	-	8.6s	📓 Noteb...	🔹 sklearn	0.849	lightgbm_r...

Figure 6.28 – AutoML advanced configuration for the Favorita forecasting sales example

Out of the 100 combinations, only 6 have an R-squared value of 0.85 or higher. Using AutoML is saving us considerable time and effort. During the experiment, MLflow tried many model types and hyperparameter tuning utilizing **Hyperopt**. This experiment is also distributed with the power of Spark, meaning we have a solid model that was tuned efficiently. We have a baseline model, and we are sure a signal can be found. From here forward, we want to aim to beat the model. Beating the model at this point is done by brute force. We improve performance by creating new features, gathering more data points, or enriching the dataset. This point is brute force. We improve performance by creating new features, gathering more data points, or enriching the dataset.

Summary

In this chapter, we discussed quick ways to create a baseline model and demonstrated how that increases productivity.

We demonstrated MLflow functionality that supports MLOps and helps track model training and tuning. We also covered more complex classification frameworks that can be used in the lakehouse. Access to these frameworks made it possible to implement a DL model in PyTorch for the Parkinson's FOG example. The openness of Databricks opens the doors for open source and proprietary innovations with API integrations, as shown by the SQL bot LLM. This integration saved time by not recreating the wheel and putting the SQL tool in the hands of our analysts sooner.

The next chapter will focus on moving our models into production.

Questions

The following questions solidify key points to remember and tie the content back to your experience:

1. Why would you use a baseline model?
2. What are examples of more advanced classification techniques?
3. When would you use LLM models, such as OpenAI's ChatGPT or **Dolly**, in your lakehouse?

Answers

After putting thought into the questions, compare your answers to ours:

1. Use a baseline model to have a simple model as a starting point to compare later and more complex models.
2. Some examples of more advanced classification techniques include DL and GANs.
3. I would use an LLM model in my lakehouse if I needed to have more advanced language techniques with my data, such as a chatbot.

Further reading

In this chapter, we pointed out specific technologies, technical features, and options. Please take a look at these resources to get deeper into areas that interest you most:

- *Introducing AI Functions: Integrating Large Language Models with Databricks SQL*: `https:// www.databricks.com/blog/2023/04/18/introducing-ai-functions- integrating-large-language-models-databricks-sql.html`
- *PyTorch on Databricks – Introducing the Spark PyTorch Distributor*: `https://www. databricks.com/blog/2023/04/20/pytorch-databricks-introducing- spark-pytorch-distributor.html`

- *Free Dolly: Introducing the World's First Truly Open Instruction-Tuned LLM*: `https://www.databricks.com/blog/2023/04/12/dolly-first-open-commercially-viable-instruction-tuned-llm`

- *Ray 2.3 release (PyPI)*: `https://pypi.org/project/ray/`

- *Ray on Spark Databricks docs*: `https://docs.databricks.com/machine-learning/ray-integration.html`

- *Announcing Ray support on Databricks and Apache Spark Clusters*: `https://www.databricks.com/blog/2023/02/28/announcing-ray-support-databricks-and-apache-spark-clusters.html`

- *Ray docs*: `https://docs.ray.io/en/latest/cluster/vms/user-guides/community/spark.html#deploying-on-spark-standalone-cluster`

7

Productionizing ML on Databricks

"Production is 80% of the work."

— *Matei Zaharia*

Once you've refined your model and have satisfactory results, you are ready to put it into production. We've now entered the field of **machine learning operations (MLOps)**! Unfortunately, this is where many data scientists and ML engineers get stuck, and it's common for companies to struggle here. Implementing models in production is much more complex than running models ad hoc because MLOps requires distinct tools and skill sets and sometimes, entirely new teams. MLOps is an essential part of the data science process because the actual value of a model is often only realized post-deployment.

You can think of MLOps as combining **DevOps**, **DataOps**, and **ModelOps**. MLOps is often divided into two parts: inner and outer loops. The inner loop covers the data science work and includes tracking various stages of the model development and experimentation process. The outer loop encompasses methods to orchestrate your data science project throughout its life cycle, from testing to staging and ultimately into production.

Fortunately, the path from model development to production doesn't have to depend entirely on another team and tool stack when using the Databricks **Data Intelligence (DI)** platform. Productionizing an ML model using Databricks products makes the journey more straightforward and cohesive by incorporating functionality such as the **Unity Catalog Registry (UC Registry)**, Databricks workflows, **Databricks Asset Bundles (DABs)**, and model serving capabilities. This chapter will cover the tools and practices for taking your models from development to production.

Here is what you will learn as part of this chapter:

- Deploying the MLOps inner loop

- Deploying the MLOps outer loop

- Deploying your model

- Applying our learning

Deploying the MLOps inner loop

In Databricks, the MLOps inner loop uses a variety of tools within the DI platform that we've already touched upon throughout this book, such as MLflow, Feature Engineering with Unity Catalog, and Delta. This chapter will highlight how you can leverage them together to facilitate MLOps from one place. MLOps is covered in even more depth by Databricks' ebook, *The Big Book of MLOps*, which we highly recommend if you wish to learn more about the guiding principles and design decisions when architecting your own MLOps solution. We use **GitHub** to help facilitate DevOps and code reproducibility. For the DataOps portion, we use **Unity Catalog** and **Delta**. These tools help us track the versions of data and the code associated with the features created. This is the data reproducibility piece of DataOps. We use Delta time travel to query data from previous versions of the same table in the short term. For long-term reproducibility, we recommend saving the training dataset as a Delta table and logging the table path with the `mlflow.log_input()` method. The upstream sources of the feature tables we create are automatically tracked by UC lineage.

Registering a model

Let's jump into model registries and their role in productionalization. A model registry is a centralized model store that helps manage the entire model life cycle, including versioning or aliasing, CI/CD integration, webhooks, and notifications. In Databricks, the UC Registry extends the governance features of Unity Catalog to the model registries, including centralized access control, auditing, lineage, and model discovery across workspaces. The UC Registry is a centralized repository for your models and their chronological lineage. This means that the experiment and experiment run that created each respective model are linked to the respective code and data source. Once you are satisfied with your ML model, the first thing to do is register it in Databricks under your central model registry. A registered model is a logical grouping of a model's version history. The UC Registry tracks different model versions, including each version's training data, hyperparameters, and evaluation metrics. A model rarely, if ever, has only one version. In addition to experimentation of model types and hyperparameter values, there are also cases where we want to experiment with different versions of a model. We can refer to these different model versions using model aliases. For example, deploying different versions simultaneously can be helpful for A/B testing; we'll cover this in more detail in the *Model inference* section. With the UC Registry, you can easily create and manage multiple model aliases, making it easier to track changes, compare performance, and revert to earlier versions if needed.

Collaborative development

The UC Registry provides a collaborative model development environment, enabling teams to share and review models. This collaboration is also tracked, allowing multiple teams or leads to stay abreast of the model development process. Team or project leads can also require documentation before allowing a model to continue through the life cycle. We find it easier to add snippets of documentation throughout the project rather than trying to remember everything and take the time to write it all down afterward.

The UC Registry allows you to tag models and model versions. In the Streaming Transactions project, we use tags to track the validation status of a model. The approval process can be automated or may require human interaction. An approval process can ensure that models are high quality and meet business requirements.

Figure 7.1 shows a screenshot of the UC Model Registry. Note that there are built-in locations for tags, aliases, and comments:

Figure 7.1 – The UC Model Registry UI shows each model version

The UC Registry is tightly integrated with the DI platform. This provides a single technical stack – a unified environment for moving a model through experimentation to deployment. The seamless integration lets you leverage other Databricks components such as Databricks Notebooks, Databricks Jobs, Databricks Lakehouse Monitoring, and Databricks Model Serving.

Next, let's move on to product features that support the outer loop process.

Deploying the MLOps outer loop

The ML life cycle looks different for different use cases. However, the set of tools available in the Databricks platform makes it possible to automate as you like and supports your MLOps. The outer loop connects the inner loop products with the help of Workflows, Databricks Terraform Provider, REST API, DABs, and more. We covered automating the tracking process through MLflow Tracking and the UC Registry. The UC Registry is tightly integrated with the Model Serving feature and has a robust API that can easily be integrated into the automation process using webhooks. Each of these features can play a role in automating the ML life cycle.

Workflows

Databricks Workflows is a flexible orchestration tool for productionizing and automating ML projects. Workflows help the ML life cycle by providing a unified way to chain together all aspects of ML, from data preparation to model deployment. With Databricks Workflows, you can designate dependencies between tasks to ensure tasks are completed in the required order. These dependencies are visualized with arrows connecting the tasks, as shown in *Figure 7.2*:

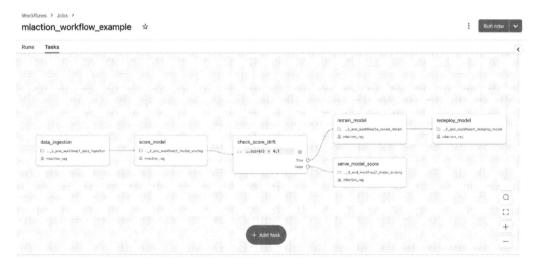

Figure 7.2 – A Databricks workflow with five tasks, with the feature
engineering task having two dependencies

Tasks in a workflow are not limited to notebooks. In *Chapter 3*, we prepared a DLT pipeline to prepare data in the Bronze layer, and DLT pipelines can be a workflow component. Additional objects, such as JAR files, Python scripts, and SQL, can be tasks within a workflow, as shown in *Figure 7.3*:

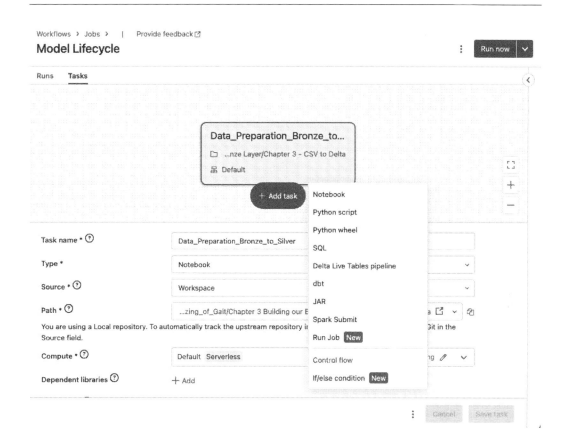

Figure 7.3 – Examples of objects that can be used as tasks within a workflow

Workflows are robust and play a key role in automating work within Databricks. DABs are another tool for productionization in Databricks.

DABs

DABs are a way to bring uniformity and standardization to the deployment approach for all data products built on the Databricks platform. They are an **Infrastructure as Code (IaC)** approach to managing your projects, allowing developers to outline a project's infrastructure and resources using a YAML configuration file. DABs are especially useful for managing complex projects that involve a lot of collaborators and require automation. Where **continuous integration and continuous deployment (CI/CD)** is necessary, DABs are a wonderful way to manage ML pipeline resources across environments and to help your team follow best practices throughout the development and productionalization processes.

Under the hood, DABs are collections of Databricks artifacts (including jobs, DLT pipelines, and ML models) and assets (for example, notebooks, SQL queries, and dashboards). These bundles are managed through YAML templates that are created and maintained alongside source code. You can build DAB YAML files manually or use templates to automate. You can also build custom templates for more complex processing tasks.

Using DABs requires the Databricks CLI. We discussed installing the CLI in *Chapter 2* if you want to review it again. Also, DABs are fairly new and not incorporated into the projects. However, great resources are listed in *Further reading* that cover this new product feature in depth.

REST API

Everything you can do in the UI can be accomplished via the API as well. The UI is great for exploring product features and building workflows for the first time. For example, we automated the process after building out our AutoML experiment in the UI. Additionally, we saw how secrets are completely contained in the API and not available via the UI. As we'll see in the next section, it is possible to deploy your models via the API.

Deploying your model

Deploying a model can be done in many ways, depending on the use case and data availability. For example, deployment may look like packaging a model in a container and deploying it on an endpoint or model that runs daily in a production workflow to provide predictions in tables that can be consumed by applications. Databricks has product features to pave the way to production for all inference types.

Model Inference

We've walked through the methods and tools that help you set up your model in production, and finally, you have a model ready for inference! But one key question you should consider as part of this process is how your model should be used. Do you need the results once a day? Is the model powering an application that requires real-time results? Your model's purpose will help you decide the type of deployment you need. You've seen the words "batch" and "streaming" a few times in this chapter already, so let's quickly define what those mean in the context of model inference:

- **Batch inference**: Batch inference (also known as offline inference) refers to a job that generates predictions on a group (or "batch") of data all at once. Batch jobs are scheduled to run on a specified cadence, such as once a day. This type of inference is best when there are no/low-latency requirements and allows you to take advantage of scalable compute resources.

- **Streaming inference**: Streaming inference (also known as online inference) refers to a job that generates predictions on data as it is streamed. This is possible in the Databricks platform via Delta Live Tables.

- **Real-time inference**: Real-time inference (also known as model serving) refers to the process of exposing your models as REST API endpoints. This enables universally available, low-latency predictions and is especially useful when deploying models that generate predictions required by real-time applications.

All these options are available via the Databricks UI. Let's use the Favorita Store example again. Perhaps we've met with our beverages business team, and they would like to see weekly forecasts to help decide how much of each product they should purchase. We will opt for batch inference since we only need to produce an updated forecast once a week. It just takes a few clicks to set up a model for batch processing. Follow the *Applying our learning* section of the Favorita Sales dataset for detailed instructions on deploying your model for batch inference.

Model serving

Let's dive deeper into real-time inference or **model serving**. The process of model serving can be complex and costly, involving additional tools and systems to achieve real-time needs. Fortunately, deploying a registered model as an endpoint only takes a single click from the Databricks platform! Because model serving is tightly integrated with MLflow, the path from development to production is much faster. Using a model registered in the MLflow Model Registry, Databricks automatically prepares a production-ready container and deploys the container to serverless compute.

It's also easy to deploy models via API, as shown here. A forecasting problem doesn't make much sense as a model serving use case, so let's consider instead the MIC problem we've been working on throughout this book. We will use model serving to serve our classification model in real time. The following example code snippet creates an endpoint that serves a version of a model named `asl_model`:

```
POST /api/2.0/serving-endpoints

{
  "name": "lakehouse-in-action-endpoint",
  "config":{
   "served_models": [{
     "model_name": "asl_model",
     "model_version": "1",
     "workload_size": "Small",
     "scale_to_zero_enabled": true
   }]
  }
}
```

Figure 7.4 – Deploying a model through a serving endpoint

Model serving lets you build workflows around model endpoints, which provides plenty of flexibility in terms of model deployment. For example, an organization may want to A/B test two or more models. Model serving makes it easy to deploy multiple models behind the same endpoint and distribute traffic among them. In another pattern, you can deploy the same model behind multiple endpoints. The following is an example of the UI and the analysis you can perform when A/B testing models:

Figure 7.5 – Model serving gives us the flexibility to A/B test models deployed behind the same endpoint

Get ready to follow along in your own Databricks workspace as we review the *Chapter 7* code project by project.

Applying our learning

Let's use what we have learned to productionalize our models.

Technical requirements

Here are the technical requirements needed to complete the hands-on examples in this chapter:

- On-demand features require the use of DBR ML 13.1 or higher.
- RAG and CV parts require DBR ML 14.2 and higher.
- Python UDFs are created and governed in UC; hence, Unity Catalog must be enabled for the workspace – no shared clusters.

- The Streaming Transactions project uses `scikit-learn==1.4.0rc1`. The notebooks that need it install it.

- The Streaming Transactions project, again, performs better with parallel compute. We'll use the multi-node cluster from *Chapter 5*. See *Figure 7.6* for the multi-node CPU configuration:

Figure 7.6 – Multi-node CPU cluster configuration (on AWS)

Project – Favorita Sales forecasting

In this chapter, we discussed using managed MLflow and the UC Model Registry to register and prepare models for deployment. We'll start by walking through the UI, so please open the following notebooks and a tab within the Experiments UI page:

- `CH7-01-Registering the Model`

- `CH7-02-Batch Inference`

As a reminder, in *Chapter 6*, we ran experiments to find a baseline model, and you can review those experiments from the Experiments UI page in Databricks. To follow along in your workspace, please open the Experiments UI page from *Chapter 6*, as shown in *Figure 7.7*:

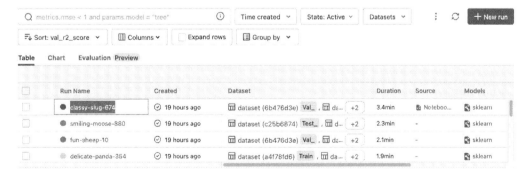

Figure 7.7 – The Experiments UI page for exploring the experiment runs

For the sake of the project, we will move forward as though the best baseline model is the model we want in production. To productionalize the model, follow these steps:

1. On the AutoML experiment page, click on the best run (the run at the top when sorting by the evaluation metric in descending order). This will open the run details page. As shown in *Figure 7.8*, there are four tabs – **Overview**, **Model metrics**, **System metrics**, and **Artifacts**:

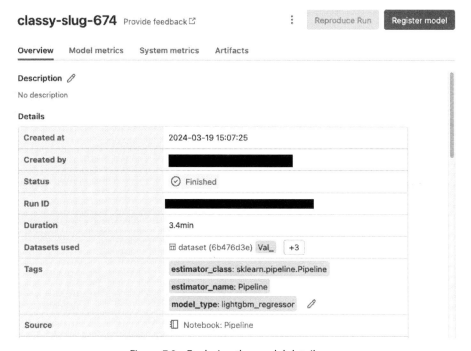

Figure 7.8 – Exploring the model details page

2. Click **Register model** in the top corner. This opens a dialogue box where you can register the model in the workspace or UC Model Registry. Of course, we want to use Unity Catalog. Selecting Unity Catalog provides the code to register the model via API. This code is already included in the CH7-01-Registering the Model notebook. When running the notebook in your workspace, you must update the runs:/ URL in the notebook before executing it:

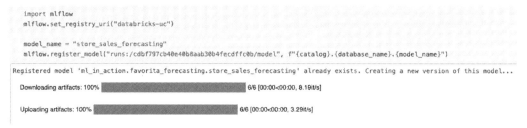

Figure 7.9 – Registering a new model

3.   While still in your notebook, execute the final cell a second time. This creates a second version of the same model.

4.   Navigate to the `favorita_forecasting` database in Unity Catalog. Selecting the **Models** tab opens a new UI, as shown in *Figure 7.10*:

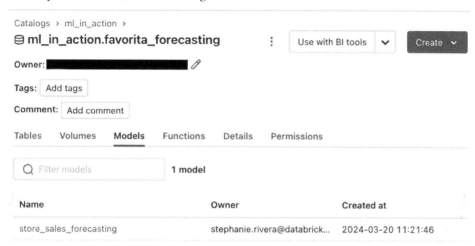

Figure 7.10 – Viewing the model in Unity Catalog

5.   Select the forecasting model. You'll notice that we have two versions of the model. Add an alias to each: **champion** and **challenger** are common to indicate the current best model and the newer version being considered to replace the current best model:

Figure 7.11 – Assigning aliases to identify model status

Now, it's time to think about how we want to deploy this model. Since this is a sales forecasting use case that's predicting 10+ days in advance, real-time inference doesn't make the most sense.

6.   Open `CH7-02-Batch Inference` to run inference on the test set. Notice that in *Figure 7.12*, we define `model_uri` using the alias rather than the model version number:

```
import mlflow
from pyspark.sql.functions import struct, col
mlflow.set_registry_uri("databricks-uc")
model_name = "store_sales_forecasting"

logged_model = f"models:/{model_name}@Champion"

# Load model as a Spark UDF.
loaded_model = mlflow.pyfunc.spark_udf(spark, model_uri=logged_model)

df = sql("SELECT * FROM test_set")

# Predict on a Spark DataFrame.
df.withColumn('predictions', loaded_model(struct(*map(col, df.columns))))
```

Figure 7.12 – Batch forecasting on the test set using the Champion model

This inference code will always run inference on the data provided using the Champion model. If we later determine that an updated version is better, we can change the model alias and run the correct model without making any code changes to the inference code.

The next practical step is to set up a workflow on a schedule. Please refer to the streaming project to see this demonstrated. This wraps up the end of this project. In *Chapter 8*, we will use the Favorita Sales data to show how easily a SQLbot can be created using the Foundational Model API.

Project – Streaming Transactions

We have much to do to wrap up the Streaming Transactions project! We will build our model, wrap it, validate it, and implement batch inference. To accomplish this, we'll begin ingesting the labels into a different table. This allows us to set up the inference table and merge the actual labels after the predictions happen. We will create two workflows: *Production Streaming Transactions* and *Production Batch Inference and Model Retraining*.

As with any project, we must refine the previously written code as we work toward production. The notebooks that look familiar from earlier in this book may have some minor updates, but most of the code remains unchanged.

Before we jump in, let's remember where we are and where we are going by taking a quick look at the project pipeline:

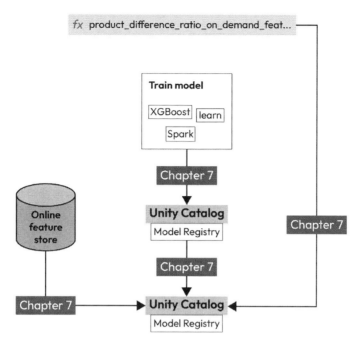

Figure 7.13 – The project pipeline for the Production Streaming Transactions project

To follow along in your workspace, please open the following notebooks:

- `CH7-01-Generating Records`
- `CH7-02-Auto Loader`
- `CH7-03-Feature Engineering Streams`
- `CH7-04-Update Maximum Price Feature Table`
- `CH7-05-Wrapping and Logging the Baseline Model`
- `CH7-06-Wrapping and Logging the Production Model`
- `CH7-07-Model Validation`
- `CH7-08-Batch Inference`
- `CH7-09-Production Batch Inference`
- `CH7-10-Auto Label Loader`
- `mlia_utils/transactions_funcs.py`
- `production_streams.yaml`
- `model_retraining_n_inference_workflow.yaml`

We recommend using a multi-node CPU cluster for this project. The first four notebooks (CH7-01 through CH7-04) are nearly identical to their previous versions in *Chapter 6*, but the *Chapter 7* versions all point to the production rather than the development catalog. Table names are parameterized in widgets so that they can be set in workflows. Here is a list of the essential notebook-specific changes that have been made to the first four notebooks:

- CH7-01-Generating Records: Labels and transactions are now being written to separate folders. The data generation components have also been moved to the transactions_funcs file in the utils folder.

- CH7-02-Auto Loader: The label column is no longer being added to the transactions table. For production, we ensure that the table being written to has delta.enableChangeDataFeed = true before the stream starts. If the table property is set after the stream starts, the stream is interrupted and will require a restart. Lastly, if the table property is never set, Lakehouse Monitoring is negatively impacted and will not support continuous monitoring.

- CH7-03-Feature Engineering Streams: Similar to the CH7-02-Pipeline Auto Loader notebook, table properties are set before any data is written.

- CH7-04-Update Maximum Price Feature Table: The code is cleaned up for a step toward production. Specifically, the feature table is updated rather than created once it exists.

You will need transaction data in the production catalog to create the model. Note the new setup variable, $env=prod. The pipeline workflow notebooks – that is, CH7-01, CH7-02, and CH7-03 – are ready to be added to a workflow in the jobs section of Databricks. Start by clicking the **Workflows** icon on the left-side menu bar. Then, click **Create job**. We have provided you with a YAML file, production_streams.yaml, to guide you. Note that in the YAML file and *Figure 7.14*, the tasks do not depend on one another:

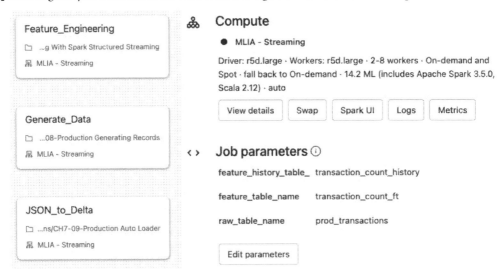

Figure 7.14 – The task DAG (left) and some settings (right) for the Production Streaming Transactions job

As shown in *Figure 7.14*, you can use the compute cluster shown in *Figure 7.6* for the job and the other notebooks. Also, we chose to add parameters at the job level rather than the individual tasks. You can now easily generate the data needed to build the model.

We will use `training_set`, which we created in *Chapter 6*, to train an updated version of the model. Recall that logging a model in Unity Catalog packages the feature metadata with the model. Hence, at inference time, it automatically looks up features from feature tables provided in the specified training set. We added this spec to the `CH7-05-Wrapping and Logging the Baseline Model` and `CH7-06-Wrapping and Logging the Production Model` notebooks. We will not go through these notebooks separately. The difference between them is that the baseline model is trained on data in the development catalog. Then, the model is re-trained in production using production data from the inference table.

We know that we don't have an inference table yet. Don't worry – it's coming! Going back to `training_set`, being able to match up the features is only useful if we have feature values. We use the time boundaries of our feature table to ensure that the raw transactions being used for training have feature values. Also, we require the label column to be present, as shown in *Figure 7.15*:

```
ft_name = "product_3minute_max_price_ft"

if not spark.catalog.tableExists(ft_name) or spark.table(tableName=ft_name).isEmpty():
  raise Exception("problem")
else:
  min_time = sql(f"SELECT MIN(LookupTimestamp) FROM {ft_name}").collect()[0][0]
  max_time = sql(f"SELECT MAX(LookupTimestamp) FROM {ft_name}").collect()[0][0]
  raw_transactions_df = sql(f"""
    SELECT Amount,CustomerID,actual_label as Label,Product,TransactionTimestamp FROM {table_name}
    WHERE TransactionTimestamp >= '{min_time}' AND TransactionTimestamp <= '{max_time}' AND actual_label IS NOT NULL
    """)
```

Figure 7.15 – Defining the feature lookups for the inference model

The transactions shown in *Figure 7.15* come from the inference table, `packaged_transaction_model_predictions`, which was created in `CH7-08-Batch Inference`. The baseline model does something similar with the `raw_transactions` table. The baseline model also sets the model description, as shown in *Figure 7.16*:

```
import pandas as pd
import mlflow
mlflow.set_registry_uri("databricks-uc")

model_name = "packaged_transaction_model"
full_model_name = f'{catalog}.{database_name}.{model_name}'
model_description = "MLflow custom python function wrapper around a LightGBM model with embedded
pre-processing. The wrapper provides data preprocessing so that the model can be applied to input
dataframe directly without training/serving skew. This model serves to classify transactions as 0/1 for
learning purposes."

model_artifact_path = volume_model_path + model_name
dbutils.fs.mkdirs(model_artifact_path)
```

Figure 7.16 – Setting the model description

We are now ready to focus on the model. Let's walk through the rest of the process:

1. Set the model registry to Unity Catalog with `mlflow.set_registry_uri("databricks-uc")`.

2. Use `pip` to save a `requirements.txt` file.

3. Create a PyFunc wrapper for `TransactionModelWrapper`.

Most of the code for `TransactionModelWrapper` should look familiar to those who have created a model using Sklearn. The initialization function, `__init__(self, model, X, y, numeric_columns, cat_columns)`, accepts a model and DataFrames. The data preprocessing for training and inference data is standardized within the wrapper. `TransactionModelWrapper` consists of four methods: `init`, `predict`, `preprocess_data`, and `fit`.

The initialization method does the following:

1. Splits the data into train and test sets.

2. Initializes and fits `OneHotEncoder` for the categorical feature columns provided.

3. Initializes and fits `StandardScaler` for the numerical feature columns provided.

4. Applies the `preprocess_data` method to the training and test data.

5. Defines an `evaluation` method to calculate the log loss on the X and y sets provided.

6. Invokes the `evaluation` method on preprocessed test data.

7. Defines and invokes the `_model_signature` method to easily provide the signature when logging the model.

The `predict` method calls the `preprocess_data` (*Figure 7.17*) method on the input DataFrame before performing and returning the prediction. This method is used to process the training data and the inference data, ensuring identical preprocessing for predictions:

```
@staticmethod
def preprocess_data(df, numeric_columns,fitted_scaler,cat_columns, encoder):
    if "TransactionTimestamp" in df.columns:
        try:
            df = df.drop("TransactionTimestamp",axis=1)
        except:
            df = df.drop("TransactionTimestamp")
    one_hot_encoded = encoder.transform(df[cat_columns])
    df = pd.concat([df,one_hot_encoded],axis=1).drop(columns=cat_columns)
    df["isTimeout"] = df["isTimeout"].astype('bool')
    ## scale the numeric columns with the pre-built scaler
    if len(numeric_columns):
        ndf = df[numeric_columns].copy()
        df[numeric_columns] = fitted_scaler.transform(ndf[numeric_columns])
    return df
```

Figure 7.17 – The preprocessing method for the model

As shown in *Figure 7.17*, the fitted numeric scaler and one-hot encoder are passed as input. This protects against skew between the training and inference features. Notice how `TransactionTimestamp` is dropped. This is done because after the features from the feature tables are present, we no longer need a timestamp. The input DataFrame can be a Spark or pandas DataFrame. This is why we need different syntax to drop the timestamp column.

In the following command cell, you customize `mlflow.autolog` and start the MLflow experiment for training, testing, wrapping, and logging the model. You will use `mlflow.evaluate` to handle the evaluation process. The logging process is easy – you call `log_model` with the model name, wrapped model, `pyfunc` flavor, and previously created training set. This process also registers the model in Unity Catalog. The last thing in this notebook is a quick test that's performed on the predict function showing how to pass in the Spark context with the input data. You are now ready to validate the model.

Next, focus on the `CH7-07-Model Validation` notebook, which checks that the input model has the correct metadata so that it's ready for production. This notebook can be used to test any model. Ideally, you will add numerous checks, including the ability to predict and possibly test the accuracy of specific slices of data. For example, you could check the model performance on each product or geography. You can pass those columns with tags when slices need testing.

Collect the model details, as shown in *Figure 7.18*. Notice the use of the `util` function, which is imported in a previous cell from `mlia_utils.mlflow_funcs import get_latest_model_version`:

```
model_details = mlfclient.get_registered_model(model_name)
model_version = str(get_latest_model_version(model_name))
model_version_details = mlfclient.get_model_version(name=model_name, version=model_version)
```

Figure 7.18 – Using the mlfclient and util functions to access the model details

Each time you train and log the model, a new model version is created. Using tags, you can indicate which model version(s) must be tested and validated before deployment:

```
assert 'validation_status' in model_version_details.tags.keys(), f"the model, model={model_name},
specfied does not have validation_status tag"
if model_version_details.tags['validation_status'] == 'passed_tests':
  dbutils.notebook.exit("No validation needed!")

assert model_version_details.tags['validation_status'] == 'needs_tested', f"the latest version,
version={model_version}, of model, model={model_name} is not tagged as validation_status=needs_tested"
```

Figure 7.19 – Assertions to ensure the model needs to be tested

As shown in *Figure 7.20*, you need an informative model description for all production models. We recommend that you include information about the use case the model is used for. Metadata hygiene is becoming increasingly important as companies want to leverage generative AI on internal data. This is because LLMs use the metadata fields to find relevant information in the models:

```
if model_details.description == "":
  print("No model description found. Please add a model description to pass this test.")
  validation_results['description'] = 0
elif len(model_details.description) < 15:
  print("Model description is too short. Perhaps include a note about the business impact.")
  validation_results['description'] = 0
else:
  validation_results['description'] = 1
```

Figure 7.20 – Validating that a model description is present

Similar to what's shown in *Figure 7.20*, the notebook checks for tags. These are examples to get you started. This is an ideal section to expand on the current code and continue adding validation results and update tags:

```
if sum(validation_results.values()) == len(validation_results.values()):
  mlfclient.set_model_version_tag(name=model_name, key="validation_status", value="passed_tests",
  version=model_version)
  print(f"Success! Your model, {model_name} version {model_version}, passed all tests.")
else:
  mlfclient.set_model_version_tag(name=model_name, key="validation_status", value="failed_tests",
  version=model_version)
  print(f"Fail! Check the results to determine which test(s) the model failed. {validation_results}")
```

```
Success! Your model, ml_in_prod.synthetic_transactions.packaged_transaction_model version 8, passed all tests.
```

Figure 7.21 – Processing the results of the validation tests

With a tested model, you can progress to inference; see the CH7-08-Batch Inference notebook. Review the examples of performing batch inference on a DataFrame (*Figure 7.22*) and a JSON data string:

```
from databricks.feature_engineering import FeatureEngineeringClient
from mlia_utils.mlflow_funcs import get_latest_model_version
import mlflow
mlflow.set_registry_uri("databricks-uc")
fe = FeatureEngineeringClient()

scoring_df = sql("SELECT * FROM raw_transactions ORDER BY TransactionTimestamp DESC").drop("Label").limit(100)

print(f"Scoring model={model_name} version={get_latest_model_version(model_name)}")

scored = fe.score_batch(
  model_uri=f"models:/{model_name}/{get_latest_model_version(model_name)}",
  df=scoring_df,
  env_manager="conda"
)

display(scored)
```

Figure 7.22 – Loading and scoring the model by performing batch inference on a DataFrame

Now, look at the code in CH7-09-Production Batch Inference. The substantial changes include scoring_df, which is the DataFrame we apply our model to for predictions. Notice that in *Figure 7.23*, the min_time and max_time variables provide boundaries for the transactions, ensuring the batch feature values have been calculated. Additionally, the inference table provides a boundary that prevents duplicate prediction calculations:

```
min_time = sql(f"SELECT MIN(LookupTimestamp) FROM {ft_name}").collect()[0][0]
max_time = sql(f"SELECT MAX(LookupTimestamp) FROM {ft_name}").collect()[0][0]

if not spark.catalog.tableExists(inference_table) or spark.table(tableName=inference_table).isEmpty
():
  scoring_df = sql(f"""
                   SELECT Amount,CustomerID,Product,TransactionTimestamp FROM {table_name}
                   WHERE TransactionTimestamp <= '{max_time}' AND TransactionTimestamp >= '
                   {min_time}'
                   """)
  sql(f"""
      CREATE TABLE IF NOT EXISTS {inference_table}
      (Amount FLOAT, CustomerID INT, Product STRING, TransactionTimestamp TIMESTAMP,
      transactionCount INT, isTimeout BOOLEAN, MaxProductAmount FLOAT, MaxDifferenceRatio FLOAT,
      prediction DOUBLE, model_version STRING, actual_label INT) USING delta TBLPROPERTIES (delta.
      enableChangeDataFeed = true)
      """)
else:
  last_inf_time = sql(f"SELECT MAX(TransactionTimestamp) FROM {inference_table}").collect()[0][0]
  scoring_df = sql(f"""
                   SELECT Amount,CustomerID,Product,TransactionTimestamp FROM {table_name}
                   WHERE TransactionTimestamp <= '{max_time}' AND TransactionTimestamp >= '
                   {min_time}'
                   AND TransactionTimestamp > '{last_inf_time}'
                   """)
```

Figure 7.23 – The scoring_df query's configuration

The inference table in CH7-08 needs to be updated to fit the requirements for the inference table monitoring provided by Lakehouse Monitoring. This means adding the model_version and actual_label columns. The actual_label column is set to NULL so that it is clear the value has not been updated yet; see *Figure 7.24*:

```
scored = fe.score_batch(
  model_uri=f"models:/{model_name}/{model_version}",
  df=scoring_df
)
scored.withColumn("model_version",lit(model_version))\
  .withColumn(colName="actual_label",col=lit(None))\
  .write.mode('append').format('delta').saveAsTable(inference_table)
```

Figure 7.24 – The addition of the model version and actual label columns

These two additional columns for the inference table are requirements for Lakehouse Monitoring. The `InferenceLog` monitor comes with autogenerated dashboards. However, you need to populate the table. Begin by creating a bronze table for the transaction labels. The Auto Loader is back again, focusing on labels; see CH7-10-Auto Label Loader and *Figure 7.25*. In the notebook, the `transaction_labels` table was created; this is similar to the code from *Chapter 3*. In *Figure 7.25*, you can use the CDF and CDC Delta features to update the new inference table with the ground truth label:

```
def merge_stream(df, i):
  df.createOrReplaceTempView("labels_cdc_microbatch")

  df._jdf.sparkSession()\
    .sql(f"""MERGE INTO {inference_table} target
      USING
      (SELECT CustomerID, TransactionTimestamp, Label as actual_label
      FROM labels_cdc_microbatch) as source
      ON source.CustomerID = target.CustomerID
      AND source.TransactionTimestamp = target.TransactionTimestamp
      WHEN MATCHED THEN UPDATE SET target.actual_label == source.actual_label
      """)

if spark.catalog.tableExists(inference_table):
  (stream.writeStream
    .foreachBatch(merge_stream)
    .option("checkpointLocation", volume_file_path+inference_table+"/checkpoint_cdc")
    .trigger(availableNow=True)
    .start()
  )
```

Figure 7.25 – Merging transaction labels into the inference table

You now have a bronze table and the ability to merge new labels into the inference table. However, the inference table is still empty. So, let's create a workflow job, as shown in *Figure 7.26*, to generate predictions every 15 minutes:

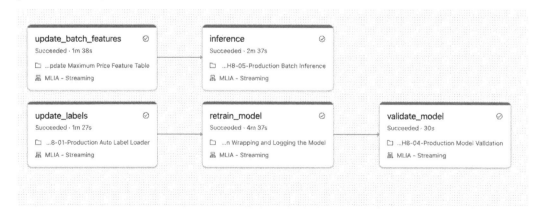

Figure 7.26 – The DAG for the inference (upper) and model retraining (lower) job

Walk through the two workflow paths, starting with the upper path. The batch features are updated, thus providing feature data for inference. The data is ready for predictions, and the inference task can begin.

As its first task, the lower path updates labels. It adds the latest data to the `transaction_labels` table and merges all new labels that match previous predictions into the inference table. Skip forward beyond the first iteration and the inference table contains not only previous predictions but also the labels for those predictions. Model training is performed using the updated table containing the features. Retraining the model only occurs if there is data in the inference table, as shown in *Figure 7.27*. The retraining process is, of course, followed by validation when needed. The validation notebook exits when it detects that the latest version of the model has already been tested:

```
if not spark.catalog.tableExists(table_name) or spark.table(tableName=table_name).isEmpty():
    dbutils.notebook.exit("No inference table exists yet")
```

Figure 7.27 – The retraining notebook exits if there is no data to retrain on

Create the workflow job shown in *Figure 7.29*. You can reference the configuration for the job in the `model_retraining_n_inference_workflow.yaml` file. The workflow automatically provides the lineage of all upstream and downstream tables. You can see these in *Figure 7.26*. This saves us time on documentation:

∨   Upstream tables read by this job (4)

⊞   ml_in_prod.synthetic_transactions.packaged_transaction_model_predictions

⊞   ml_in_prod.synthetic_transactions.prod_transactions

⊞   ml_in_prod.synthetic_transactions.product_3minute_max_price_ft

⊞   ml_in_prod.synthetic_transactions.transaction_count_history

∨   Downstream tables written to by this job (3)

⊞   ml_in_prod.synthetic_transactions.packaged_transaction_model_predictions

⊞   ml_in_prod.synthetic_transactions.product_3minute_max_price_ft

⊞   ml_in_prod.synthetic_transactions.transaction_labels

Figure 7.28 – The workflow table lineage

All that is left is to run both workflows simultaneously. After letting both run for a bit (don't forget to schedule the Production Batch Inference and Model Retraining workflow), you should have a screen that looks similar to what's shown in *Figure 7.29*:

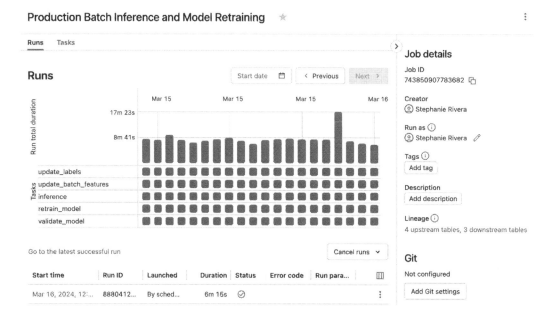

Figure 7.29 – The historical view of successful job runs

You now have all of the pieces to productionize this project.

Project – multilabel image classification

We currently have a working image classification model that we trained and evaluated in *Chapter 6*. Now, let's add some infrastructure around our code to serve our model and make it available to downstream applications and, ultimately, our end users. To follow along in your workspace, please open the following notebooks:

- Ch7-01-Create_Final_Wrapper_Production
- Ch7-02-Serve_In_Production

We'll start by creating our model class wrapper. This wrapper includes two functions, `feature_extractor` and `predict`. The `feature_extractor` function is required because otherwise, our fine-tuned model won't contain the same preprocessing step that's used during fine-tuning and would, therefore, not be consistent during serving. Of course, you can simply serve your original model if you do not need to make any custom modifications to your model and only need the raw format outputs:

```python
from io import BytesIO
import torchvision

class CVModelWrapper(mlflow.pyfunc.PythonModel):
    def __init__(self, model):
        # instantiate model in evaluation mode
        model.to(torch.device("cpu"))
        self.model = model.eval()

    def feature_extractor(self, image, p=0.5): …

    def predict(self, context, images): …
```

Figure 7.30 – Creating the model class wrapper

The `feature_extractor` function, which transforms an image into the format required by the served model, is the same code we used to score the model in *Chapter 6*. Let's dive into the prediction part; it's similar to what we created in *Chapter 6* to score our model.

The `predict` function is similar to the one we used to score our model in *Chapter 6* using `pandas_udf`. Note that we are not only returning the predicted label but also a label corresponding to it in a dictionary format (this isn't required, but we wanted to show the output format's flexibility):

```python
class CVModelWrapper(mlflow.pyfunc.PythonModel):
    def __init__(self, model):
        # instantiate model in evaluation mode
        model.to(torch.device("cpu"))
        self.model = model.eval()

    def feature_extractor(self, image, p=0.5): ...

    def predict(self, context, images):
        id2label = {
            0: 'buildings',
            1: 'forest',
            2: 'glacier',
            3: 'mountain',
            4: 'sea',
            5: 'street'
            }
        with torch.set_grad_enabled(False):

            # assuming this is a DataFrame
            pil_images = torch.stack([self.feature_extractor(row[0]) for _, row in images.iterrows()])
            pil_images = pil_images.to(torch.device("gpu"))
            outputs = self.model(pil_images)
            preds = torch.max(outputs, 1)[1]
            probs = torch.nn.functional.softmax(outputs, dim=-1)[:, 1]
            labels = [id2label[pred] for pred in preds.tolist()]

            return pd.DataFrame(
                        data=dict(
                            label=preds,
                            labelName=labels
                            )
                        )
```

Figure 7.31 – Including the feature_extractor and predict functions in the model class wrapper

Now, we are ready to wrap our fine-tuned model from *Chapter 4* into the wrapper. To do this, we must load the artifact from MLflow and pass it to the pre-created CVModelWrapper class:

```
2    import os
3    import mlflow
4    from mlflow.store.artifact.models_artifact_repo import ModelsArtifactRepository
5    from mlia_utils.cv_clf_funcs import select_best_model
6
7    experiment_path = f"/Users/{current_user}/intel-clf-training_action"
8    local_path = select_best_model(experiment_path)
9
10   requirements_path = os.path.join(local_path, "requirements.txt")
11   if not os.path.exists(requirements_path):
12     dbutils.fs.put("file:" + requirements_path, "", True)
13
14   device = "cuda" if torch.cuda.is_available() else "cpu"
15   loaded_model = torch.load(local_path+"/data/model.pth", map_location=torch.device(device))
16
17   wrapper = CVModelWrapper(loaded_model)
```

Figure 7.32 – Loading our model from the existing MLflow experiment

Let's test whether our wrapper is functioning as expected. To do so, we must encode a few images (as the model serving accepts strings and cannot accept images and convert them yet) and save them into a pandas DataFrame. Then, we must use our model wrapper to get a prediction:

```
1    import base64
2    import pandas as pd
3
4    images = spark.read.format("delta").load(val_delta_path).take(25)
5
6    b64image1 = base64.b64encode(images[0]["content"]).decode("ascii")
7    b64image2 = base64.b64encode(images[1]["content"]).decode("ascii")
8    b64image3 = base64.b64encode(images[3]["content"]).decode("ascii")
9    b64image4 = base64.b64encode(images[4]["content"]).decode("ascii")
10   b64image24 = base64.b64encode(images[24]["content"]).decode("ascii")
11
12   df_input = pd.DataFrame(
13       [b64image1, b64image2, b64image3, b64image4, b64image24], columns=["data"])
14
15   df = wrapper.predict("", df_input)
16   display(df)
```

Figure 7.33 – Using our model wrapper to create predictions on a few images

Next, we will use MLflow to log and serve the model via Databricks Model Serving:

```
1    import mlflow
2    # Set the registry URI to "databricks-uc" to configure
3    # the MLflow client to access models in UC
4    mlflow.set_registry_uri("databricks-uc")
5    model_name = f"{catalog}.{database_name}.cvops_model_mlaction"
6
7    from mlflow.models.signature import infer_signature,set_signature
8    img = df_input['data']
9    predict_sample = df[['label', 'labelName']]
10   # To register models under UC you require to log signature for both
11   # input and output
12   signature = infer_signature(img, predict_sample)
13
14   print(f"Your signature is: \n {signature}")
15
16   with mlflow.start_run(run_name=model_name) as run:
17       mlflowModel = mlflow.pyfunc.log_model(
18           artifact_path="model",
19           python_model=wrapper,
20           input_example=df_input,
21           signature=signature,
22           registered_model_name=model_name,
23       )
24   ##Alternatively log your model and register later
25   # mlflow.register_model(model_uri, "ap.cv_ops.cvops_model")
```

Figure 7.34 – Logging and running models using MLflow

During the production phase, you will usually operate on the aliases and the latest model version, so here, we'll simulate setting the alias, Champion, to the best-performing model and getting the latest model version to be deployed:

```
from mlflow import MlflowClient
import mlflow

mlflow.set_registry_uri('databricks-uc')
client = MlflowClient()
model_name = f'{catalog}.{database_name}.cvops_model_mlaction'

client.set_registered_model_alias(model_name, "Champion", 1)

model_version_uri = f"models:/{model_name}@Champion"
# Or another option: model_version_uri = f"models:/{model_name}/1"
loaded_model_uc = mlflow.pyfunc.load_model(model_version_uri) # runiid / model_registry_name+version
# champion_version = client.get_model_version_by_alias("prod.ml_team.iris_model", "Champion")
latest_model = client.get_model_version_by_alias(model_name, "Champion")
```

Figure 7.35 – Loading our champion model

Next, we must create our model serving endpoint using the Databricks SDK. You could also create your endpoint using the UI. If you decide to use the SDK, you must create a configuration file for your endpoint. The following example is for a CPU container with a small workload size. If you are unfamiliar with this option, please check out *Create model serving endpoints* in the *Further reading* section:

```python
import mlflow
from mlia_utils.mlflow_funcs import *

# Create or update serving endpoint
from databricks.sdk import WorkspaceClient
from databricks.sdk.service.serving import EndpointCoreConfigInput, ServedModelInput

serving_endpoint_name = "cvops_model_mlaction_endpoint"
latest_model_version = get_latest_model_version(model_name)


w = WorkspaceClient(host=db_host, token = db_token)

endpoint_config = EndpointCoreConfigInput(
    name=serving_endpoint_name,
    served_models=[
        ServedModelInput(
            model_name=model_name,
            model_version=latest_model_version,
            workload_size="Small",
            scale_to_zero_enabled=True
        )
    ]
)
```

Figure 7.36 – Setting config input for the endpoint to serve our model

Once the settings have been provided, you are ready to deploy or update your endpoint if it already exists:

```python
import os
serving_endpoint_url = f"{db_host}/ml/endpoints/{serving_endpoint_name}"

try:
    w.serving_endpoints.get(serving_endpoint_name)
    print(f"Updating the endpoint {serving_endpoint_url} to version {latest_model_version}, this will take a few minutes to package and
    deploy the endpoint...")
    w.serving_endpoints.update_config_and_wait(served_models=endpoint_config.served_models, name=serving_endpoint_name)
except:
    print(f"Creating the endpoint {serving_endpoint_url}, this will take a few minutes to package and deploy the endpoint...")
    w.serving_endpoints.create_and_wait(name=serving_endpoint_name, config=endpoint_config)

displayHTML(f'Your Model Endpoint Serving is now available. Open the <a href="/ml/endpoints/{serving_endpoint_name}">Model Serving Endpoint
page</a> for more details.')
```

Your Model Endpoint Serving is now available. Open the Model Serving Endpoint page for more details.

Figure 7.37 – Deploying a new endpoint if it does not exist or updating the existing one

Keep in mind that if your endpoint does not exist, it will take a while to deploy:

Figure 7.38 – UI example while the GPU endpoint is deploying/updating

Now, we can score our model. Again, for simplicity and reusability, we are covering the serving call into a `score_model` function:

```
def create_tf_serving_json(data):
  return {'inputs': {name: data[name].tolist() for name in data.keys()} if isinstance(data, dict) else data.tolist()}

def score_model(dataset):
  url = f"{db_host}/serving-endpoints/{serving_endpoint_name}/invocations"
  headers = {'Authorization': f'Bearer {db_token}', 'Content-Type': 'application/json'}
  ds_dict = {'dataframe_split': dataset.to_dict(orient='split')} if isinstance(dataset, pd.DataFrame) else create_tf_serving_json(dataset)
  data_json = json.dumps(ds_dict, allow_nan=True)
  response = requests.request(method='POST', headers=headers, url=url, data=data_json)
  if response.status_code != 200:
    raise Exception(f'Request failed with status {response.status_code}, {response.text}')
  return response.json()
```

Figure 7.39 – Defining a model scoring function

Lastly, we must score our model using our model scoring function, as shown in *Figure 7.40*:

```
score_model(df_input)
```

Figure 7.40 – Scoring our model

Here is an example of scoring under the UI page:

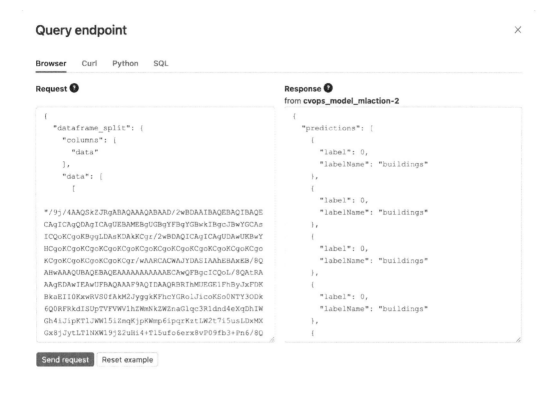

Figure 7.41 – Scoring our model under the UI page of the Databricks Model Serving

Now that our model is ready for production, we can train and create it, designate our champion model, serve it on an endpoint, and score. The next steps might include setting up a monitor to track image pixel distributions, the number of images, label distributions, and the distribution of the response. We will talk more about model monitoring in *Chapter 8*.

Project – retrieval augmented generation chatbot

In the previous chapter, we completed our chatbot and tested it out in a notebook. It might be tempting to jump to the final deployment step immediately, but that would involve skipping a critical step in the process – evaluation! Evaluating projects for correctness before providing them to the end users should always be part of the development process. However, it can be especially tricky to build automated evaluation solutions for newer technologies and techniques, such as when working with LLMs. This is a continually developing area of research, and we recommend reading Databricks' recommendations on *Best Practices for LLM Evaluation* for more information (linked in *Further reading*). We'll walk through the MLflow evaluation capability to evaluate the RAG chatbot we've built.

To follow along in your workspace, please open the following notebooks:

- `CH7-01-GetData`
- `CH7-02-Evaluating_ChatBot`

Loading the ground truth labels

We'll start in the first notebook, `CH7-01-GetData`. To evaluate our model, we must have ground truth labels – that is, the correct answers. This generally involves human effort to write out some typical questions you expect users to ask your chatbot and the answers you expect your chatbot to respond with. To simplify this process, we created a file containing 35 sample questions and the corresponding human-generated answers for this project, saved to `Questions_Evaluation.csv`. Let's load this file and examine the question and answer pairs:

```
import pandas as pd

df_evaluation = pd.read_csv("/Volumes/ml_in_action/rag_chatbot/files/Questions_Evaluation.csv").dropna().
drop(columns=["id_question"])
df_eval = spark.createDataFrame(df_evaluation)
display(df_eval)
```

Figure 7.42 – Reading our pre-created evaluation set

Take a look at some of the records to get a sense of the questions a user might ask and the expected answers. You can also add your own examples to augment the evaluation data further:

question_asked	answer_given
How does the choice between rules and standards impact content moderation on social media platforms?	Rules can provide clear guidelines for content moderators to follow, reducing the need for human involvement an potentially lowering error costs. However, rules may not be effective in addressing complex or dynamic issues, su hate speech, and may require frequent updates to remain effective. Standards, on the other hand, can provide fle for content moderators to adjust their policies to specific contexts, but may require more human involvement and potentially increase error costs d...
What are large language models (LLMs) and how do they differ from other generative AI models?	Large language models (LLMs) are artificial intelligence models that can process and produce various forms of se data, including but not limited to natural language. They differ from other generative AI models as they can be tra using a range of architectures and are not limited to transformer-based models. LLMs can generate a wide range sequences, such as assembly language, protein sequences, and chess games.

Figure 7.43 – Question-answer pair examples

Let's save these examples to a Delta table named `evaluation_table`. That way, if a new `Question_Evaluation.csv` file with different examples is uploaded, you can append the new examples to the existing table without risking losing the original data:

```
%sql
--Note that we need to enable Change Data Feed on the table to create the index
CREATE TABLE IF NOT EXISTS evaluation_table (
  id_question BIGINT GENERATED BY DEFAULT AS IDENTITY,
  question_asked STRING,
  answer_given STRING,
  pdf_name STRING,
  article_name STRING
  ) TBLPROPERTIES (delta.enableChangeDataFeed = true);
```

Figure 7.44 – Creating evaluation_table to store the question/answer pairs

Upon saving the table, we are now ready to evaluate our model:

```
df_eval.write.mode("append").saveAsTable(f"{catalog}.{database_name}.evaluation_table")
```

Figure 7.45 – Saving thequestions_evaluation.csv data to a Delta table

Setting up the evaluation workflow

We're now ready to open the second notebook, CH7-02-Evaluating_ChatBot, and evaluate our chatbot against the ground truth labels we saved to evaluation_table. Let's briefly discuss how we will compare our model's outputs to the human-generated answers. While there is plenty of ongoing research in the realm of automated LLM evaluation methods, we will focus on one technique in particular: *LLM-as-a-judge*. This method brings in a second LLM to evaluate the performance of the first, automating the tedious task of comparing the generated answer to the true answer, something a human would traditionally have to do. Follow these steps:

1. To use an LLM as a judge, we must load the original model we created in *Chapter 6*:

```
import mlflow
from mlia_utils.mlflow_funcs import *
from pyspark.sql.functions import col, udf, length, pandas_udf, explode

os.environ['DATABRICKS_TOKEN'] = dbutils.secrets.get("mlaction", "rag_sp_token")
model_name = f"{catalog}.{database_name}.mlaction_chatbot_model"

model_version_to_evaluate = get_latest_model_version(model_name)
mlflow.set_registry_uri("databricks-uc")
rag_model = mlflow.langchain.load_model(f"models:/{model_name}/{model_version_to_evaluate}")
```

Figure 7.46 – Loading mlaction_chatbot_model as rag_model

2. Now, we must run a quick test to verify that our RAG model works as expected:

```
1   question = "What is GPT ?"
2   dialog = {"query": question}
3   rag_model.invoke({"query":"What is GPT? "})["result"]
```

'\nGenerative Pre-trained Transformers (GPTs) are a type of artificial intelligence model that uses machine learning to generate human-like text based on input data. They are a subset of a broader category of technologies known as general-purpose technologies (GPTs), which have the potential to significantly impact a wide range of industries and applications. GPTs are capable of performing a variety of tasks, including text generation, translation, summarization, and question answering. They are trained on large amounts of text data and can generate coherent and contextually relevant responses to a wide range of prompts. GPTs have the potential to significantly impact the labor market by automating certain tasks and potentially creating new types of work.'

Figure 7.47 – Verifying our loaded model works as expected

3. Next, we must use our RAG chatbot to generate answers for all of the example questions we stored in `evaluation_table`. These responses are what we will compare against the ground truth answers. We'll build a `pandas_udf` function to make this part run faster:

```
1   import mlflow
2   from mlia_utils.mlflow_funcs import *
3   from pyspark.sql.functions import col, udf, length, pandas_udf, explode
4
5   os.environ['DATABRICKS_TOKEN'] = dbutils.secrets.get("mlaction", "rag_sp_token")
6   model_name = f"{catalog}.{database_name}.mlaction_chatbot_model"
7
8   model_version_to_evaluate = get_latest_model_version(model_name)
9   mlflow.set_registry_uri("databricks-uc")
10  rag_model = mlflow.langchain.load_model(f"models:/{model_name}/
    {model_version_to_evaluate}")
11
12  @pandas_udf("string")
13  def predict_answer(questions):
14      def answer_question(question):
15          dialog = {"query": question}
16          return rag_model.invoke(dialog)['result']
17      return questions.apply(answer_question)
```

Figure 7.48 – Creating a function to receive a question and return an answer using our RAG model

We used Llama-2-70b for our judge, but you could use GPT-4 or any other LLM you prefer (though we cannot guarantee satisfactory results!). Our code leverages the Databricks Foundational Model API, which we also used in *Chapter 3* when creating the embeddings of ArXiv article text chunks. As a reminder, the Databricks Foundation Model APIs provide direct access to state-of-the-art open models from a serving endpoint, allowing you to incorporate high-quality generative AI models into your application without the need to maintain your model deployment. We call the Llama-2-70b endpoint in *Figure 7.49*:

```
1   from mlflow.deployments import get_deploy_client
2   deploy_client = get_deploy_client("databricks")
3   endpoint_name = "databricks-llama-2-70b-chat"
4   #Let's query our external model endpoint
5   answer_test = deploy_client.predict(endpoint=endpoint_name, inputs={"messages":
    [{"role": "user", "content": "What is GPT?"}]})
6   answer_test['choices'][0]['message']['content']display(spark.table
    ('evaluation_dataset'))
```

Figure 7.49 – Testing the Foundation Model endpoint for Llama-2-70b

4. Next, we must build a DataFrame from the `evaluation_table` questions and answers. If you have added many more question/answer examples to this dataset, you may want to downsample the number of questions and speed up the prediction process. Then, we must call our UDF, `predict_answer`:

```
1   df_qa = (spark.read.table('evaluation_table')
2               .selectExpr('question_asked as inputs', 'answer_given as targets')
3               .where("targets is not null")
4               #.sample(fraction=0.005, seed=40) # if your dataset is very big you
            could sample it
5               )
6
7   df_qa_with_preds = df_qa.withColumn('preds', predict_answer(col('inputs'))).cache()
```

Figure 7.50 – Building a DataFrame with questions and ground
truth answers, and adding RAG chatbot answers

5. Now that we have our DataFrame with the chatbot's responses to each question, we must save this to a Delta table. We'll continue to reference the DataFrame throughout the rest of this code, but this way, we won't have to generate the chatbot's responses again if we want to query this data in the future:

```
1   df_qa_with_preds.write.saveAsTable(f"{catalog}.{database_name}.
    evaluation_table_preds")
```

Figure 7.51 – Writing our evaluation DataFrame to a new table

6. As we mentioned at the beginning of this section, we are using MLflow's Evaluate capability to facilitate our model evaluation. Before we evaluate our RAG chatbot, let's load the methods and verify how MLflow Evaluate works by default. First, we must load the "answer correctness" metric, which we will use as-is:

```python
1    from mlflow.metrics.genai.metric_definitions import answer_correctness
2    from mlflow.metrics.genai import make_genai_metric, EvaluationExample
3
4    # Because we have our labels (answers) within the evaluation dataset, we can evaluate the answer correctness as part
     of our metric. Again, this is optional.
5    answer_correctness_metrics = answer_correctness(model=f"endpoints:/{endpoint_name}")
6    print(answer_correctness_metrics)
```

```
Example Input:
How is MLflow related to Databricks?

Example Output:
MLflow is a product created by Databricks to enhance the efficiency of machine learning processes.

Additional information used by the model:
key: targets
value:
MLflow is an open-source platform for managing the end-to-end machine learning (ML) lifecycle. It was developed by Databricks, a
company that specializes in big data and machine learning solutions. MLflow is designed to address the challenges that data scie
ntists and machine learning engineers face when developing, training, and deploying machine learning models.

Example score: 4
Example justification: The output provided by the model is mostly correct. It correctly identifies that MLflow is a product crea
ted by Databricks. However, it does not mention that MLflow is an open-source platform for managing the end-to-end machine learn
ing lifecycle, which is a significant part of its function. Therefore, while the output is mostly accurate, it has a minor omiss
ion, which is why it gets a score of 4 according to the grading rubric.
```

Figure 7.52 – Viewing the answer correctness metrics

The out-of-the-box metrics are good, but professionalism is also an important criterion for our use case, so we'll create a custom professionalism metric. *Figure 7.53* shows how to use the make_genai_metric() function to build out our professionalism evaluation metric:

```
professionalism = make_genai_metric(
    name="professionalism",
    definition=(
        "Professionalism refers to the use of a formal, respectful, and appropriate style of communication that is "
        "tailored to the context and audience. It often involves avoiding overly casual language, slang, or "
        "colloquialisms, and instead using clear, concise, and respectful language."
    ),
    grading_prompt=(
        "Professionalism: If the answer is written using a professional tone, below are the details for different scores: "
        "- Score 1: Language is extremely casual, informal, and may include slang or colloquialisms. Not suitable for "
        "professional contexts."
        "- Score 2: Language is casual but generally respectful and avoids strong informality or slang. Acceptable in "
        "some informal professional settings."
        "- Score 3: Language is overall formal but still have casual words/phrases. Borderline for professional contexts."
        "- Score 4: Language is balanced and avoids extreme informality or formality. Suitable for most professional contexts. "
        "- Score 5: Language is noticeably formal, respectful, and avoids casual elements. Appropriate for formal "
        "business or academic settings. "
    ),
    model=f"endpoints:/{endpoint_name}",
    parameters={"temperature": 0.0},
    aggregations=["mean", "variance"],
    examples=[professionalism_example],
    greater_is_better=True
)
```

Figure 7.53 – Adding a custom professionalism metric

7. As you can see from `grading_prompt`, we've designed this metric to give a score between one and five, where a score of one identifies text as casual and a score of five evaluates text as noticeably formal. This is a powerful tool to evaluate your model based on criteria that are important to your business use case. You can modify the template according to your needs. We must also add examples of the metric, as defined in *Figure 7.54*:

```
1   # Adding custom professionalism metric
2   professionalism_example = EvaluationExample(
3       input="What is MLflow?",
4       output=(
5           "MLflow is like your friendly neighborhood toolkit for managing your machine
            learning projects. It helps "
6           "you track experiments, package your code and models, and collaborate with
            your team, making the whole ML "
7           "workflow smoother. It's like your Swiss Army knife for machine learning!"
8       ),
9       score=2,
10      justification=(
11          "The response is written in a casual tone. It uses contractions, filler words
            such as 'like', and "
12          "exclamation points, which make it sound less professional. "
13      )
14  )
```

Figure 7.54 – Adding an example for the custom professionalism metric

8. With our professionalism metric, let's run the model evaluation using MLfLow. To run an evaluation, we can call `mlflow.evaluate()` against the pandas DataFrame containing the questions, ground truth answers, and chatbot-generated answers. We'll include the answer correctness and professionalism metrics as extra metrics. The following code will calculate many other metrics in addition to the two we specified, such as token count, toxicity, and Automated Readability Index grade (the approximate grade level required to comprehend the text):

```
1   from mlflow.deployments import set_deployments_target
2
3   set_deployments_target("databricks")
4
5   #This will automatically log all
6   with mlflow.start_run(run_name="chatbot_rag") as run:
7       eval_results = mlflow.evaluate(data = df_qa_with_preds.toPandas(), # evaluation
        data,
8                                       model_type="question-answering", # toxicity and
                                        token_count will be evaluated
9                                       predictions="preds", # prediction column_name from
                                        eval_df
10                                      targets = "targets",
11                                      extra_metrics=[answer_correctness_metrics,
                                        professionalism])
12
13  eval_results.metrics
```

Figure 7.55 – Running an MLflow experiment with mlflow.evaluate()

Once we've run the experiment, the metrics can be accessed in our notebook and via the UI so that we can easily see how our chatbot is performing in terms of accuracy and professionalism.

Evaluating the chatbot's responses

First, let's look at the MLfLow UI in Databricks to compare the results between the human-generated and chatbot-generated responses. To do so, navigate to the **Experiments** page and open the experiment matching your notebook's name (in this case, CH7-02-Evaluating Chatbot). Then, navigate to the **Evaluation** tab. We're using this view to see some examples of how closely the bot's answers match what we would expect to see, but it is also particularly useful when you want to test and compare outputs across different models or chunking strategies:

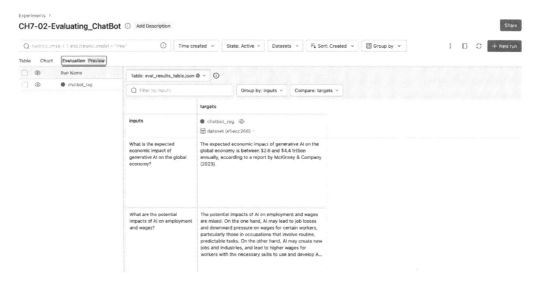

Figure 7.56 – Using the Evaluation view in Databricks MLflow

Take a look at a few examples from the evaluation dataset. We'll see that our model, according to a quick human assessment, is performing reasonably well. Of course, this form of evaluation isn't scalable, so let's dig into the other metrics as well. We'll use the common visualization library, plotly, to take a closer look at our model results. First, we'll look at the distribution of token counts in our chatbot's responses:

```
1  import plotly.express as px
2  px.histogram(df_genai_metrics, x="token_count", labels={"token_count": "Token Count"}, title="Distribution of Token Counts
   in Model Responses")
```

Distribution of Token Counts in Model Responses

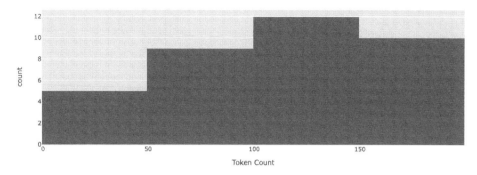

Figure 7.57 – Plotting token counts from our chatbot's responses

While interesting, what we care about here are the two metrics we discussed earlier: correctness and professionalism. Let's take a look at the distribution of the correctness scores:

```
1  # Counting the occurrences of each answer correctness score
2  px.bar(df_genai_metrics['answer_correctness/v1/score'].value_counts(), title='Answer Correctness Score Distribution')
```

Answer Correctness Score Distribution

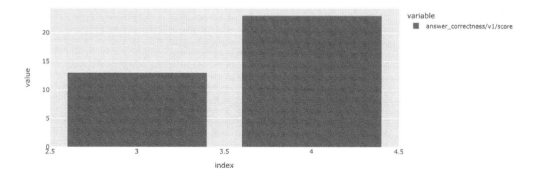

Figure 7.58 – Plotting the correctness score distribution

Let's also view the professionalism score distribution. Our distribution is threes and fours, which means the tone is most often "borderline professional." This is how we defined it in our custom metric:

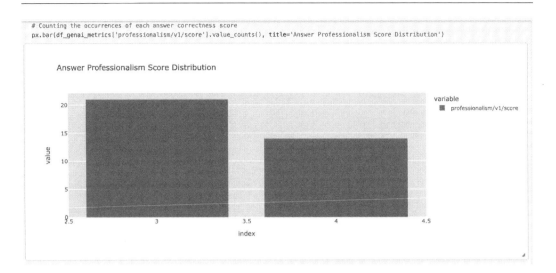

Figure 7.59 – Plotting the professionalism score distribution

Overall, our model is looking good! If we're satisfied with the accuracy and professionalism scores, we can mark this model as ready for production by giving it a production alias:

```
1   client = MlflowClient()
2   client.set_registered_model_alias(name=model_name, alias="Production",
    version=model_version_to_evaluate)
```

Figure 7.60 – Aliasing our model to show it is production-ready

With that, we evaluated our chatbot by creating predictions from our question-and-answer dataset, created a custom evaluation metrics to evaluate the professionalism of each response, and visualized information about our model outputs. In the last chapter, we will demonstrate how to build a Gradio app so that you can bring your RAG chatbot to your end users!

Summary

Implementing models in production can be challenging, but with tools designed to support productionizing models and automating the MLOps process, it is much easier. In this chapter, we looked at using the UC Model Registry to manage the life cycle of an ML model. We highlighted MLflow and how it can be used to create reproducible, modularized data science workflows that automatically track parameters and performance metrics. We also discussed techniques for calculating features at the time of inference. To make the end-to-end MLOps process more manageable, we showed how to use workflows and webhooks to automate the ML life cycle. We also showed how to serve models and make inferences using MLflow and the Databricks platform.

In the last chapter, *Monitoring, Evaluating, and More*, we will look at monitoring our data and ML models within the Databricks Lakehouse so that you can get the most value from your data.

Questions

Let's test ourselves on what we've learned by going through the following questions:

1. Can more than one model be in production simultaneously? When would you want to use two models in production?
2. What component of MLflow could you use to route approvals?
3. Can you use an MLflow API to serve your model?

Answers

After putting some thought into the preceding questions, compare your answers to ours:

1. Yes, having multiple models in production simultaneously is possible, and this is appropriate for use cases such as comparing models in a challenger/champion test or running A/B tests.
2. The UC Model Registry can be used to route approvals.
3. The Model Serving API within MLFlow can be used for model serving.

Further reading

This chapter discussed tools and technologies to help productionize ML. Please take a look at these resources to dive deeper into the areas that interest you most – and help you get more of your ML projects into production!

*   *Best Practices for Using Structured Streaming in Production - The Databricks Blog*: `https://www.databricks.com/blog/streaming-production-collected-best-practices`
*   *The big book of machine learning use cases*: `https://www.databricks.com/resources/ebook/big-book-of-machine-learning-use-cases`
*   *Databricks Model Serving*: `https://www.databricks.com/blog/2023/03/07/announcing-general-availability-databricks-model-serving.html`
*   *Create and manage serving endpoints using Mlflow*: `https://docs.databricks.com/en/machine-learning/model-serving/create-serving-endpoints-mlflow.html`
*   *Model Evaluation in MLFLow*: `https://www.databricks.com/blog/2022/04/19/model-evaluation-in-mlflow.html`

- *The big book of MLOps*: `https://www.databricks.com/resources/ebook/the-big-book-of-mlops`

- *Databricks Asset Bundles - Programmatically define, deploy, and run Databricks jobs, Delta Live Tables pipelines, and MLOps Stacks using CI/CD best practices and workflows*: `https://docs.databricks.com/en/dev-tools/bundles/index.html`

- *Model Registry Webhooks*: `MLflow Model Registry Webhooks on Databricks`

- *Webhooks*: `https://docs.databricks.com/en/mlflow/model-registry-webhooks.html`

- *CI/CD workflows with Git and Databricks Repos - Use GitHub and Databricks Repos for source control and CI/CD workflows*: `https://docs.databricks.com/en/repos/ci-cd-techniques-with-repos.html`

- *Continuous integration and delivery using GitHub Actions - Build a CI/CD workflow on GitHub that uses GitHub Actions developed for Databricks*: `https://docs.databricks.com/en/dev-tools/ci-cd/ci-cd-github.html`

- *CI/CD with Jenkins on Databricks – Develop a CI/CD pipeline for Databricks that uses Jenkins*: `https://docs.databricks.com/en/dev-tools/ci-cd/ci-cd-jenkins.html`

- *Orchestrate Databricks jobs with Apache Airflow – Manage and schedule a data pipeline that uses Apache Airflow*: `https://docs.databricks.com/en/workflows/jobs/how-to/use-airflow-with-jobs.html`

- *Service principals for CI/CD – Use service principals instead of users with CI/CD systems*: `https://docs.databricks.com/en/dev-tools/ci-cd/ci-cd-sp.html`

- *DFE client*: `https://docs.databricks.com/en/machine-learning/feature-store/python-api.html#use-the-clients-for-unit-testing`

- *Unity*: `https://docs.databricks.com/en/udf/unity-catalog.html`

- *Best Practices for LLM Evaluation of RAG Applications, Part 1*: `https://www.databricks.com/blog/LLM-auto-eval-best-practices-RAG`

- *Best Practices for LLM Evaluation of RAG Applications, Part 2*: `https://www.databricks.com/blog/announcing-mlflow-28-llm-judge-metrics-and-best-practices-llm-evaluation-rag-applications-part`

- *Create model serving endpoints*: `https://docs.databricks.com/en/machine-learning/model-serving/create-manage-serving-endpoints.html`

8
Monitoring, Evaluating, and More

"Focus on how the end-user customers perceive the impact of your innovation – rather than on how you, the innovators, perceive it." — Thomas A. Edison

Congratulations, you've made it to the final chapter! We've come a long way, yet there is still more to explore in Databricks. As we wrap up, we will take another look at Lakehouse Monitoring. We'll focus on monitoring model inference data. After all the work you've put in to build a robust model and push it into production, it's essential to share the learnings, predictions, and other outcomes with a broad audience. Sharing results with dashboards is very common. We will cover how to create visualizations for dashboards in both the new Lakeview dashboards and the standard Databricks SQL dashboards. Deployed models can be shared via a web application. Therefore, we will not only introduce Hugging Face Spaces but also deploy the RAG chatbot using the Gradio app in *Applying our learning*. Lastly, we'll demonstrate how analysts can invoke LLMs via SQL AI Functions! By the end of this chapter, you will be ready to monitor inference data, create visualizations, deploy an ML web app, and use the groundbreaking DBRX open source LLM with SQL.

Here is the roadmap for this chapter:

- Monitoring your models
- Building gold layer visualizations
- Connecting your applications
- Incorporating LLMs for analysts
- Applying our learning

Monitoring your models

The ML lifecycle does not end at deployment. Once a model is in production, we want to monitor the input data and output results of the model. In *Chapter 4*, we explored two key features of Databricks Lakehouse Monitoring integrated with Unity Catalog: Snapshot and TimeSeries profiles. Snapshot profiles are designed to provide an overview of a dataset at a specific point in time, capturing its current state. This is particularly useful for identifying immediate data quality issues or changes. On the other hand, TimeSeries profiles focus on how data evolves over time, making them ideal for tracking trends, patterns, and gradual changes in data distributions.

Expanding on these capabilities, Databricks also provides an Inference profile, tailored for monitoring machine learning models in production. This advanced profile builds upon the concept of TimeSeries profiles, adding critical functionalities for comprehensive model performance evaluation. It includes model quality metrics, essential for tracking the accuracy and reliability of predictions over time. It also records predictions and, optionally, ground truth labels, directly comparing expected and actual outcomes. This functionality is key for identifying model drift, where shifts in input data or the relationship between inputs and outputs occur.

Inference Tables in Databricks further bolster this monitoring capability. They contain essential elements such as model predictions, input features, timestamps, and potentially ground truth labels. Building a monitor on top of InferenceTables with the corresponding `InferenceLog` allows us to monitor model performance and data drift continuously.

In the event of drift detection, immediate actions should be taken – data pipeline verification or model retraining and evaluation are recommended. These steps ensure the model adapts to new data patterns, maintaining accuracy and effectiveness. Continuous monitoring against your baseline and cross-model versions is a strategy to adopt when trying to ensure a stable process across various deployed solutions.

Figure 8.1 is a code sample for creating an Inference monitor with model quality metrics using the `InferenceLog` profile type. This illustrates a practical application of this monitoring setup. We specify the `schedule` argument to make sure that this monitor is refreshed hourly.

```
lm.create_monitor(
    table_name=f"{catalog}.{database_name}.packaged_transaction_model_predictions",
    profile_type=lm.InferenceLog(
        timestamp_col="TransactionTimestamp",
        granularities=["5 minutes","30 minutes","1 hour"],
        model_id_col="model_version",
        prediction_col="prediction",
        label_col="actual_label",
        problem_type="classification"
    ),
    slicing_exprs=["Product","CustomerID"],
    schedule=lm.MonitorCronSchedule(
        quartz_cron_expression="0 0 * * * ?", # schedules a refresh every hour
        timezone_id="MST",
    ),
    output_schema_name=f"{catalog}.{database_name}"
)
```

Figure 8.1 – Creating an Inference profile monitor that refreshes hourly

Model monitoring is an effective way to ensure your models are working for you as expected. We hope this gets you thinking about how you use monitoring in your MLOPs process.

Next, we'll learn about ways to create dashboards.

Building gold layer visualizations

The gold layer in your lakehouse is the consumption-ready layer. In this layer, final transformations and aggregations crystallize the insights within your data so it is ready for reporting and dashboarding. Being able to share your data with an audience is critical, and there are several options for doing so in the DI Platform. In fact, both Lakeview and Databricks SQL dashboards allow you to transform and aggregate your data within visualizations. Let's walk through how to do that.

Leveraging Lakeview dashboards

Lakeview dashboards in Databricks are a powerful tool for creating data visualizations and sharing insights hidden in data. Visualizations can be made in the English language, making dashboard creation available to more users. To create a Lakeview dashboard, first click **Dashboards** in the left-hand navigation bar, and then open the **Lakeview Dashboards** tab. You will see a **Create Lakeview dashboard** button at the top right of the screen. Clicking this will open a canvas to create your dashboard. The canvas is where the visualization magic happens. It includes an enhanced visualization library to bring your data to life and makes it easy to add widgets for interactive filtering. The **Data** tab, shown in *Figure 8.2*, is where you can define your dataset with SQL or simply by selecting a table.

For example, you could select the ml_in_action.favorita_forecasting.train_set table. This creates a dataset by selecting all records from the provided table. Notice how we do not *have to* write any SQL or create aggregates in order to visualize data aggregations.

Figure 8.2 – The Data tab for adding data to your Lakeview dashboard

Once you have a dataset, return to the **Canvas** tab. Select the **Add a visualization** button found on the blue bar toward the bottom of your browser window. This gives you a widget to place on your dashboard. Once placed, your widget will look similar to *Figure 8.3*.

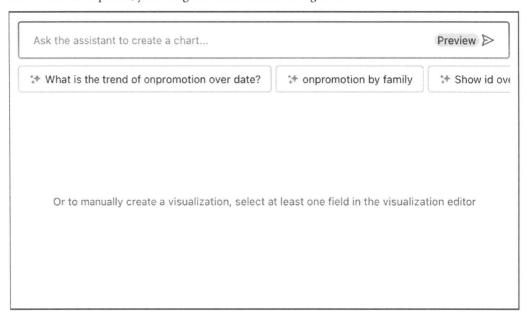

Figure 8.3 – A new Lakeview widget

In the new widget, you can manually create a visualization using the options on the right-side menu. Alternatively, Databricks Assistant can help you rapidly build a chart using just English. You can write your own question, or explore the suggested queries. We selected the suggested question *What is the trend of onpromotion over date?* to automatically generate a chart, and *Figure 8.4* is the result.

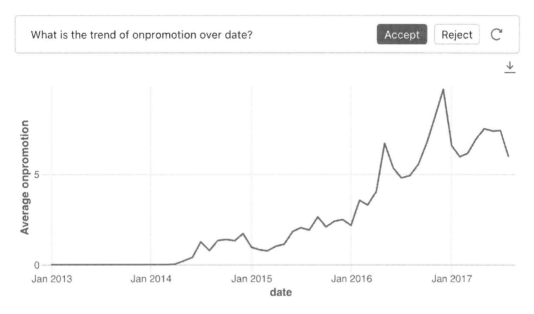

Figure 8.4 – English text generated Lakeview widget

When you are ready to share your dashboard, you can publish it! The engine powering Lakeview dashboards is optimized for performance, driving faster interactive charts for your data. It's also powerful enough to handle streaming data. Furthermore, Lakeview dashboards are unified with the DI Platform through Unity Catalog, providing data lineage. They are designed for easy sharing across workspaces, meaning users in other workspaces can access your curated dashboard.

Visualizing big data with Databricks SQL dashboards

Lakeview dashboards are the future of Databricks. However, you can also build dashboards with **Databricks SQL** (**DBSQL**). The SQL editor built into the DI Platform is another way to quickly create visualizations. With a single `select` statement, you can produce the data and use it for multiple visualizations.

> **Note**
>
> To recreate *Figure 8.5* in your own workspace, you will want to uncheck the **LIMIT 1000** box. There is still a limit for the visualizations of 64,000 rows. The best way to get around this is by filtering or aggregating.

Figure 8.5 is an example visualization we created from a simple SQL query against the *Favorita Store Sales* data.

```
1 | select * from lakehouse_in_action.favorita_forecasting.training_set
```

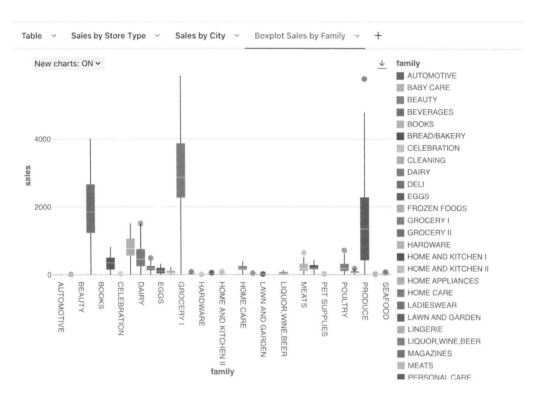

Figure 8.5 – After executing the select statement in the DBSQL editor,
we create the visualizations without writing any code

Suppose your dataset has categorical variables that you want to use to filter and compare features, as with the *Favorita* sales data. You can add filters within the DBSQL editor without revising the query. To add a filter, click the + and choose either **filter** or **parameter**. Both options provide widgets for filtering, as shown in *Figure 8.6*. You can use the widgets with any visualizations or dashboards associated with the query.

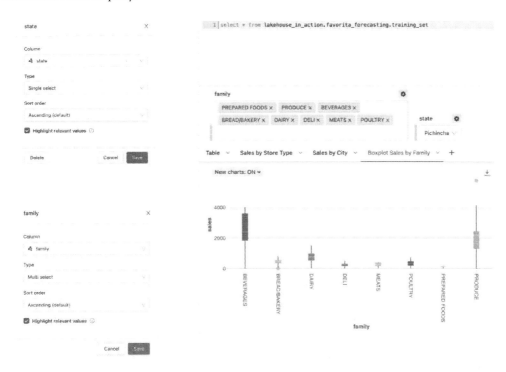

Figure 8.6 – (L) The configuration for the state and family filter; (R) the
result of adding two filters to the Favorita sales query

The dashboard functionality shown in *Figure 8.7* is built into Databricks SQL as a way to present the charts and other visualizations created from one or many queries.

Figure 8.7 – A dashboard with charts created from the Favorita sales data query

The built-in visualization capabilities of DBSQL are a quick way to explore data without connecting to an external dashboarding or data visualization tool.

Next, we'll look at an example of using Python **User-Defined Functions** (**UDFs**) for reusable Python code within DBSQL.

Python UDFs

Python UDFs are a way to create reusable snippets of code in Python, and these can be used in DBSQL. In this example, we'll create a UDF for sales analysts to redact information in a customer record. Line five indicates the language syntax for the function is Python between $$ signs:

```
 2  --Create a SQL UDF
 3  CREATE FUNCTION redact(a STRING)
 4  RETURNS STRING
 5  LANGUAGE PYTHON
 6  AS $$
 7  import json
 8  keys = ["phone", "email"]
 9  obj = json.loads(a)
10  for k in obj:
11    if k in keys:
12      obj[k] = "REDACTED"
13  return json.dumps(obj)
14  $$;
15
16  -- Grant execute so sales analysts can use the SQL UDF
17  GRANT EXECUTE ON sales.customer_db.redact TO sales-analysts
18
19  --Members of the sales-analyst group can use the redact UDF in their SQL expressions
20  -- Using the redact UDF to remove phone and email from the contact_info field
21  SELECT customer_id, redact(contact_info) FROM sales.customer_db.customer_data
```

Figure 8.8 – Creating a Python UDF in DBSQL

UDFs are defined and managed as part of Unity Catalog. Once a UDF is defined, you can give teams the ability to execute the UDF using GRANT EXECUTE.

```
 2  --Create a SQL UDF
 3  CREATE FUNCTION redact(a STRING)
 4  RETURNS STRING
 5  LANGUAGE PYTHON
 6  AS $$
 7  import json
 8  keys = ["phone", "email"]
 9  obj = json.loads(a)
10  for k in obj:
11    if k in keys:
12      obj[k] = "REDACTED"
13  return json.dumps(obj)
14  $$;
15
16  -- Grant execute so sales analysts can use the SQL UDF
17  GRANT EXECUTE ON sales.customer_db.redact TO sales-analysts
18
19  --Members of the sales-analyst group can use the redact UDF in their SQL expressions
20  -- Using the redact UDF to remove phone and email from the contact_info field
21  SELECT customer_id, redact(contact_info) FROM sales.customer_db.customer_data
```

Figure 8.9 – Granting permissions for the sales-analysts groups to execute a UDF

In this SQL query, we are applying the `redact` UDF to the `contact_info` field.

```
2  --Create a SQL UDF
3  CREATE FUNCTION redact(a STRING)
4  RETURNS STRING
5  LANGUAGE PYTHON
6  AS $$
7  import json
8  keys = ["phone", "email"]
9  obj = json.loads(a)
10 for k in obj:
11   if k in keys:
12     obj[k] = "REDACTED"
13 return json.dumps(obj)
14 $$;
15
16 -- Grant execute so sales analysts can use the SQL UDF
17 GRANT EXECUTE ON sales.customer_db.redact TO sales-analysts
18
19 --Members of the sales-analyst group can use the redact UDF in their SQL expressions
20 -- Using the redact UDF to remove phone and email from the contact_info field
21 SELECT customer_id, redact(contact_info) FROM sales.customer_db.customer_data
```

Figure 8.10 – Using the Python UDF in a SQL query

Now that we have the basics for visualizing data and applying Python UDFs in SQL, let's cover a couple of tips and tricks.

Tips and tricks

This section covers our tips and tricks related to DBSQL. Some tips apply to DBSQL and Lakeview, but not all:

- **Use managed compute (a.k.a. serverless compute) when possible**: Query performance using Databricks' SQL warehouses is record-setting, as mentioned in *Chapter 1*. The new managed compute for DBSQL puts the new first query performance at roughly 10 seconds. This means that idle time has drastically been reduced, which translates into cost savings.

- **Use a subquery as a parameter filter**: In your query visualizations and dashboards, you can prepopulate drop-down filter boxes. You can do this by creating and saving a query in the SQL editor. For example, you could create a query that returns a distinct list of customer names. In *Figure 8.11*, we select a query called **Customer Name Lookup Qry** as a subquery to filter the query visualization by customer name. Therefore, we can filter on **Customer** using a drop-down list.

Customer   ✕

* Keyword | Customer |

* Title | Customer |

Type | Query Based Dropdown List   ⌄ |

Query | Customer Name Lookup Qry   ⌄ |
             Select query to load dropdown values from

             ☐ Allow multiple values

                                              Cancel   OK

Figure 8.11 – Using a subquery as a parameter for a query

- **Schedule report delivery**: If you have users who want to receive an up-to-date dashboard regularly, you can schedule the refresh and have it sent to subscribers. For DBSQL dashboards, remember to turn off **Enabled** when you are developing so that users don't get too many updates.

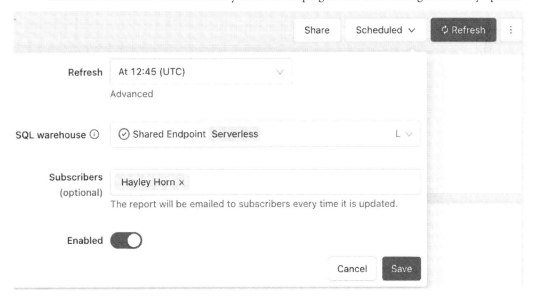

Add schedule

Settings   Subscribers

Schedule

Every | Day   ⌄ | at | 18   ⌄ | : | 47   ⌄ |

☐ Show cron syntax

Timezone

| America/Denver   DST ⌄ |

Cancel   **Create**

Figure 8.12 – Scheduling a dashboard report with subscribers (T) DBSQL (B) Lakeview

- **Speed up development with Databricks Assistant**: As we covered in *Chapter 4*, Databricks Assistant is an AI-based interface that can help generate, transform, fix, and explain code. The Assistant is context-aware, meaning it uses Unity Catalog to look at the metadata of your tables and columns, personalized in your environment. In *Figure 8.13*, we ask the Assistant to help write a query with syntax for grouping. It sees the metadata of the **Favorita Stores** table and provides code specific to that table and the column of interest.

Figure 8.13 – Using Databricks Assistant for help writing a query

- **Be informed**: Keep an eye out for important data changes with alerts. Use SQL to calibrate the alert and schedule the condition evaluation at specific intervals through the UI shown in *Figure 8.14*. You can use HTML to create a formatted alert email.

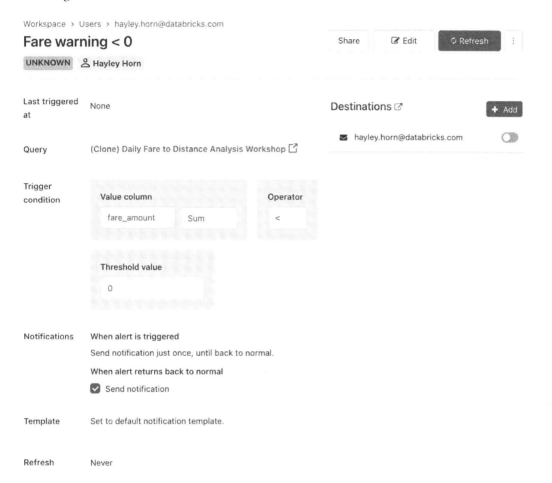

Figure 8.14 – Scheduling alerts to trigger when certain conditions are met

- **Use tags to track usage**: When creating a new SQL warehouse, use tags to code your warehouse endpoint with the correct project. Tagging is a great way to understand usage by project or team. System tables contain the information for tracking usage.

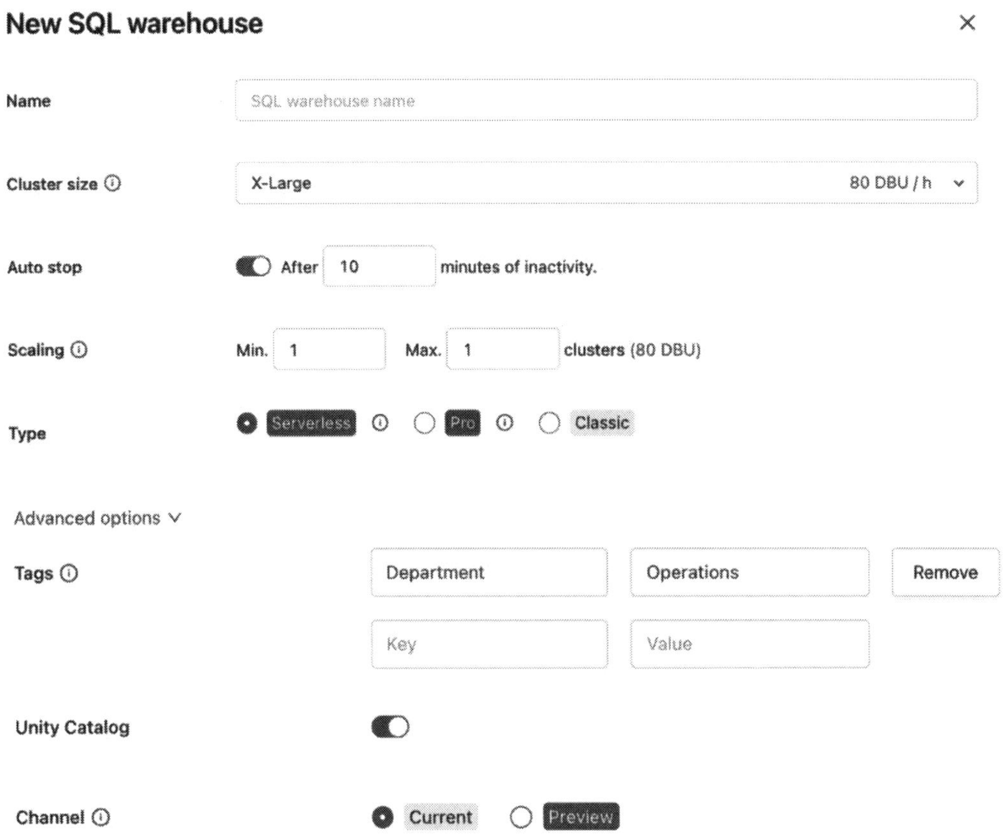

Figure 8.15 – Using tags to connect an endpoint to a project

Next, you'll learn how to connect your models to applications.

Connecting your applications

You can deploy your model anywhere using Databricks Model Serving, which is how you deployed your RAG chatbot model in *Chapter 7*. In this section, we will introduce how to host ML demo apps in **Hugging Face** (**HF**). Having an easy way to host ML apps allows you to build your ML portfolio, showcase your projects at conferences or with stakeholders, and work collaboratively with others in the ML ecosystem. With HF Spaces, you have multiple options for which Python library you use to create a web app. Two common ones are Streamlit and Gradio.

We prefer Gradio. It is an open source Python package that allows you to quickly build a demo or web application for your machine learning model, API, or any arbitrary Python function. You can then share a link to your demo or web application in just a few seconds using Gradio's built-in sharing features. No JavaScript, CSS, or web hosting experience is needed – we love it!

We will walk you through deploying a chatbot to an HF Space in the *Applying our learning* section's RAG project work.

Incorporating LLMs for analysts with SQL AI Functions

There are many use cases where you can integrate an LLM, such as DBRX or OpenAI, for insights. With the Databricks Data Intelligence Platform, it's also possible for analysts who are most comfortable in SQL to take advantage of advances in machine learning and artificial intelligence.

Within Databricks, you can use **AI Functions**, which are built-in SQL functions to access LLMs directly. AI Functions are available for use in the DBSQL interface, SQL warehouse JDBC connection, or via the Spark SQL API. In *Figure 8.16*, we are leveraging the Databricks SQL editor.

> **Foundational Models API**
>
> The storage and processing of data for Databricks-hosted foundation models occur entirely within the Databricks Platform. Importantly, this data is not shared with any third-party model providers. This is not necessarily true when using the External Models API, which connects you to services such as OpenAI that have their own data privacy policies. Keep this in mind when you are concerned about data privacy. You may be able to pay for a tier of service that restricts the use of your data.

Let's do some simple emotion classification. Since the three datasets we've been working with don't include any natural language, we'll create a small dataset ourselves first. You can also download a dataset (such as the Emotions dataset from Kaggle) or use any other natural language source available to you:

1. First, let's explore the built-in AI_QUERY DBSQL function. This command will send our prompt to the remote model configured and retrieve the result. We're using Databricks' DBRX model, but you can use a variety of other open source and proprietary models as well. Open up the Databricks SQL editor and type in the code as shown in *Figure 8.16*. Let's write a query to give us a sample sentence that we can classify.

Figure 8.16 – Crafting a prompt using the AI_QUERY function

2. If you don't have a dataset ready and don't want to download one, you can build a function to generate a dataset for you, as shown here. We're expanding on the prompt from *Step 1* to get several sentences back in JSON format.

```
Run (1000)  ∨   mandy_baker_demo_catalog . ai_demos ∨

1  CREATE OR REPLACE FUNCTION GENERATE_EMOTIONS_DATA(num_records INT DEFAULT 5)
2  RETURNS array<struct<eid:long, emotion:string>>
3  RETURN
4  SELECT FROM_JSON(
5        AI_QUERY(
6              'databricks-dbrx-instruct',
7              CONCAT('You are helping create a training dataset of sentences expressing a variety of emotions.
8                    Generate a sample dataset of ', num_records, ' rows that contains the following columns:
9                    "eid" (random long) and "sentence".
10
11                   Each record should be a sentence expressing one of these emotions:
12                   Joy, Love, Anger, Fear, Sadness, or Surprise.
13
14                   Just write the sentence, do not name the emotion or provide additional information.
15
16                   *** Example: I had a really great day today. ***
17                   *** Example: I feel blue. ***
18
19                   Give me JSON only. No text outside JSON. No explanations or notes.
20                   [{"eid":<long>, "sentence":<string>}]')),
21                   "array<struct<eid:long, sentence:string>>")
22
```

Figure 8.17 – Creating a function to generate fake data

3. Now use the GENERATE_EMOTIONS_DATA function to build a small dataset. After a quick review of the data, it looks like we have a good sample of emotions.

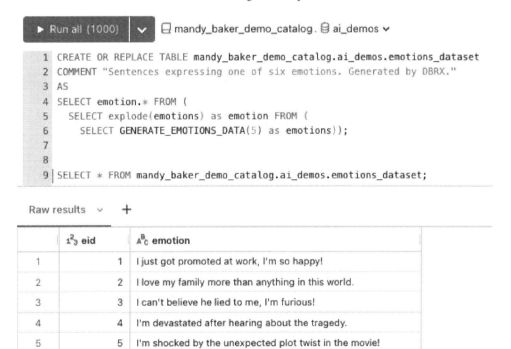

```
Run all (1000)  ∨   mandy_baker_demo_catalog . ai_demos ∨

1  CREATE OR REPLACE TABLE mandy_baker_demo_catalog.ai_demos.emotions_dataset
2  COMMENT "Sentences expressing one of six emotions. Generated by DBRX."
3  AS
4  SELECT emotion.* FROM (
5    SELECT explode(emotions) as emotion FROM (
6      SELECT GENERATE_EMOTIONS_DATA(5) as emotions));
7
8
9  SELECT * FROM mandy_baker_demo_catalog.ai_demos.emotions_dataset;
```

Raw results ∨   +

	eid	emotion
1	1	I just got promoted at work, I'm so happy!
2	2	I love my family more than anything in this world.
3	3	I can't believe he lied to me, I'm furious!
4	4	I'm devastated after hearing about the tragedy.
5	5	I'm shocked by the unexpected plot twist in the movie!

Figure 8.18 – Generating fake emotion data

4. Now, we're going to write a function called CLASSIFY_EMOTION. We're using the AI Function AI_QUERY again, but this function will use a new prompt asking the model to classify a given sentence as one of six emotions.

```
1  CREATE OR REPLACE FUNCTION CLASSIFY_EMOTION(sentence string)
2  RETURNS array<struct<emotion_class:string>>
3  RETURN
4  SELECT FROM_JSON(
5      AI_QUERY(
6          'databricks-dbrx-instruct',
7          CONCAT(
8              'A human wrote this sentence. We classify sentences by emotion for further analysis.
9              Extract the following information:
10               - classify the emotion as ["SADNESS", "JOY", "LOVE", "ANGER", "FEAR", "SURPRISE"]
11
12              Return JSON ONLY. No other text outside the JSON. JSON format:
13              {
14                  "emotion_class": <entity sentiment>,
15              }
16
17              Sentence:', sentence)},
18              "array<struct<emotion_class: STRING>>");
```

Figure 8.19 – Creating a function to classify sentences by emotion

5. Let's call our function to evaluate an example sentence and take a look at the results.

```
1  select classify_emotion("I am shocked by how easy it is to use SQL AI Functions!") as emotion_class;
```

emotion_class
> [{"emotion_class":"SURPRISE"}]

Figure 8.20 – Calling the CLASSIFY_EMOTION function

6. Finally, to classify all records in a table, we call the CLASSIFY_EMOTION function on the records in our table and view the results.

Figure 8.21 – Calling the CLASSIFY_EMOTION function on a table

SQL AI Functions are a great way to put the power of LLMs in the hands of SQL users. Solutions like SQL AI Functions still require some technical knowledge. Databricks is researching ways to allow business users direct access to data, with less upfront development required to get your team moving even faster. Keep an eye out for exciting new product features that remove the programming experience barrier to unlock the value of your data!

Applying our learning

Let's use what we have learned to build a SQL chatbot using the Favorita project's table metadata, monitor the streaming transaction project's model, and deploy the chatbot that we have assembled and evaluated.

Technical requirements

The technical requirements needed to complete the hands-on examples in this chapter are as follows:

- The SQLbot will require OpenAI credentials.

- We will use the Databricks Secrets API to store our OpenAI credentials.

- You will need a **personal access token** (**PAT**) to deploy your web app to HF. See *Further reading* for detailed instructions.

Project: Favorita store sales

Let's build a simple **SQLbot** using OpenAI's GPT to ask questions about our Favorita Sales tables. Please note that while this section continues to use the *Favorita Store Sales* data, it is not a continuation of the earlier project work. In this example, you'll create instructions on how the bot can ask for a list of tables, get information from those tables, and sample data from the tables. The SQLbot will be able to build a SQL query and then interpret the results. To run the notebooks in this example, you will need an account with OpenAI on the OpenAI developer site and request a key for the OpenAI API.

To follow along in your own workspace, please open the following notebook:

`CH8-01-SQL Chatbot`

Keeping secret API keys in your Databricks notebook is far from best practice. You can lock down your notebook access and add a configuration notebook to your `.gitignore` file. However, your ability to remove people's access may not be in your control, depending on your role. Generally, the permissions of admins include the ability to see all code. The OpenAI API key ties back to your account and your credit card. Note that running the notebook once cost us $0.08.

We added our API key to Databricks secrets. The Secrets API requires the Databricks CLI. We set up our CLI through Homebrew. If you haven't already, we suggest getting Secrets set up for your workspace. This may require admin assistance. Start by installing or updating the Databricks CLI. You know the CLI is installed correctly when you get version v0.2 or higher. We are working with `Databricks CLI v0.208.0`.

We followed these steps to set up our API key as a secret:

1. Create a scope:

    ```
    databricks secrets create-scope dlia
    ```

2. Create a secret within the scope:

    ```
    databricks secrets put-secret dlia OPENAI_API_KEY
    ```

3. Paste your API key into the prompt.

Once your secret is successfully saved, we can access it via `dbutils.secrets` in our notebooks.

We are all set up to use OpenAI via the API now. We do not have to worry about accidentally committing our API or a coworker running the code, not knowing it costs you money.

Next, let's focus on creating our SQLbot notebook, step by step, beginning with the setup:

1. First, we install three libraries: `openai`, `langchain_experimental`, and `sqlalchemy-databricks`.

2. To create a connection to OpenAI, pass the secret we set up previously and open a `ChatOpenAI` connection.

3. In *Figure 8.22*, we create two different models. The first is the default model and the second uses GPT 3.5 Turbo.

```
from langchain_openai import OpenAI
from langchain_openai import ChatOpenAI
import os

os.environ['OPENAI_API_KEY'] = dbutils.secrets.get(scope="dlia", key="OPENAI_API_KEY")
llm = OpenAI(temperature=0)
chat = ChatOpenAI(model_name="gpt-3.5-turbo")
```

Figure 8.22 – OpenAI API connection

4. The setup file does not set your schema variable. Define your schema; we chose `favorita_forecasting`. We have been using `database_name` rather than a schema. However, we specify the database we want to ask SQL questions against, which is different.

```
1    schema = "favorita_forecasting"
2
3    table_schemas = spark.sql(
4    f"""
5    select
6      *
7    from
8      system.information_schema.columns
9    where
10     table_catalog = '{catalog}'
11     and table_schema = '{schema}'
12   order by
13     table_name,
14     ordinal_position;
15   """
16   )
```

```
18    table_schemas = table_schemas.drop(
19            "table_catalog",
20            "table_schema",
21            "ordinal_position",
22            "character_octet_length",
23            "numeric_precision",
24            "numeric_precision_radix",
25            "numeric_scale",
26            "datetime_precision",
27            "interval_type",
28            "interval_precision",
29            "identity_start",
30            "identity_increment",
31            "identity_maximum",
32            "identity_minimum",
33            "identity_cycle",
34            "is_system_time_period_start",
35            "is_system_time_period_end",
36            "system_time_period_timestamp_generation",
37            "is_updatable"
38    )
```

Figure 8.23 – (L) Collecting the table schema and system information
schema; (R) dropping unnecessary and repetitive columns

5.   Next, we create two helper functions. The first function organizes the schema information
     provided, `table_schemas`, creating a table definition. The second collects two rows of
     data as examples.

```
1    def table_def(table):
2        table_schema = table_schemas.drop("table_name").where(f'table_name = "{table}"')
3
4        return f"Table Schema for {table}: \ncolumn_index" + table_schema.toPandas().to_csv(
5            sep="|"
6        )
7
8    def table_records(table):
9        records = spark.sql(f"select * from {catalog}.{schema}.{table} limit 2")
10
11        return f"Example records for {table}: \ncolumn_index" + records.toPandas().to_csv(
12            sep="|"
13        )
```

Figure 8.24 – Helper functions for organizing table information

6. Iterate through the table and column data, leveraging our helper functions to format the SQL database input.

```
1   metadata = {}
2   table_list = []
3
4   for row in table_schemas.select("table_name").distinct().collect():
5       tbl = row['table_name']
6       table_list.append(tbl)
7       meta = table_def(tbl) + '\n\n' + table_records(tbl)
8       metadata[tbl] = meta
```

Figure 8.25 – Iterating through the tables and leveraging the helper functions

7. We now have all of our data ready to be able to create a SQL database for OpenAI to talk to. You will need to edit endpoint_http_path to match the path of an active SQL warehouse in your workspace. The database is passed to both the default OpenAI model and the GPT 3.5 model.

```
from sqlalchemy.engine import create_engine
from langchain.sql_database import SQLDatabase
from langchain_experimental.sql import SQLDatabaseChain

table = table_list

databricks_token = dbutils.notebook.entry_point.getDbutils().notebook().getContext().apiToken().get()
workspace_url = spark.conf.get("spark.databricks.workspaceUrl")
# Obtain this from a SQL endpoint under "Connection Details", HTTP Path
endpoint_http_path = "/sql/1.0/warehouses/5ab5dda58c1ea16b"

engine = create_engine(
    f"databricks+connector://token:{databricks_token}@{workspace_url}:443/{database_name}",
    connect_args={"http_path": endpoint_http_path, "catalog": catalog}
)

db = SQLDatabase(engine, schema=None, include_tables=table)
db_chain = SQLDatabaseChain.from_llm(llm, db, verbose=True)
chat_chain = SQLDatabaseChain.from_llm(chat, db, verbose=True)
```

Figure 8.26 – Create a database for OpenAI to query containing only the information we provided

With the setup complete, we can now interact with our SQL chatbot models! Let's start with a basic question: *Which store sold the most?*

In *Figure 8.27*, we run both models on the question and get back two different answers.

```
> Entering new  chain...
Which store sold the most?
SQLQuery:SELECT store_nbr, SUM(transactions) AS total_transactions FROM favorita_transactions
GROUP BY store_nbr ORDER BY total_transactions DESC LIMIT 5;
SQLResult: [(44, 7273093), (47, 6535810), (45, 6201115), (46, 5990113), (3, 5366350)]
Answer:Store 44 sold the most with 7273093 transactions.
> Finished chain.

'Store 44 sold the most with 7273093 transactions.'


> Entering new  chain...
Which store sold the most?
SQLQuery:SELECT store_nbr, SUM(sales) AS total_sales
FROM train_set
GROUP BY store_nbr
ORDER BY total_sales DESC
LIMIT 1
SQLResult: [(44, 62087553.25008899)]
Answer:Store number 44 sold the most with a total sales of 62,087,553.25
> Finished chain.

'Store number 44 sold the most with a total sales of 62,087,553.25'
```

Figure 8.27 – The SQL chatbot model's responses to our question "Which store
sold the most?". (T) db_chain.run(question) (B) chat_chain.run(question)

As new versions of OpenAI's GPT model are released, the results and behavior of your SQLbot may change. As new models and approaches become available, it is good practice to test them and see how the changes impact your work and the results of your chatbot. Leveraging MLflow with your SQLbot experiment will help you track and compare the different features and configurations throughout your production process.

Project -streaming transactions

You are ready to wrap up this project. The production workflow notebooks are the CH7-08-Production Generating Records, CH7-09-Production Auto Loader, and CH7-10-Production Feature Engineering components in the workflow job created in *Chapter 7*. You will run that same job once the new workflow is in place. To follow along in your own workspace, please open the following notebook: CH8-05-Production Monitoring

In the CH8-05-Production Monitoring notebook, you create two monitors – one for the prod_transactions table and one for the packaged_transaction_model_predictions table. See *Figure 8.28* for the latter.

```
lm.create_monitor(
    table_name=f"{catalog}.{database_name}.packaged_transaction_model_predictions",
    profile_type=lm.InferenceLog(
        timestamp_col="TransactionTimestamp",
        granularities=["5 minutes","30 minutes","1 hour"],
        model_id_col="model_version",
        prediction_col="prediction",
        label_col="actual_label",
        problem_type="classification"
    ),
    slicing_exprs=["Product","CustomerID"],
    schedule=lm.MonitorCronSchedule(
        quartz_cron_expression="0 0 * * * ?", # schedules a refresh every hour
        timezone_id="MST",
    ),
    output_schema_name=f"{catalog}.{database_name}"
)
```

Figure 8.28 – The inference table monitor

Congratulations! The streaming project is complete. We encourage you to add improvements and commit them back to the repository. Here are a few possible examples: add more validation metrics to the validation notebook, incorporate the inference performance results into the decision to retrain, and make adjustments to the configuration of data generation to simulate drift.

Project: retrieval-augmented generation chatbot

To follow along in your own workspace, please open the following notebooks and resources:

- CH8-app.py
- CH8-01-Deploy Your Endpoint with SDK
- The **Hugging Face Spaces** page

First, we need to ensure our chatbot is deployed using Model Serving, as shown in *Figure 8.30*. Here, we are using the fastest way by going through the UI of the Model Serving page. To follow along and serve, we are selecting the registered model that we registered in *Chapter 7*. Select the latest version – in our case, it's version 4. For this demo project, we expect minimal concurrency so the endpoint will have only four possible concurrent runs and will scale to 0 when no traffic is available. We are enabling inference tables under the same catalog to track and potentially further monitor our payload. We are not going to demonstrate in this chapter how to set a monitor or data quality pipeline for the RAG project, as it was demonstrated for the streaming project. We encourage you to apply it on your own!

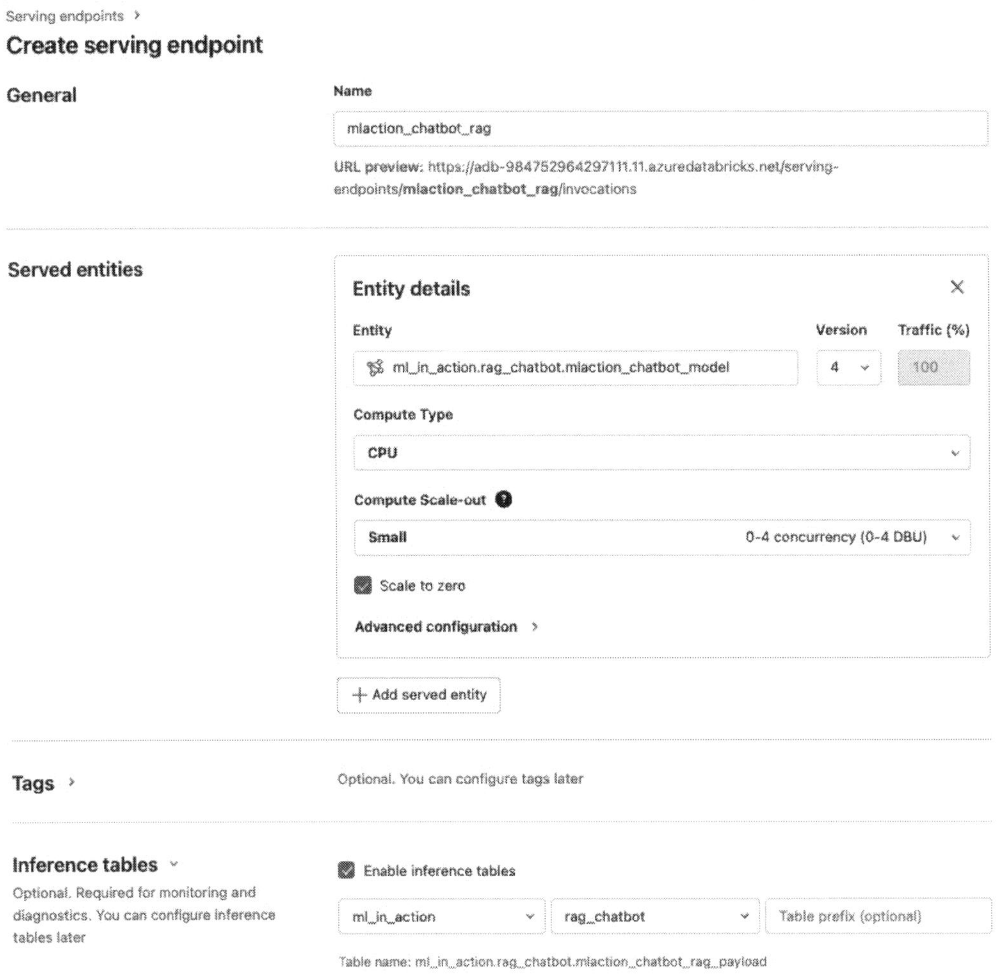

Serving endpoints ›

Create serving endpoint

General

Name

mlaction_chatbot_rag

URL preview: https://adb-984752964297111.11.azuredatabricks.net/serving-
endpoints/**mlaction_chatbot_rag**/invocations

Served entities

Entity details   ✕

Entity   Version   Traffic (%)

🐙 ml_in_action.rag_chatbot.mlaction_chatbot_model   4 ⌄   100

Compute Type

CPU   ⌄

Compute Scale-out ❓

Small   0-4 concurrency (0-4 DBU) ⌄

☑ Scale to zero

Advanced configuration ›

+ Add served entity

Tags ›   Optional. You can configure tags later

Inference tables ⌄   ☑ Enable inference tables

Optional. Required for monitoring and
diagnostics. You can configure inference   ml_in_action ⌄   rag_chatbot ⌄   Table prefix (optional)
tables later

Table name: ml_in_action.rag_chatbot.mlaction_chatbot_rag_payload

Figure 8.29 – Example of the Model Serving deployment via UI

In order for your application to be able to connect to the resources attached to it, such as Vector Search, the endpoint requires you to provide additional configurations to the endpoint such as your PAT and host under **Advanced configuration**:

Advanced configuration ⌄

Environment Variables

| DATABRICKS_TOKEN | {{secrets/mlaction/rag_sp_token}} | ✕ |
| DATABRICKS_HOST | {{secrets/mlaction/rag_sp_host}} | ✕ |

Figure 8.30 – Advanced configuration requirements

> **Note**
>
> You could also use the Databricks SDK service to deploy your endpoints. If you are interested in seeing how to use SDK deployment, please use the notebook attached under `CH8 - 01 -Deploy Your Endpoint with SDK`.

Jump over to the Hugging Face Spaces website. Instructions on how to deploy your first HF Space are explained very well on the main page of HF Spaces, so we will not duplicate them here. We would like to highlight that we are using a free deployment option of Spaces with 2 CPUs and 16 GB of memory.

When you deploy your Space, it will look like this:

Figure 8.31 – Empty Hugging Face Space

We would like to highlight a few things that are important in order to connect to your chatbot, which is served in real time with Databricks Model Serving. To connect the chatbot to your HF Space, you must set `API_TOKEN` and an `API_ENDPOINT`. Here's how to set these values:

1. Go to **Settings** in the HF Space you created.

2. Scroll down to **Variables and secrets**.

3. Set your API_ENDPOINT as the URL from the REST API provided on the Databricks Model Serving page.

4. Set your API_TOKEN using a personal access token generated by Databricks. This is required to connect to the endpoint.

Figure 8.32 – Example of Variables and secrets on HF Spaces

5. Once this is set, you are ready to bring your Gradio web app script into your HF Space.

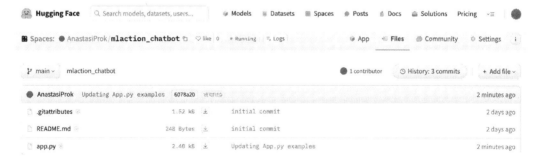

Figure 8.33 – Example of Variables and secrets on HF Spaces

6. When your endpoint is ready, jump back to your HF Space.

7. Go to the **Files** tab under the pre-created Space and click **+Add File**.

8. Now add CH8-app.py that was given to you for *Chapter 8* – you can create your own web application. Feel free to experiment with the design according to your business needs.

Let's talk a bit about the `respond` function in the `CH8-app.py` file – see *Figure 8.34*, which is passed to our app's UI chatbot. The `respond` function, in this case, is the caller of your deployed endpoints, where we do not just send and receive responses but also can shape the format of the input or output. In our case, the endpoint expects to receive a request in the format of a JSON with field inputs with the questions within a list, while the output is a JSON with field predictions.

```python
import itertools
import gradio as gr
import requests
import os
from gradio.themes.utils import sizes


def respond(message, history):

    if len(message.strip()) == 0:
        return "ERROR the question should not be empty"

    # Set your secrets under HF secrets for your Space
    local_token = os.getenv('API_TOKEN')
    local_endpoint = os.getenv('API_ENDPOINT')

    if local_token is None or local_endpoint is None:
        return "ERROR missing env variables"

    # Add your API token to the headers
    headers = {
        'Content-Type': 'application/json',
        'Authorization': f'Bearer {local_token}'
    }

    # Pay attenction to what your model expects as schema format
    q = {"inputs": [message]}
    try:
        response = requests.post(
            local_endpoint, json=q, headers=headers, timeout=100)
        response_data = response.json()
        response_data=response_data["predictions"][0]

    except Exception as error:
        response_data = f"ERROR status_code: {type(error).__name__}"


    return response_data
```

Figure 8.34 – The respond function written in the Gradio app

To create a chatbot, as was mentioned in the introduction section, we are using a simple example from Gradio where we add options such as the title of our application, a description, and example questions. *Figure 8.35* shows the full code.

```
theme = gr.themes.Soft(text_size=sizes.text_sm,radius_size=sizes.radius_sm, spacing_size=sizes.spacing_sm,)

demo = gr.ChatInterface(
    respond,
    chatbot=gr.Chatbot(show_label=False, container=False, show_copy_button=True, bubble_full_width=True),
    textbox=gr.Textbox(placeholder="Ask me a question",
                container=False, scale=7),
    title="Ml in Action LLM RAG demo - Chat with Mixtral from Foundational Databricks model serving endpoint",
    description="This chatbot is a demo example for the llm chatbot. <br>This content is provided as a LLM RAG educational example, without support.
    It is using Mixtral, can hallucinate and should not be used as production content.<br>Please do not use this for production.",
    examples=[["Can LLM's impact wages and how ?"],
              ["Will AI impact work forces in the US ? "],
              ["Can LLM's impact wages and how ?"],],
    cache_examples=False,
    theme=theme,
    retry_btn=None,
    undo_btn=None,
    clear_btn="Clear",
)
```

Figure 8.35 – The Gadio app.py interface for your LLM

The chatbot is now available in a more user-friendly interface, as shown in *Figure 8.36*.

Figure 8.36 – The interface for your chatbot application

Let's ask a few questions to make sure our RAG chatbot is providing correct results.

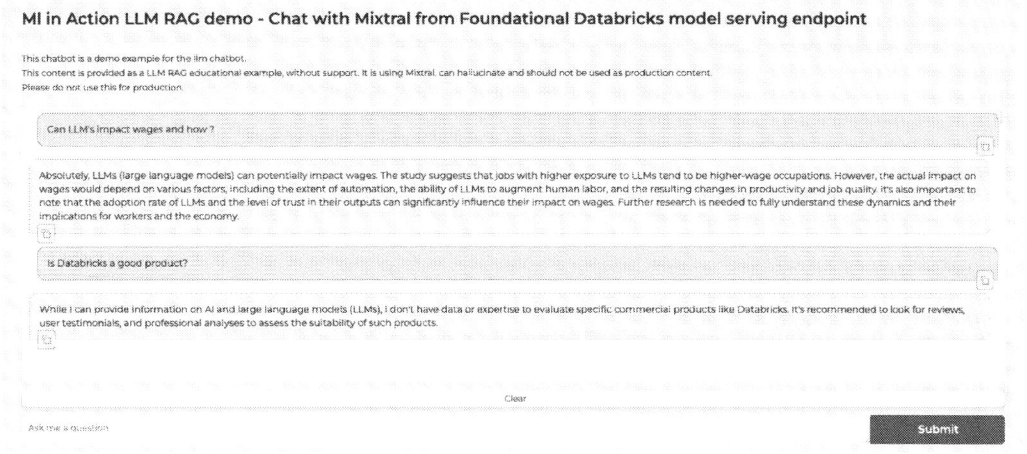

MI in Action LLM RAG demo - Chat with Mixtral from Foundational Databricks model serving endpoint

This chatbot is a demo example for the llm chatbot.
This content is provided as a LLM RAG educational example, without support. It is using Mixtral, can hallucinate and should not be used as production content.
Please do not use this for production.

Can LLM's impact wages and how ?

Absolutely, LLMs (large language models) can potentially impact wages. The study suggests that jobs with higher exposure to LLMs tend to be higher-wage occupations. However, the actual impact on wages would depend on various factors, including the extent of automation, the ability of LLMs to augment human labor, and the resulting changes in productivity and job quality. It's also important to note that the adoption rate of LLMs and the level of trust in their outputs can significantly influence their impact on wages. Further research is needed to fully understand these dynamics and their implications for workers and the economy.

Is Databricks a good product?

While I can provide information on AI and large language models (LLMs), I don't have data or expertise to evaluate specific commercial products like Databricks. It's recommended to look for reviews, user testimonials, and professional analyses to assess the suitability of such products.

Clear

Ask me a question   Submit

Figure 8.37 – Examples of chatbot answers from our RAG application

If the responses look good, your application is ready to be used!

Summary

Sharing insights from your models is an important way to get value from your machine learning practice. Using dashboards as a medium for sharing your information is an accessible way to communicate insights to business users and teams outside of the data science team. In this chapter, we discussed how to build the gold layer, tips on presenting your data using DBSQL dashboards, taking advantage of innovations such as OpenAI models in DBSQL, and how you can share data and AI artifacts through Databricks Marketplace to get the most value from your enterprise data.

We hope you have had a chance to get hands-on with building your lakehouse. From exploration, cleaning, building pipelines, and building models to finding insights hidden in your data, all the way to sharing insights – it's all doable on the Databricks Platform. We encourage you to take the notebooks and experiment! The authors would love to hear feedback, and whether this has been helpful on your journey with the Databricks Platform.

Questions

Let's test ourselves on what we've learned by going through the following questions:

1. What are some differences between the gold layer and the silver layer?
2. What is one way you could set an alert to identify that a table has an invalid value?

3. Why would you choose to use an external dashboarding tool?

4. If you use a language model through an API such as OpenAI, what are some considerations about the data you send via the API?

5. What are some reasons a company would share data in Databricks Marketplace?

Answers

After putting thought into the questions, compare your answers to ours:

1. The gold layer is more refined and aggregated than the silver layer. The silver layer powers data science and machine learning, and the gold layer powers analytics and dashboarding.

2. You can monitor the values of a field and send an email alert when the value is invalid.

3. Sometimes companies use multiple dashboarding tools. You might need to provide data in a dashboard a team is accustomed to using.

4. If I were a language model through an API, I would be cautious about sending sensitive data, including PII, customer information, or proprietary information.

5. A company might share data in Databricks Marketplace in order to monetize the data or make it available externally for people to use easily and securely.

Further reading

In this chapter, we pointed out specific technologies, technical features, and options. Please look at these resources to get deeper into the areas that interest you most:

- *Databricks SQL Statement Execution API*: `https://www.databricks.com/blog/2023/03/07/databricks-sql-statement-execution-api-announcing-public-preview.html`

- *Power to the SQL People: Introducing Python UDFs in Databricks SQL*: `https://www.databricks.com/blog/2022/07/22/power-to-the-sql-people-introducing-python-udfs-in-databricks-sql.html`

- *Actioning Customer Reviews at Scale with Databricks SQL AI Functions*: `https://www.databricks.com/blog/actioning-customer-reviews-scale-databricks-sql-ai-functions`

- *Databricks sets the official data warehousing performance record*: https://dbricks.co/benchmark

- *Databricks Lakehouse and Data Mesh*: `https://www.databricks.com/blog/2022/10/10/databricks-lakehouse-and-data-mesh-part-1.html`

- *Hugging Face*: `https://huggingface.co/spaces`

- *Gradio*: `https://www.gradio.app/`

- *Hugging Face Spaces*: `https://huggingface.co/docs/hub/en/spaces-overview`

- *Databricks Lakehouse monitoring documentation*: `https://api-docs.databricks.com/python/lakehouse-monitoring/latest/databricks.lakehouse_monitoring.html#module-databricks.lakehouse_monitoring`

- Databricks personal access token authentication `https://docs.databricks.com/en/dev-tools/auth/pat.html`

Index

Packtpub.com

Subscribe to our online digital library for full access to over 7,000 books and videos, as well as industry leading tools to help you plan your personal development and advance your career. For more information, please visit our website.

Why subscribe?

- Spend less time learning and more time coding with practical eBooks and Videos from over 4,000 industry professionals

- Improve your learning with Skill Plans built especially for you

- Get a free eBook or video every month

- Fully searchable for easy access to vital information

- Copy and paste, print, and bookmark content

Did you know that Packt offers eBook versions of every book published, with PDF and ePub files available? You can upgrade to the eBook version at packtpub.com and as a print book customer, you are entitled to a discount on the eBook copy. Get in touch with us at customercare@packtpub.com for more details.

At www.packtpub.com, you can also read a collection of free technical articles, sign up for a range of free newsletters, and receive exclusive discounts and offers on Packt books and eBooks.

Other Books You May Enjoy

If you enjoyed this book, you may be interested in these other books by Packt:

Data Lakehouse in Action

Pradeep Menon

ISBN: 978-1-80181-593-2

- Understand the evolution of the Data Architecture patterns for analytics
- Become well versed in the Data Lakehouse pattern and how it enables data analytics
- Focus on methods to ingest, process, store, and govern data in a Data Lakehouse architecture
- Learn techniques to serve data and perform analytics in a Data Lakehouse architecture
- Cover methods to secure the data in a Data Lakehouse architecture
- Implement Data Lakehouse in a cloud computing platform such as Azure
- Combine Data Lakehouse in a macro-architecture pattern such as Data Mesh

Azure Databricks Cookbook

Phani Raj , Vinod Jaiswal

ISBN: 97-81-78980-971-8

- Build a modern data warehouse with Delta tables and Azure Synapse Analytics
- Create real-time dashboards in Databricks SQL
- Implement data governance with Unity Catalog
- Build end-to-end data processing pipelines for near real-time data analytics
- Integrate Azure DevOps for version control as well as for deploying and productionizing solutions with continuous integration and continuous deployment (CI/CD) pipelines
- Enhance Azure Databricks with OpenAI and Microsoft Fabric integration for cutting-edge data solutions

Packt is searching for authors like you

If you're interested in becoming an author for Packt, please visit `authors.packtpub.com` and apply today. We have worked with thousands of developers and tech professionals, just like you, to help them share their insight with the global tech community. You can make a general application, apply for a specific hot topic that we are recruiting an author for, or submit your own idea.

Share Your Thoughts

Now you've finished *Databricks ML in Action*, we'd love to hear your thoughts! Scan the QR code below to go straight to the Amazon review page for this book and share your feedback or leave a review on the site that you purchased it from.

`https://packt.link/r/1-800-56489-9`

Your review is important to us and the tech community and will help us make sure we're delivering excellent quality content.

Download a free PDF copy of this book

Thanks for purchasing this book!

Do you like to read on the go but are unable to carry your print books everywhere?

Is your eBook purchase not compatible with the device of your choice?

Don't worry, now with every Packt book you get a DRM-free PDF version of that book at no cost.

Read anywhere, any place, on any device. Search, copy, and paste code from your favorite technical books directly into your application.

The perks don't stop there, you can get exclusive access to discounts, newsletters, and great free content in your inbox daily

Follow these simple steps to get the benefits:

1. Scan the QR code or visit the link below

https://packt.link/free-ebook/978-1-80056-489-3

2. Submit your proof of purchase
3. That's it! We'll send your free PDF and other benefits to your email directly

Made in the USA
Monee, IL
27 June 2024

60701507R00146